The Age of Triage

The Age of Triage

Fear and Hope in an Over-crowded World

Richard L. Rubenstein

Beacon Press   Boston

This book
is
dedicated
to

Carolyn Bullock Rubenstein,
my daughter-in-law,
and
Nicole Ann Rubenstein,
my granddaughter

Beacon Press books are published under the auspices
of the Unitarian Universalist Association,
25 Beacon Street, Boston, Massachusetts 02108
Published simultaneously in Canada by
Fitzhenry & Whiteside Limited, Toronto

(paperback) 9 8 7 6 5 4 3 2 1

Rubenstein, Richard L.
    The age of triage.

    Bibliography: p.
    Includes index.
    1. Genocide. 2. Unemployment 3. Emigration and Immigration
    4. Social Change 5. Social Darwinism
JX5418.R82 1982   304.6'5   82.9407
                                                              AACR2

ISBN 0-8070-4377-X

FOREWORD

THIS BOOK is dominated by a single concern: the fate of tens of millions of human beings whose lives have been either lost or blighted because they were unable to find a viable role in the economy and society in which they were born. This book is also a continuation of my earlier work on the destruction of the European Jews during World War II, as well as an attempt to comprehend that terrible event in a larger historical context. As such, it is the promised sequel to *The Cunning of History: Mass Death and the American Future* (1975).

My earliest work explored the theological significance of genocide. The current work explores the economic, social, and cultural forces at work in modern civilization that make for *both* unemployment and genocide. Lest it be thought that I have abandoned theology and turned exclusively to political and social analysis, I wish to state my conviction that no theological enterprise, that is, no consideration of the ultimate values that move men and women, can be adequate to its task if it ignores critical political and social theory, especially insofar as these modes of inquiry seek to comprehend the conditions under which men attempt to conduct their lives both individually and collectively.

No book is the product of a single author even when his or her name alone appears on the title page. Specialists will easily recognize the debt I owe to the authorities who have devoted their lives to the study of the areas I attempt to interpret. I freely acknowledge my indebtedness and express my gratitude to those whom I regard as my teachers, the many men and women whose historical and scientific investigations made this work possible.

In addition to the scholars whom I have met only through their works, I am profoundly indebted to a number of men, women, and institutions without whose support this work could not have been brought to completion. I wish to express my appreciation to MaryAnn Lash, Marie Cantlon, Jeffrey Smith, and the staff of Beacon Press for their support in producing this book. I am especially indebted to my editor, Marie Cantlon, who also served as the editor of *The Cunning of History.* Her counsel and, most especially, her patience are deeply appreciated.

Special mention must be made of two men, William Styron and Charles E. Merrill, Jr., without whom this book could never have come into being. Had it not been for William Styron's support of *The Cunning of History,* which was expressed both in his review in *The New York Review of Books* (June 29, 1978), and his discussion of the book in his novel *Sophie's Choice,* there would have been no sequel to *The Cunning of History.* Styron's review appeared three years after that book's publication. At the time, the book had been almost completely ignored and had sold less than 1,000 copies. As a result of Styron's support, a paperback edition was published. I am happy to report that the book has found its audience.

I am deeply indebted to Charles E. Merrill, Jr. of Boston, a friend of almost three decades. As chairman of the Board of Trustees of the Charles E. Merrill Educational and Charitable Trust, Mr. Merrill used his good offices to secure the funding of a Charles E. Merrill Discretionary Grant in Modern Jewish History and Thought to the Center for the Study of Southern Culture and Religion, now known as the Humanities Institute of the Florida State University. This grant made it possible for me to spend two summers at the Harvard College Library in the course of writing this book and one yet to appear. The grant also provided other research support for this project.

I am also grateful to President Bernard Sliger and Dr. Augustus B. Turnbull III, Vice-President for Academic Affairs, of Florida State University for the support they have given the University's Robert O. Lawton Distinguished Professors. It has been their policy to provide the Robert O. Lawton Distinguished Professors with an annual stipend for travel and research as well as time that can be devoted exclusively to research and writing. Without this program, it would have taken me several more years to complete this project. I am also indebted to Professor John Priest,

Chairman of the Department of Religion, and my colleagues in the Department for the additional time I have received for my research.

A very special word of gratitude is due to Mrs. Karen Bickley, Research Associate of the Humanities Institute, and Ms. Jan DeCosmo, Research Assistant at the Institute. Their work on behalf of the Institute and their constant encouragement have been an indispensable ingredient in the completion of this task. My heartfelt thanks are also due to Professor Leon Golden, Director of the Humanities Doctoral Program, and my colleague as Co-Director of the Humanities Institute. Because of his imaginative and insightful leadership of the doctoral program, I was enabled to offer a number of doctoral seminars in the areas of the humanities and political and social theory. The fruit of those seminars is woven into the texture of this work.

I also wish to express my thanks to Dr. Jeanne Ruppert of the Florida State University Press for her editorial advice and to the staffs of the Robert Manning Strozier Library of the Florida State University, the Harvard College Library, the Library of Congress and the Library of the Iliff School of Theology, Denver, Colorado.

Finally, I want to express my deepest gratitude to my wife and life's companion, Dr. Betty Rogers Rubenstein. No words are adequate to express all that I owe to her.

The Department of Religion and
The Humanities Institute,
Florida State University
Tallahassee

June 20, 1982

CONTENTS

1
OVERVIEW
The Revolution
of Rationality

WITH UNEMPLOYMENT RISING to its highest levels since the Great Depression in both the United States and Europe, it is once again painfully apparent that few problems confronting modern civilization have been as insidiously corrupting or as destructive of the common good as the phenomenon of mass surplus population. A surplus or redundant population is one that for any reason can find no viable role in the society in which it is domiciled. Because such people can expect none of the normal rewards of society, governments tend to regard them as potential sources of disorder and have often attempted to control them or to remove them from the mainstream of society altogether.

The modern, worldwide phenomenon of mass surplus population had its origins in the unprecedented demographic explosion that began in Europe during the eighteenth century and continues unabated to this day in the less developed countries of the world. In 1740 there were between 120 and 140 million people in Europe including European Russia. In 1913 there were 468,000,000. In addition, by 1914 there were about 250,000,000 people of European origin living outside the continent.[1]

This unprecedented explosion in the number of people can be seen as one of the most important social consequences of the triumph of an attitude of value-neutral, calculating rationality as the predominant mode of problem-solving in practical affairs. This attitude manifested itself in what historian David Landes has characterized as "the high value placed on the manipulation of the environment" which, he tells us, is composed of two elements,

1

rationality and "the Faustian sense of mastery."[2] In the words
of the German sociologist Max Weber such rationality involves
"the methodical attainment of a definitely given and practical end
by means of an increasingly precise calculation of adequate
means."[3] Landes observes that "there is good reason to believe
that rationality is a homogenous character trait, that is, that he
who is rational in one area is more likely to be rational in others."[4]
It is Landes' opinion that this rationality has religious origins, an
opinion he shares with Weber. Weber held that the radical monotheism of the Bible, with its tendency to desacralize the natural
order and to secularize the political order, is one of the earliest
and most influential expressions of the rationalization motif in
human affairs.[5] According to Weber, a principal consequence of
biblical religion was the "disenchantment of the world" *(Entzaü-
berung der Welt)*. Where such disenchantment takes place, "there
are no mysterious forces that come into play, but rather one can, in
principle, master all things by calculation."[6] I would add that the
related phenomena of rationalization, secularization, and the disenchantment of the world Weber saw as derivative of biblical monotheism are specifically derivative of the biblical theology of cove-
nant and election which proclaims God alone to be sovereign. By
rejecting all intermediary authorities and powers that might sub-
vert or divert Israel from its covenantal obligation, this theology
had a secularizing effect on the way reality was apprehended and
mastered. For the believer God alone is sacred. Since no spirits
exist to be appeased, rationality can replace magic as the fundamental mode of problem-solving in all areas of human activity.[7]
    Landes further asserts that the rationalizing spirit was com-
plemented by a "Faustian ethic" which he defines as "a sense of
mastery over nature and things." As Landes observes, the spirit
of rationality and the Faustian ethic reinforced each other:
"mastery entailed the adaptation of means to ends; and attention of means to ends was the precondition of mastery."[8] It is
interesting to note that the German poet Goethe completed the
first part of *Faust* at almost the same time as his friend Hegel
completed what was perhaps his greatest work, *Phenomenology
of the Spirit*. The *Phenomenology* was completed in 1806; *Faust,*

Part I, appeared in 1808. In the *Phenomenology* Hegel gave expression to his conviction that all of nature and history constitute the dynamic unfolding of Reason as the underlying unitary reality of all things. Hegel also identified his own age as the era in which Reason had finally come to self-conscious realization. Thus, as Reason was in the process of becoming triumphant in the realm of practical affairs, Hegel identified the underlying substance of all things as the expression of the evolution of self-conscious Reason.[9]

One of the most important social consequences of the triumph of practical or instrumental Reason was that man's ability to produce a surplus of both food and manufactured goods was vastly enhanced. Yet, there is great irony in this achievement for *by producing a surplus, men take the first step in making themselves superfluous.* The rational division of labor rests upon humanity's ability to produce a surplus. The division of labor also enlarges that capacity, making it possible for ever fewer people to produce an ever greater output of goods and services.

Even before the publication of the *Phenomenology* Hegel understood the connection between surplus goods and surplus people. Writing in 1803 about the evolving worldwide division of labor that was beginning to make it possible for factories in England to supply cheap manufacturing goods to people in Asia, Hegel observed: "It thus happens that a far-away operation often affects a whole class of people who have hitherto satisfied their needs through it [their own craftsmanship]; all of a sudden it [the distant manufacture of cheap goods] limits their work, makes it redundant and useless."[10]

Hegel saw that cheap manufactured goods could destroy the native craft industries of the lands to which they were exported, thereby rendering the native craftsmen superfluous. He also saw that as modern industry and commerce developed, they were bound to have a destabilizing effect on the community in which they arose. In 1820 he wrote that it was inherent in the nature of what he called civil society *(bürgerliche Gesellschaft),* what we today would identify as modern bourgeois society, to overproduce both goods and people.[11] Foreseeing that this would lead to the growth of a class of economic outcasts — an underclass within the heart of society — he described this process in a passage that has an amazingly contemporary ring to it:

> When the standard of living of a large mass of people falls below a subsistence level — a level regulated automatically as the one necessary for a member of the society — and when there is a consequent loss of the sense of right and wrong, of honesty and the self-respect which makes a man insist on maintaining himself by his own work, the result is the creation of a rabble of paupers.[12]

Elsewhere, Hegel observed that, as labor's productivity increased, a point would be reached at which more goods would be produced than could be consumed. This would force factory owners to cut back the number of people they employed. As the number of unemployed grew, society would be faced with a problem for which Hegel saw no solution save emigration. Hegel was dubious about welfare assistance for the unemployed with or without a work requirement. Without a work requirement, public assistance was likely to intensify the poor's sense of dependence and lack of self-respect. On the other hand, if the unemployed were compelled to produce goods for a saturated market, they would only aggravate the problem that made them unemployed to begin with. Discussing the futility of work-relief, Hegel observed:

> As an alternative, they [the poor] might be given subsistence directly through being given work, i.e. the opportunity to work. In this event the volume of production would be increased, but the evil consists precisely in an excess of production and the lack of a proportionate number of consumers who are themselves also producers, and thus it is simply intensified by both of the methods...by which it is sought to alleviate it. It hence becomes apparent that despite an excess of wealth civil society is not rich enough, i.e. its own resources are insufficient to check excessive poverty and the creation of a penurious rabble.[13]

Unable to resolve its most dangerous social problems, the tendency to overproduce goods and people while underproducing consumers, civil society is, according to Hegel, driven to seek foreign markets for the disposition of the goods and foreign lands for the disposition of the people. Although Hegel explicitly cited England as an example of this development, it is clear from his text that he regarded the problem as intrinsic to bourgeois society as such.[14] Concerning the overproduction of goods and the need for foreign markets, Hegel wrote: "The inner dialectic of civil society thus drives it...to push beyond its limits and seek markets, and so its necessary means of subsistence in foreign lands which are either deficient in the goods it has overproduced, or else generally backward in industry,"[15] and concerning surplus people: "Civil society is thus driven to found colonies. Increase in population alone has this effect, but it is due in particular to the appearance of a number of people who cannot secure the satisfaction of their own needs by their own labor once production rises above the requirements of consumers."[16]

Writing as he did in the early decades of the nineteenth century, Hegel already understood one of the most ironic and potentially tragic consequences of the triumph of instrumental rationality, namely, that mankind's collective ingenuity could act as an anonymous, indifferent force that would exclude an ever-increasing number of men and women from productive work and, hence, a meaningful life in the communities in which they were born. Nevertheless, Hegel did not consider what might happen when new territories were no longer available to absorb the world's surplus people. As we have seen, Hegel did foresee that the rationalization of the economy and society would almost inevitably lead to what we today would regard as mild strategies of population elimination such as emigration and colonization, but he could not possibly have foreseen how widespread the problem or how draconian the administrative measures employed in dealing with it might become.

An important aspect of both the rationalization of the economy and society and the rise of the phenomenon of surplus population in modern times has been the development of a universal money economy. Unfortunately, as money came to be the measure of all that is real, people without money became unreal. Thus Hegel wrote:

> The object is here something that has meaning according to its [money] value, not for itself, not in relation to the need...A person is real to the extent to which he has money

...The formal principle of reason is to be found here...it is the abstraction from all particularity, character, historicity, etc., of the individual.[17]

If, however, "a person is real to the extent that he has money," then a person without money is fated to have no social reality and, ultimately, perhaps no reality at all. As early as 1651, Thomas Hobbes argued that the market alone determines the worth of a man:

> The Value, or Worth of a man, is as of all other things, his Price; that is to say, so much as would be given for the use of his Power: and therefore not absolute but a thing dependent on the need and judgement of another...And as in other things, so in men, not the seller, but the buyer determines the Price. For let a man (as most men do,) rate themselves [sic] at the highest Value they can; yet their true Value is no more than it is esteemed by others.[18]

The world Hobbes describes is one in which a man's labor power is a commodity offered for sale and a man's worth is no more nor less than the market price of that labor power. In a passing remark Hobbes observes, "For a man's Labor also is a commodity exchangeable for benefit, as well as any other thing."[19] If, however, Hobbes is correct, those whose labor fetches no price will be regarded as worthless. Thus, as the economy and society became ever more rationalized, a development which was already under way during Hobbes's lifetime, it was inevitable that money would become more real than people.

Moreover, a money economy is both rationalizing and desacralizing. Where such an economy is fully operative, nothing whatsoever can legitimately be valued according to any standard other than money. Everything is disenchanted and everything is regarded as having its price. In a perfectly rational money economy, no extrinsic value, not even the laws of a God of justice and morality can function as a credible restraint on the absolutely free functioning of the marketplace. This is implied in Weber's observations concerning the nature of a money economy:

> The market community as such is the most impersonal re-

lationship of practical life into which human beings can enter with one another. . . The reason for the impersonality of the market is its matter-of-factness, its orientation to the commodity and only to that. Where the market is allowed to follow its own tendencies, its participants do not look towards the persons of each other but only towards the commodity; there are no obligations of brotherliness or reverence, and none of those spontaneous human relations that are sustained by personal unions. They all would just obstruct the free development of the bare market relationship. . .[20]

Weber concludes his observations with a restrained comment in which we can discern his own judgment concerning the economic and social transformations that have yielded the modern world: "Such absolute depersonalization is contrary to all elementary forms of human relations."[21]

The depersonalization brought about by the modern rationalizing consciousness has long been the subject of serious reflection by social theorists. The late Benjamin Nelson has described the transition to the modern period as one "from tribal brotherhood to universal otherhood."[22] Others have characterized the transformation as having involved a shift from *Gemeinschaft*, a type of organic social relationship of those who share common origins, morals, beliefs and inherited institutions, to *Gesellschaft*, a type of relationship characterized by the rational and impersonal pursuit of self-interest on the part of isolated, self-seeking individuals bound to each other solely by contractual relations (Ferdinand Tonnies and Max Weber).[23] Other formulations include the shift from mechanical to organic solidarity (Durkheim), and from a traditional subsistence economy to a self-regulating market economy (Karl Polanyi). Every major social theorist has stressed the revolutionary character of the transformation. Polanyi has described it as follows:

The industrial revolution was merely the beginning of a revolution as extreme and radical as ever inflamed the minds of sectarians, but the new creed was utterly materialistic and believed that all human problems could be resolved given an

unlimited amount of material commodities...All transactions are turned into money transactions — a market
system, self-regulating, must be allowed to function — for
the first time the natural and human substance of society
are turned into commodities. Everything is for sale and
nothing has any worth other than its market price.[24]

Nevertheless, not one of these theorists has made his central
concern the question of whether those historical events which have
involved mass population elimination in modern times are an
intrinsic rather than an accidental feature of the modernization
process. It is this author's considered opinion that both the rise
of large-scale surplus populations and the various strategies that
have been employed to eliminate them are in fact intrinsic to the
modernization process.

Population elimination programs can be of varying degrees of
severity. The least radical have involved revocation of the target
population's customary rights of land tenure, as has occurred
whenever peasants have been evicted in order to facilitate the shift
from subsistence farming to the raising of a cash crop for the
market. More radical programs have involved the segregation or
incarceration of target populations. These have taken the form
of the compulsory settlement in reservations, ghettos, almshouses,
and concentration or slave-labor camps. Even more radical
measures have involved expulsion from one's homeland. Modern
mass warfare can also have large-scale population reduction as
one of its unstated purposes, although population elimination programs are not necessarily related to the disasters of war.[25] In a
modern economy the "overproduction" of people and goods can
often be regarded as a greater threat to economic and political
stability than their destruction. Obsolescence and destruction can
form the basis of future prosperity, as indeed was the case in both
Germany and Japan after World War II. A surplus of either goods
or people can lead to mass unemployment and depression. The
most radical form of population elimination is, of course, outright extermination.

It is my conviction that both the "overproduction" of people
and programs for their elimination are an intrinsic rather than

an accidental feature of modern civilization in both capitalist and communist societies. In support of this view, a number of historical situations are examined in this book in which economic rationalization had the effect of bringing about the elimination of large numbers of people from their native communities. Some were fortunate enough to establish themselves in new communities that could absorb their energies and their skills. Others were not so fortunate. Nevertheless, their story is important to us because the conditions that led to their misfortune have not disappeared. On the contrary, from its very inception modern civilization has all too frequently found it difficult to achieve a viable fit between the number of people seeking work and the work available.

The historical situations we explore do not by any means exhaust the subject. Of necessity, much has been omitted. Nevertheless, the situations have been chosen for their relevance to an understanding of the problem of population redundancy in the present and as it is likely to confront us in the future. Little is presented that is not known to historians or to literate readers. What may be new is the perspective from which well-known facts are considered. I have attempted not so much a discovery of new material as a rereading of old material in the light of the deliberate, systematic, mass destruction of human beings by legally constituted governments in the twentieth century. In the light of the rereading I hope to demonstrate the continuity of this century's state-sponsored programs of population elimination with older, less radical programs going back to the time of England's Tudor monarchs. If we understand that all of the policies had a single objective, namely, the removal of a target population from a given community, we will see that the varying means used to attain the objective do not represent discontinuous instances of large-scale human suffering but are alternative attempts to solve a common problem, one of getting rid of people whom governments perceive to be without function or otherwise undesirable. When seen in that light all of the situations we examine can be understood as chapters of a single tragic story, the end of which is not yet before us.

Moreover, even the threat of nuclear weapons cannot be divorced from the problem of mass population redundancy. A world in which ever more millions are permanently locked out of the rewards and constraints of normal society is one in which men and women may arise whose values and actions are utterly idiosyncratic and unpredictable. Were some of their number to gain possession of nuclear weapons, a not implausible scenario, it would be impossible to predict what they might do with them. Surplus people are not necessarily people without talent or education. On the contrary, there are times when people have been rendered redundant because of their ability. Many of the most important scientists who enabled the United States to develop nuclear weapons were considered refuse and targeted for elimination by National Socialist Germany. Similarly, Palestinian Arabs are among the most highly educated of all Arabs. As contemporary terrorism demonstrates, people who have no viable place in their native communities can become exceedingly dangerous. Incidentally, one of the most potentially dangerous groups of surplus people are unemployed intellectuals who have the capacity persuasively to express their resentments against a social system which has rejected them.

The following are some of the historical situations that are relevant to our story:

THE ENCLOSURE MOVEMENT IN ENGLAND AND ITS SOCIAL CONSEQUENCES

The Acts of Enclosure in England have been called "the revolution of the rich against the poor."[26] They were a series of legal and political acts extending from the sixteenth to the nineteenth century that had the effect of consolidating uneconomic small peasant holdings by evicting large numbers of peasants from their ancient domiciles and thereby creating the basis for capitalist agriculture in England. By destroying the customary rights of the lower stratum of the English peasantry, the enclosures facilitated the transformation of the peasants into a landless agricultural and industrial proletariat whose livelihood was dependent upon the uncertain availability of wage labor in an impersonal money economy.

The enclosure movement can thus be seen as the first significant example of both the creation of a surplus population and the removal of that population from its original domicile by legal means. As such, the movement is an important part of our story and is examined in some detail.

THE FAMINE YEARS IN IRELAND, 1846–1848

The Irish famine of 1846 to 1848 was one of the greatest demographic catastrophes of the nineteenth century. The Irish lost a greater proportion of their population as a consequence of the famine than did any other nationality in modern times, save the Jews and the Armenians and, more recently, the Kampucheans. Had the famine been solely a natural disaster, there would be little reason to include it in our story. However, to this day there is debate concerning whether high British officials in charge of famine relief practiced a calculated program of genocide by withholding adequate aid and by taking administrative measures that prevented Ireland from helping itself. It is the opinion of this author that the Irish catastrophe can be seen as the outcome of an early attempt by a modern government systematically to eliminate a population it deemed undesirable. Having been indifferent to the fate of their own peasants in the enclosures, many of the same British leaders had even less concern for the fate of the peasants of a people they regarded as a conquered enemy. Moreover, the role of the British government in the Irish famine anticipates its behavior in (a) forcibly preventing Jews from escaping from Nazi-occupied Europe in order to reach a haven from extermination in Palestine and (b) refusing all measures that would have directly assisted Jewish resistance to the Holocaust in Eastern Europe. In neither the Irish nor the Jewish tragedies did the British government initiate the chain of events which led to the demographic catastrophe. However, in both cases it appears to have taken advantage of an opportunity not initially of its own making.

THE ARMENIAN GENOCIDE

The deliberate decision taken by the Turkish government during World War I to transform Turkish society by means of the systematic extermination of Turkey's Armenian Christian population anticipates the destruction of the European Jews in method, scope and intent. The homeland of the Armenians was located in a border region partly within the Russian and partly within the Turkish empires. By the beginning of the twentieth century an Armenian diaspora had developed in which the literate and linguistically competent Armenians performed roles in commerce and the professions in the urban centers of the Ottoman empire similar to those performed by the Jews in the less developed parts of Europe. As has so often been the case elsewhere, on the eve of Turkey's entrance into the modern world, commerce and the professions were largely in the hands of nonindigenous minorities, predominantly the Greeks, Jews, and Armenians. However, the Armenian role in the business and financial world of the Ottoman empire was rendered especially hazardous by the dependence of the Turkish military and bureaucratic elite upon the Armenians for credit for personal and institutional needs.[27] Where debtors are members of a weak minority, they often run the risk of being eliminated as a means of canceling the debts.

As a result of the Russo-Turkish War of 1877-1878, in which the Turks were badly beaten, Russia gained possession of three districts in Turkish Armenia. For reasons of its own Russia claimed to be the "protector" of the Christian populations of Turkey both in the Balkans and Armenia, a claim that the Turks saw as a threat to the territorial integrity of their empire. In the case of the Armenians, the situation was further aggravated by the fact that the Armenians dwelt on both sides of the Russo-Turkish border. The last Sultan of the Ottoman empire, Abdul Hamid, who reigned from 1876 to 1909, was angered by reports that some Armenians had welcomed the invading Russians during the 1877-1878 war. Abdul Hamid considered the Armenians a community whose loyalty was suspect and whose geographic location made them a danger to his declining empire.

Abdul Hamid's actions made matters worse. He systematically disarmed the Armenians while arming their hostile neighbors, the Moslem Kurds.[28] As a means of self-protection, some Armenians joined revolutionary secret societies. This development was not unwelcome to Abdul Hamid since it gave him a pretext for taking action against the Armenian population as a whole.[29] In 1894 the Kurds and regular Turkish troops began a series of attacks against the Armenians which continued for two years and culminated in three days of slaughter by Turkish mobs of between five and eight thousand Armenians in Constantinople from August 26 to 29, 1896. Unlike the slaughter in the distant provinces of Turkish Armenia, the carnage in the capital city could not be hidden. As a result of diplomatic pressure, Abdul Hamid finally issued orders ending the violence. It is estimated that in the two-year period about 300,000 Armenians were murdered.[30]

Even by twentieth-century standards, Abdul Hamid's slaughter of the Armenians was a major assault by a legally constituted state on one of its own subject-populations. By comparison, the Russian pogroms against the Jews, which started in 1881 and continued with varying degrees of intensity until 1921, were far less deadly. However, both the Armenian massacres under Abdul Hamid and the Russian pogroms achieved an important objective of their instigators: the size of the target population was materially reduced through emigration. Although some Armenians emigrated to North America, more entered Russia. As Jews were terrorized into leaving Russia in large numbers, a smaller but influential group of Armenians were seeking refuge in that country.

In 1908 the modernizing and seemingly progressive Young Turks overthrew Abdul Hamid's corrupt and backward regime. In the ensuing revolutionary enthusiasm, most Armenians made an understandable but deadly miscalculation. Unlike the empire's other Christian minorities, they welcomed the new regime. They mistakenly assumed that the overthrow of a corrupt and inefficient government by one that was less corrupt and more rational augured well for their own community. They could not foresee that the Young Turks, many of whom had been trained in European universities, were speedily to prove even less tolerant of diversity and infinitely more efficient and murderous than the old regime. Whereas Abdul Hamid was content to murder and terrorize the Armenians in large-scale pogroms, the Young Turks planned and executed a systematic program of outright genocide using the power of the state and the cover of war to kill the largest number of people with least effort and least visibility. One of the many documents in which the objective of the Turkish government was frankly spelled out was a telegram dated September 15, 1915, to the Police Office of Aleppo from Taalat Bey, a member of the ruling triumvirate:

> It has already been reported that by the order of the Committee [of Union and Progress] the Government has determined completely to exterminate the Armenians living in Turkey. Those who refuse to obey this order cannot be regarded as friends of the Government. Regardless of the women, children or invalids, and however deplorable the methods of destruction may seem an end is to be put to their existence [i.e., the Armenians] without paying any heed to feeling or conscience.
> Minister for the Interior,
Taalat.[31]

One can easily imagine Heinrich Himmler sending a letter similar in spirit and tone to his subordinates in the SS.

Actual genocide began in April 1915 with the rounding up and deportation of Armenian men in one Armenian population center after another. Like many Jews in World War II, the Armenians were at first deceived into thinking they were being mobilized for wartime labor service. The men were usually imprisoned for several days, after which they were marched out of town and massacred. Later women, children, and older men were also deported. The violence done to the women often involved rape and mutilation. In June 1915, the government began to use the railroads to expedite deportation and extermination. Freight cars were used to carry thousands of persons to remote areas where they were left to starve to death while being assaulted by the ravages of nature and human malice. Many were, of course, murdered outright. The Armenian deportees were among the first men and women in the twentieth century to learn that human rights are inseparable from political status. Having been effectively deprived of political status by their own government, there was no abuse that could not with impunity be inflicted upon them.

The extermination operation was thoroughly modern in spirit and implementation from the initial planning stage to its execution.[32] Mass extermination was advocated in the planning sessions as the appropriate "scientific" response to the universal struggle of the races for survival.[33] This type of Social Darwinist legitimation for genocide was to be used by the National Socialists in World War II. The operation was meticulously planned. The government counted on the inability of the British, who had just withdrawn from Gallipoli after suffering 213,980 casualties in battle, to frustrate their plan. As a wartime ally of imperial Germany, the Turks knew there would be no interference from that quarter. Quite the contrary: the Turkish army and much of the bureaucracy had been trained by the Germans. Without the organizational skills gained from the training, it is doubtful that the Turks could have been as efficient as they were. Above all, the Young Turks had a reliable, centralized bureaucratic network. Taalat Bey did not entrust the assignment to old-fashioned provincial bureaucrats. Instead he sent out Young Turk officials to act as his personal representatives and, when necessary, to punish governors and local bureaucrats who, for reasons of greed or compassion, failed to carry out orders. There was even a special organization with responsibility for organizing the massacres. At the local level, there were death squads who were given the name of "Butcher Battalions."[34]

One of the most comprehensive reports ever written on the subject of the Armenian genocide is that which Viscount James Bryce assembled in 1916 in partnership with the historian Arnold Toynbee. Bryce concluded his report with an observation concerning the slaughter: "It was a deliberate, systematic attempt to eradicate the Armenian population throughout the Ottoman Empire and it has certainly met with a very large measure of success."[35]

The destruction of the European Jews had yet to take place

when Viscount Bryce wrote. The Turks had introduced a new dimension in the way a modern government could treat an unwanted minority, but the full power of the state to dispose of its citizens had yet to be revealed. In 1975 Michael Arlen, a writer of Armenian extraction, wrote about the slaughter of his people from the perspective of the accumulated mass violence of the twentieth century, called by Arlen "a Lear among centuries." Arlen commented: "There is every reason to believe that this harnessing of modern technology to political mass murder began with the instance of the Turks and the Armenians."[36] The Turkish government had successfully used its wartime control of communication and transportation to murder more than 1,000,000 of its Armenian citizens. The Armenian population was reduced to about half of its prewar size.

The Armenian genocide can also be seen as a cold-blooded step taken by the Turkish government as part of its program of national modernization. Modernization has often involved homogenization, which governments have sought to achieve through centralized uniform compulsory education and the segregation, expulsion, or extermination of those groups that do not fit in. In his celebrated essay on bureaucracy, in which he identified bureaucratization as a crucial aspect of the rationalization of modern society, Weber also observed that one of the most important social consequences of bureaucracy is a tendency toward the "leveling" of the population:

> Bureaucratic organization has usually come into power on the basis of a leveling of economic and social differences... Bureaucracy inevitably accompanies mass democracy, in contrast to the democratic self-government of small homogenous units: This results from its characteristic principle: the abstract regularity of the exercise of authority, which is the result of the demand for "equality before the law" in the personal and functional sense — hence, of the horror of "privilege," and the principled rejection of doing business from case to case.[37]

The political behavior of the Young Turks exemplifies Weber's observations. Before coming to power, the Young Turks offered a democratic program calling for equality before the law of all Turkish citizens, religious toleration, abolition of caste privileges, equal obligation of all citizens to perform military service, and genuine representative government. Shortly after coming to power, the Young Turk regime extended the military service obligation to Armenians, an obligation the Armenians initially welcomed. Given the "progressive" Young Turk program, the initial reaction of most minority groups to the new regime was favorable, at least on the surface. However, it was soon apparent that there were fundamental conflicts of interest between the Young Turks and the minority communities. Turkey had traditionally been ruled by the Millet system, by which each ethnic and religious group was assured that it could govern its internal affairs in accordance with its own traditions. This gave the minorities a large measure of autonomy and guaranteed the preservation of their ethnic and religious traditions. The Millet system was, however, fundamentally incompatible with the "Ottomanization" basic to the Young Turk program. The Young Turks aimed at the eventual integration of all the empire's ethnic entities in one homogenous Turkish nation. To that end they sought to make Turkish the compulsory medium of instruction in secondary education. They also declared Turkish the official language of business and commerce. Both measures were extremely difficult to maintain. Most secondary schools were American, Greek, or Armenian; most commerce was in non-Turkish hands.[38]

For the Young Turks democratization meant homogenization, whereas the minorities, especially the Armenians, took it to mean both the promise of equal opportunity and the retention of their distinctive identities. The minorities could only find a viable place within the empire if provision were made for their cultural, linguistic, and religious differences. Apparently, they did not understand that cultural pluralism runs counter to political rationalization, which, like all rationalization, is governed by the principle of "least effort." At the very least, continued maintenance of the Millet system would vastly complicate the work of the state bureaucracy.

The Young Turks' preference for democratic homogenization

was intensified by the Turkish defeat in the Balkan War of 1912. During the postwar peace negotiations, the Armenians sought guarantees from the European powers for their political status and their cultural and religious autonomy. The move infuriated the Turks. Support for the guarantees came principally from Russia, Turkey's neighbor and hereditary adversary. The guarantees were accepted pro forma by a defeated Turkey. However, as soon as World War I broke out, the Turks denounced the concessions. The Armenians then found themselves in a worse position than would have been the case had there been no foreign intervention on their behalf. Because of their commitment to national homogenization, the Young Turks were doubly resentful of the attempt to impose guarantees of minority autonomy upon them. They regarded the Armenians as disloyal and prone to seek the aid of Turkey's enemies. The Turks had no reason to believe that a victorious Russia would permit the Armenian homeland, part of which lay in Russia and part in Turkey, to remain an integral part of the Turkish empire. Moreover, loss of Turkish Armenia would have posed a far greater threat to national security than had the loss of the Balkans. If Russia gained control of Turkish Armenia, there would be few natural barriers between the Russians and the Turkish heartland or the Arabian peninsula. Russia's historic drive to control the Dardanelles would then be realizable.

Strategically, the Turks saw their problem as one of retaining territorial control over Armenia while eliminating a population that was regarded as a potential fifth column. The Armenians became a surplus people because of their geographic rather than their social location, although as modernization continued, the Armenians might well have been endangered by the rise of an indigenous Turkish middle and professional class. Moreover, it was a matter of indifference to the Turkish leaders that the vast majority of the Armenians were in no sense a threat. The Turks believed that this Christian border people could not be integrated within a homogenized Moslem nation. Since integration was impossible, the Young Turks planned to eliminate them. When Taalat Bey, Minister of the Interior and one of the chief architects of the massacres, was queried by a reporter from the *Berliner*

Tageblatt concerning the fact that innocent women and children were being slaughtered, he replied: "We have been reproached that we make no distinction between innocent Armenians and the guilty; but that is utterly impossible in view of the fact that those who are innocent today might be guilty tomorrow."[39]

Those who are innocent today might be guilty tomorrow... A similar rationale has been used wherever governments have embarked upon a program of riddance of "objective enemies." Moreover, the decision to eliminate potential as well as actual enemies has a kind of macabre rationality about it. A government leader about to embark on a program of massacre might very well reason: "Why gamble? Let us do away with the enemy once and for all while we have the chance." In actuality, this was precisely the reasoning employed by the Young Turks. The Armenians were slaughtered not for what they did but for what the Turks suspected some of them might do in the future.

THE RATIONALIZATION OF AGRICULTURE IN THE SOVIET UNION AND SOME WESTERN PARALLELS

Although the genocidal policies of Hitler's Germany are well known in the United States, the number of people murdered by the National Socialist regime is dwarfed by the number killed in the Soviet Union since the Russian Revolution, especially but by no means exclusively under Stalin. It is conservatively estimated that in the great political purges of the nineteen-thirties, the forced collectivization of Soviet agriculture, the deportations and massacres of "unreliable" nationalities, ethnic groups and former Russian prisoners of war, the abusive slave labor camps, the squandering of life in excess of all requirements of military necessity during World War II, and the persecution of intellectuals, religious believers (Jewish, Christian, Moslem and Buddhist), and other dissidents, no less than 80,000,000 Soviet citizens lost their lives as a consequence of the policies of their own government. No other state in history has ever initiated policies designed to eliminate so many of its own citizens as has the Soviet Union.[40]

Moreover, almost every responsible attempt to estimate the number of people whose deaths can be attributed to the actions of the Soviet state has erred on the conservative side. A particularly graphic example of the heedless waste of human life by Soviet authorities can be seen in the technique reported to have been used by the Russians to clear minefields during World War II. With machine guns behind them, labor battalions consisting of men and women were driven over German minefields. Their exploding bodies became human minesweepers. When the British offered the Russians modern minesweeping equipment, the Soviet chief of military procurement in London is reported to have responded without embarrassment, "We use people for that."[41] During World War II the Germans lost about 2,500,000 men on the Eastern Front. It is now estimated that between 30 and 32,000,000 Soviet citizens lost their lives during World War II. Even if 10 to 15,000,000 were killed by the Germans, an exceedingly high kill ratio, it is difficult to avoid the conclusion that far more Soviet citizens were killed as a result of the actions of their own government than those of the enemy.[42] To take but one example, Stalin held that all Soviet prisoners in Germany were traitors.[43] Solzhenitsyn was a prisoner of war in Germany and was treated as a traitor when he returned home. He was more fortunate than most returning Russian prisoners of war. Imprisoned and deported, he at least survived to tell the tale.

Although there is much to be learned from the terrible history of the Soviet Union, for our purpose it will suffice to take note of Stalin's attempt to compel the collectivization of Soviet agriculture. In 1930 Joseph Stalin initiated a program that had as its goal the sudden and total collectivization of the Soviet Union's peasant holdings. Stalin understood that, as long as agriculture remained in the hands of 25,000,000 inefficient producers, it would be impossible to create a modern industrial economy. He believed such an economy required centralized control over agricultural production, enhanced productivity, and the achievement of economies of scale through consolidation and the use of modern agricultural techniques. Moreover, an industrialized economy would require an enlarged working force that could only come from rural workers whose services had been rendered redundant by the consolidation, collectivization, and modernization of agriculture. In order to achieve his objective, Stalin was willing to sacrifice the lives of millions of Russians. Those who stood in the way of "progress" were regarded as class enemies who deserved to be liquidated. Neither he nor his followers had any moral qualms about the slaughter. "Class enemies" were not regarded as part of the same moral community. Their murder was legitimated by Stalin's reading of Marxist ideology.

Stalin rejected the kind of gradual approach that would have involved encouraging both the more efficient peasants and the kulaks, that is, "rich" peasants whose holdings required them to hire seasonal workers, to squeeze out less efficient producers. This was the path of development taken in most Western countries, but Stalin feared such a policy would create a rural bourgeoisie that could eventually become the center of strong opposition to the Communist Party. Stalin was determined to enter upon a state-sponsored program of class warfare of absolutely unprecedented magnitude. Its purpose was in his words "the liquidation of the kulaks as a class."[44]

Stalin's program involved the forcible seizure of the property of millions of Russian peasants. Five months after it began, over half of all peasant households had been collectivized. Millions of peasants resisted violently and killed their own livestock rather than permit them to become state property. A man-made famine, the first of a series, ensued which compelled Stalin to retreat temporarily. Nevertheless, by 1932 he had broken the back of his country's peasantry.[45] During World War II Stalin admitted to Churchill that 10,000,000 peasants had to be "dealt with" in the crisis and that "the great bulk" had been "wiped out."[46] As Solzhenitsyn has pointed out, millions of peasant families were uprooted from their holdings and condemned to death, enforced proletarianization, or abusive slave labor. Stalin had achieved his objective. The kulaks, and millions of less prosperous peasants, had been liquidated "as a class." It is now estimated that 22,000,000 died as a result of Stalin's attempt to collectivize Soviet agriculture.[47]

If one ignores the monumental brutality and inhumanity of Stalin's policies, admittedly an exceedingly difficult mental exercise, the forced collectivization, deportations, and mass murder can be seen as an administrative attempt rapidly and forcibly to rationalize Russian agriculture. The transformation of Russia from a country with a primitive agrarian economy, consisting of more than 25,000,000 inefficient peasant landholders, into a modern, industrialized superpower involved extraordinary changes in every aspect of Russian society. The economic and social transformations that brought England, Germany, and the United States into the modern world took place over a far longer period than in the U.S.S.R. Moreover, they were not brought about by resort to the kind of draconian police terror employed in Russia. Nevertheless, even in the West agricultural modernization was accompanied by vast social, political, and demographic dislocations. Indeed, this has been the case all over the world.

In the United States, the rationalization of agriculture was greatly expedited by the New Deal and subsequent federal administrations. The federal government instituted measures that favored large-scale agribusiness at the expense of less efficient small farmers and sharecroppers. The motivation for the federal policies was similar to that which led to the enclosures in England and agricultural collectivization in Soviet Russia. In each case, the measures taken or encouraged by the state had as their objective the achievement of economies of scale and enhanced productivity. Usually, the policies have also led to the formation of a dislocated rural surplus population whose fate varied from country to country.

In America, the impoverished blacks of the rural South were among those hardest hit by agricultural modernization. As they became superfluous to the increasingly rationalized agricultural economy, they drifted to urban centers in search of work.[48] Although migration and urbanization brought prosperity to some blacks, a significant number became part of a permanent corps of unemployed dependent for their survival on public assistance or what has been called the "underground economy."[49]

In the Soviet Union, ideology, police terror and mass murder were systematically employed to bring about agricultural modernization; in the United States modernization was brought about more gradually through economic coercion and impersonal administrative policy. America embarked upon modernization under conditions of comparative civic tranquillity and with an abundant food supply; Russia did so under conditions of acute material scarcity almost immediately after the worst civil disorders in its entire history. In Russia there was no food surplus with which a surplus population could be maintained, especially after the man-made famines that were the result of Stalin's attempts at collectivization.

To date, America's method of coping with its surplus population has been more in keeping with what can justly be called a commitment to humanitarian values, but we do not know how the United States or any other large, relatively democratic country might act under conditions of pressing material scarcity or an extended economic depression. There is, however, one respect in which the American and the Soviet experiences with surplus people are comparable. Unlike the surplus populations of nineteenth-century England, Ireland, Germany, Italy, and eastern Europe, the surplus populations of the United States and the Soviet Union have no new worlds to which they might emigrate in search of a better life.

Moreover, as America sought to cope with the problems arising out of the surplus population of its own rural areas, it was confronted with a monumental new wave of immigrants, some "legal" others "illegal," from Puerto Rico, Mexico, Cuba, Haiti, and other parts of Latin America. Many of the poorer Latin American immigrants were able to find work, often by displacing American workers who could not subsist on the wages offered for "piece work" in agriculture and light industry. When, for example, "illegal" Mexican immigrants are employed in agriculture, it is often as migrant laborers working on an hourly basis. Such precisely calculated employment constitutes an extreme form of labor rationalization. The workers share no common community with their employers. Since their contract is calculated on the basis of the shortest span of time the law permits, it is possible for the employer to determine labor costs with considerable precision and without becoming involved in more than an absolute minimum of responsibility for the employees. The relationship between worker and employer can thus be completely depersonalized and the "cash nexus" becomes the only bond between them. Often even the "cash nexus" disappears and the bond between employer and employee is reduced to threats of death or deportation. Thousands of "illegal aliens" have been forced into virtual slavery by employers who take cruel advantage of their lack of legal status.[50]

Apart from peonage, extreme depersonalization can also be furthered by the fact that employer, supervisory staff and laborers usually do not share the same religious or ethnic background. Even when employers and intermediate supervisory staff share a common background, they seldom go to the same church or share a common culture. One of the paradoxical effects of American religious freedom is the contribution it makes to the breakdown of community between rich and poor and between labor and capital. Religious voluntarism fosters denominationalism and sectarianism along class and ethnic lines.[51] This in turn facilitates both depersonalization and a cold form of economic rationalization. In the old manufacturing towns of the Northeast and the agribusinesses of the Southwest, labor is likely to be Catholic and capital Protestant. In the South, where capital and labor are usually both Protestant, employee and employer seldom go to the same church.[52]

Many employers actually prefer to use "illegal" aliens. At the beginning of the Industrial Revolution mobility of labor was deemed necessary so that a work force would be available when, where, and only as long as needed. However, as citizens, the mobile workers enjoyed some of the same political rights as their employers. By contrast, contemporary "illegal" aliens lack many of the political rights native-born workers can assert. They can be deported whenever their status is "discovered" by the Immigration and Naturalization Service. Their lack of status adds another grim element of rationality to the mobility of labor. The "illegal" immigrant's worldlessness, his lack of a legally viable place in the community in which he or she labors, constitutes the final assurance of the impersonality and rationality of the relationship between employer and worker.

The preference in some sectors of the American economy for alien rather than native workers has at least one well-known historical precedent. In the eighteen-nineties, Prussian landlords tended to prefer Polish seasonal workers to more expensive German agrarian workers who expected an annual contract and claimed many customary privileges rooted in feudalism. The landowners found it more cost-effective and "rational" to hire Poland's human surplus while German peasants departed for the cities or emigrated to North America.[53]

Partisans of the left have frequently argued that the problem of surplus population is endemic to capitalism and would ultimately be solved under a humane version of socialism. Since socialist countries as diverse as the Soviet Union, Kampuchea under Pol Pot, and the Socialist Republic of Vietnam have attempted to "solve" the problem by programs designed to eliminate the human surplus, it would appear that the problem of surplus people arises wherever the economy or society is modernized, whether under capitalism or socialism.

THE DESTRUCTION OF EUROPE'S JEWS

Although the Jews have lived in Europe as an alien presence subject to attacks of varying intensity for almost two thousand years, it was not until the latter part of the nineteenth century that anti-Semitism became an important issue in the political arena. Moreover, it was not until the twentieth century that a mass political party was able to make the elimination of the Jews a central element in its platform. The movement of the Jewish question from the periphery to the center of the European political arena coincided with the transformation of Jews from an economically complimentary to an economically competitive group within the larger community. It was the overwhelming misfortune of the Jews of most European countries that in the late nineteenth and twentieth centuries they increasingly found themselves in the untenable situation of being competitors of the indigenous lower middle class, perhaps the most insecure of all of the social classes. It was among the lower middle-class sector that radical political anti-Semitism had its most enthusiastic support.

Consisting largely of artisans and small commercial proprietors, members of the lower middle class tended to be victims rather than beneficiaries of modernization. It was exceedingly difficult, if not impossible, for undercapitalized artisans and small proprietors to compete successfully with well-financed capitalist enterprise. The lower middle class was constantly threatened with proletarianization and, in hard times, with unemployment. Whatever other reasons there may have been for the success of political anti-Semitism in bringing about the extermination of Europe's Jews, and there were many, the determination of a politically active sector of the indigenous middle class to eliminate a competing group that was regarded as alien to both the national cultural and religious consensus cannot be underestimated.

As we shall see, the Jews of Europe became a surplus population not so much because they were unemployed but because they were competitors of a group that feared its own downward mobility and unemployment. This is obviously not the whole story, but it is a part of the story that is often overlooked in accounts of the destruction of the European Jews.

One of the most important ways in which Jews were negatively affected by modernization was the manner of their extermination. I discuss that issue at length in another book to which the current work is the sequel.[54] Suffice it to say in the present context that bureaucratic and technological rationalization made it possible for the Germans to do away with as many as 10,000 people a day at a single death factory while reducing to a minimum the negative psychological effects on their own personnel. Just as modernization resulted in increased efficiency as well as economies of scale in agriculture, industry and marketing, so too unprecedented efficiency and economy were achieved in the ability to kill. Unfortunately, genocide is as much an expression of the rationalization of the economy and society as any other bureaucratically managed, assembly-line operation. It is, however, of the utmost importance that we understand that to speak of the rationality of genocide is by no means to regard the phenomenon in a positive light. On the contrary, it is to raise urgent questions concerning the long-range consequences of modernization and rationalization both in our own times and for the future.

SURPLUS PEOPLE
IN THE CONTEMPORARY WORLD

At present, the problem of surplus people shows no sign of abating. Sooner or later the current wave of unemployment will subside and government economists will declare the downturn at an end. However, if recent experience offers any guidance, the rebound will probably leave a greater proportion of the labor force without work than any previous postwar "recovery." It is, for example, highly unlikely that the American automobile industry will be able to reemploy all of the workers who have been "laid off" even were automobile production to return to its prerecession levels. The industry has no choice but to attempt to catch up with the rate of productivity per worker of the Japanese automobile industry, the most intensely automated industry of its kind in the world.[55] Moreover, computerized robot technology is as yet in its infancy. The microprocessor promises labor-saving automation of unprecedented precision, accuracy, and sophistication in the factory, the office, and the home.[56] The rationalization of production which has taken place since the inception of the Industrial Revolution is only the beginning of a development that threatens far more explosive social and economic dislocations than any we have yet experienced. One major American corporation, General Electric, has formulated the options confronting American business: *automate, emigrate,* or *evaporate.*[57] No one can foretell the full social consequences of the microprocessor revolution, but there is little reason to doubt, if current work schedules continue to be regarded as normal, unemployment may reach far more dangerous levels than even those of the Great Depression. Without rethinking its fundamental values, an automated, computerized society cannot escape unprecedented levels of population superfluity.

We are in the midst of a technological revolution which radically accelerates the pace of the revolution of rationality characterizing the entire modern period. Computerized technology threatens to render ever larger numbers of American workers unemployed at a time when a more primitive expression of the same revolution of rationality is in the process of depriving millions of Latin America's exploding population of work opportunities in their native communities. As noted, many of these people attempt to enter the United States in the hope of finding work they can no longer find at home. To take but one example of the demographic time bomb threatening American society: in 1980 the population of Mexico City, then the world's third largest city, was 15,000,000 and half of all Mexicans were under fifteen. If present trends continue, the population of Mexico City will be 31,000,000 in the year 2000. Mexico City will then be the world's largest city.[58]

Americans tend to identify high rates of unemployment with hard times and low rates with good times. Undoubtedly, employment rises in good times and falls in bad. Unfortunately, in the future, unemployment is likely to rise both in good times and in bad unless there is some drastic rethinking of the problem of work and, perhaps, the distribution of resources.

In the past, migration alleviated the problem of population redundancy. Nevertheless, Europe was seldom able to absorb its own surplus. Only the fortunate availability of the New World gave Europe's surplus the promise of a new beginning. From 1740 to 1914 the total number of people of European stock increased from about 120,000,000 to 718,000,000. As Europe industrialized, out-migration accelerated. Thus, from 1800 to 1840 between 30,000 and 40,000 people departed annually from Europe, a total of 1,500,000. In the eighteen-forties annual emigration increased to between 200,000 and 300,000. The increase was facilitated by the development of cheap and rapid transportation. It also reflected both the extraordinary population growth and the social dislocations that were taking place in Europe. Between 1841 and 1880, about 13,000,000 people left Europe. Between 1875 and

1880 there was an average annual emigration of 280,000 persons; between 1880 and 1885 the figure was 685,000; between 1885 and 1890 the annual average was 730,000. In the peak year of 1910 2,000,000 left Europe! Between 1871 and 1914 almost 35,000,000 people emigrated, mostly to the United States. Of that number about 24,000,000 became permanent settlers.[59]

Any civilization that loses as many people as Europe did between the end of the Napoleonic Wars and the beginning of World War I is a civilization in crisis. However, the crisis was somewhat disguised by the fact that there were vast areas of the earth available for European settlement and that Europeans and people of European origin enjoyed an absolute technological superiority over non-European peoples until the beginning of the twentieth century. This enabled Europe's surplus human beings: (1) to expand over very large areas of the earth with minimal resistance from the indigenous populations; (2) exploitatively to dominate most of the non-European peoples of the world, utilizing their labor and natural resources under conditions extremely favorable to the Europeans; (3) to create and maintain an industrial and technological civilization in which most of the non-European peoples were customers rather than competitors. These developments permitted a far greater expansion of the economies of the European peoples than would have been the case had all of the peoples of the world entered the technological age simultaneously. Europe's technological headstart also permitted the absorption of more Europeans in the work force than would otherwise have been the case.

Nevertheless, in spite of the never-to-be repeated advantages enjoyed by the European peoples, Europe was unable to escape the extraordinary social dislocations of two world wars, the Russian Revolution, and the smaller colonial wars. As we have noted, 2,000,000 people left Europe in the peak year of 1910, only four years before the beginning of World War I. When that war began, Europe exchanged one way of getting rid of people for another. To paraphrase Clausewitz, the wars of this century can be seen as a continuation of population elimination "by other means." In excess of 100,000,000 people have been killed by human violence in the wars and revolutions of the twentieth century, a disproportionately large proportion being European.[60] Moreover, these social dislocations led Europeans to establish some of the most radical and murderous political systems the world has ever known, National Socialism and Stalinist bolshevism. Only the pressure of extreme crisis could have permitted societies such as Germany and Russia to submit to regimes as radical as those of Hitler and Stalin.

Unfortunately, the problem of population redundancy that plagued industrializing Europe for so long is now plaguing most of the developing and developed nations of the world alike. And the world today is a very different place from what it was even a decade ago. The peoples of European origin are no longer technologically superior to non-European peoples, especially the peoples of the Orient. For the past two centuries, the peoples of European origin were numerically inferior but technologically superior to the peoples of the East. Within the foreseeable future, the peoples of the Orient are likely to enjoy both numerical and technological superiority. At present Japanese technology is more or less the equal of that of any nation in the world. If Japan's mammoth investment in advanced computer technology pays off, it may shortly become the world's most technologically advanced nation. Nor are the Japanese the only Asian people who are transforming themselves into an advanced technological civilization. Ten "newly industrializing countries" have been identified by the Organization for Economic Cooperation and Development (OECD) as possessing a growing capacity to compete with the so-called "developed" nations. The list contains only four countries with non-European cultural origins: the Republic of Korea (South Korea), the Republic of China (Taiwan), Singapore, and Hong Kong. With a total of approximately 58,000,000 people, these four have a share of the world's manufactured exports that is one-third higher than that of the other six nations on the OECD list: Brazil, Mexico, Spain, Portugal, Greece and Yugoslavia. These have a population of about 247,000,000. Moreover, the growth rate of the Asian communities is far higher than their rivals', all of whom have European cultural roots.[61]

Clearly, the countries of noncommunist Asia have demonstrated a phenomenal capacity to compete with the West in developing a type of civilization that was originally endogenic to the West and exogenic to Asia. This is a fact of awesome significance for the future of the world, especially when one considers the long-range economic and technological potentialities of the People's Republic of China. Is there any reason to believe that the mainland Chinese are fated to be irreversibly committed for all time to an ideology that, whatever it may promise, limits that nation's growth and productivity? Between 1960 and 1977 the average annual growth rates of the Gross National Product of both the People's Republic of China and the Democratic Peoples Republic of Korea (North Korea) exceeded that of all other communist countries save Romania.[62] Is there any reason to believe that were the people of the mainland to adopt a more flexible economic and political system they would prove less capable of industrial and technological development than have the other nations of Asia? Can we begin to contemplate how the world might be transformed were the billion people of mainland China to achieve a level of productivity that begins to approach Japan's?

Even to ask such questions must give us pause. The transformations they imply in the economic, social, political and cultural relations of the major world communities would constitute a revolution of world-historical proportions. No person would remain unaffected. Moreover, most world-historical revolutions have been accompanied by large-scale demographic violence. As we contemplate the ongoing technological transformation of post-Confucian Asia, we earnestly hope that such a transformation can be achieved without bloodshed. Unfortunately, the historical record does not offer solid assurance that such hopes can be fulfilled.

Whatever the outcome of the ongoing technological transformation of Asia, there is a sense in which the peoples of European origin have reached an impasse in their attempts to solve the problem of population redundancy by exporting it, a strategy that even the United States pursued as long as its frontier moved westward. The technological revolution is in the process of becoming universal. As it does, manufactured goods made in such countries as South Korea and Singapore compete successfully in the world market with Japanese, European, and North American products. Even today, Korean-made automobiles are beginning to compete in parts of the Middle East and Latin America and Taiwan has initiated steps to produce automobiles for export to the United States, Europe, and Japan.[63]

It is one of the supreme tragedies of the twentieth century that, more than any other political leader of his time, Adolf Hitler understood the time had come, or would soon come, when Europe would no longer be able to solve its problem of surplus people by emigration. Hitler's "solution" included genocide and wars of enslavement and extermination. He also had as little compunction about eliminating those Germans he considered superfluous as he did Jews, a fact demonstrated by his "euthanasia" program.[64] Moreover, his "solution" was "rational" in the narrowly defined sense in which we use the term, namely, the most efficient, economical and morally neutral method of solving a "problem."[65] As such, genocide represents the ultimate expression of the revolution of rationality with which the problem of population redundancy began in the first place. Given the strictly formal nature of instrumental rationality, given further its indifference to moral values, it is unfortunately possible to imagine plausible scenarios in which, in a time of acute social stress, decision-makers in a desacralized society conclude that genocide is the most rational means of "solving" the problem of surplus people.[66] Put differently, as long as impersonal, value-free, cost-benefit calculations form the basis of large-scale decision-making by anonymous state functionaries, there may come a time when the functionaries may conclude that the "benefits" of a program of mass population elimination outweigh the "costs." Such reflections may appear extreme at first glance. Let us, however, remember that more than 100,000,000 people have perished through human violence in this century. The apocalypse is not a future event conjured up by paranoids and religious fanatics. It has already happened to millions.

In view of the mass extermination inflicted on human beings by governments as diverse as the Third Reich, the Soviet Union,

Turkey under the Young Turks, and Kampuchea under the Khmer Rouge, no person can be certain that the world has witnessed the last of such horrors. However, at least in warfare and weapon making, practical reason may have reached its limits. Mass destruction only makes sense to a warring power if it can survive as a viable society. Nuclear warfare renders such an outcome uncertain. Moreover, just as technological competence is in the process of becoming universalized, so too the ability to acquire if not to construct nuclear weapons is in the process of being universalized. Hence, scenarios involving the solution of the problem of surplus people through wars of extermination seem less credible than they did before the end of World War II. Any large-scale war now entails the very real possibility that nuclear weapons could terminate all life on earth, if not as a direct result of the initial assaults on population centers then as a result of the predictable aftereffects.[67]

Our current difficulties can best be described as having an "end-of-the-road" character to them and there no longer is any easy way out. The social and demographic problems confronting us are cumulative. It is no exaggeration to say that they have been gathering for centuries. They are not the result of some relatively short-term economic crisis that can be solved by applying appropriate fiscal policy or by the self-correcting movement of the business cycle. In the past we could manage things by changing our locations. If we are to survive we have only the option of changing ourselves.

2

THE ENCLOSURE MOVEMENT IN ENGLAND AND ITS SOCIAL CONSEQUENCES
The Tudor Period

THE ENCLOSURE MOVEMENT in England was one of the earliest and most enduring attempts on the part of a state to use its legal and administrative power to effect the involuntary removal of large numbers of its subjects from their native habitations and way of life.[1] As such, the enclosures can also be seen as one of the earliest large-scale programs of population elimination in modern times. Moreover, there is, as we shall see, a thread of continuity linking the English program of population elimination that deprived hundreds of thousands, if not millions, of peasants of their homes and the more radical state-sponsored programs of the twentieth century which have removed target populations from the human world altogether. Most of the facts we cite are well known. Their significance has been debated by economists, sociologists and political scientists for a very long time. Nevertheless, in the light of the demographic violence of the twentieth century, the facts may take on an altered, perhaps even a sinister, meaning that they could not have had before the age of the Gulags and the death camps.

The act of enclosing consisted in the marking-off of land with a fence or a boundary, frequently a hedge or a poling. A

Parliamentary Act of Enclosure was normally a private act, that is, an act on behalf of a private person, authorizing the "enclosure" of common land in a particular location. Such Acts had the legal effect of extinguishing common rights and converting common land, or in some cases land encumbered with the right of private use, into private property that was at the exclusive disposal of its owner.[2] As early as the Statutes of Merton (1235) and Westminster (1285), manorial lords were empowered to enclose portions of the adjacent wasteland, land outside the manor not yet brought into cultivation, provided such land was needed by the lord's free tenants.[3] Before the Tudors, enclosures did not as a rule create severe social problems. The movement with which we are concerned did. It consisted of a series of actions initiated by the English landowning class from the beginning of the sixteenth to the middle of the nineteenth century that resulted in the conversion of common arable fields, pastureland, and meadow into the exclusive private property of the lord of the manor.

Peasants who possessed no documented right of tenancy were in the worst position. And, in an age in which literacy was sparsely distributed, there were many such peasants. After their holdings had been enclosed, they were subject to summary eviction with little or no compensation.[4] Over the years, hundreds of thousands of commoners, who had been born into a world in which they had "a share and a place," were compelled to abandon their homes and become landless laborers.

Still, the story has two sides. The enclosures have been defended by a number of both conservative and Marxist writers on English land policy.[5] In spite of the fact that the enclosures brought about the destruction of the English peasant class, the movement laid the foundations for the modernization and rationalization of British agriculture. Thus, in addition to anticipating the state-sponsored programs for the elimination of surplus people of our own age, the enclosures can also be seen as the forerunner of a worldwide movement toward the weeding out of uneconomic peasant holdings, their consolidation into cost-effective larger units, and the transformation of the majority of the world's peasants into a propertyless mass wholly dependent upon wage labor in an insecure and brutally impersonal money economy. It would, however, be a serious mistake to regard the loss of economic security as the most important deprivation experienced by the dispossessed peasants. Their loss of status was part of a more generalized loss of social, cultural, ethical and religious moorings that everywhere accompanied the passing of traditional society. According to the English historian W. E. Tate, the enclosures originated in the dissatisfaction of the manorial lords with the "rigid and inelastic" open-field system that prevented them from exacting the best return from their land.[6] The open-field system itself dates back to the time when the land was originally brought into cultivation before the idea of private property had fully developed. Since the entire community had participated in the work of clearing, all members were regarded as entitled to a share in the land.[7] However, by the time of the Tudor enclosures, English legal theory had come to regard the property of the village as belonging to the lord of the manor. It also regarded the peasant landholders as his tenants. Some contemporary historians believe the theory to have been erroneous.[8] Whatever its factual status, the theory was to have awesome historical consequences because it provided the legal basis for both the enclosures and the wholesale eviction of entire villages.

The original open-field village was in Tate's words "a self-contained social and economic unit based on production for subsistence not for the market."[9] In addition to arable land, the peasant landholders needed pastureland for summer grazing and meadow for the production of hay in the winter. Before the introduction of artificial phosphates, meadowland was limited and it was impossible to create new meadow. Hence, the meadow was considered too valuable to be the private possession of any single individual. By custom, every person had the right to its use in proportion to his holdings of arable land.[10]

The arable land itself was originally divided into two or three large fields to facilitate crop rotation. These fields were divided into furlongs, which were further subdivided into long narrow strips known as selions. Originally, most peasants had the right to an equal number of strips, but in the course of time some peasant families acquired more land than others.[11]

Peasant landholders were roughly divided into three categories: freeholders, leaseholders, and customary tenants. Freeholders possessed the strongest claim to their holdings since the terms of their tenancy were documented and could not be unilaterally altered by the landlord. Leaseholders had a weaker claim. Their terms of occupancy could not be altered for the duration of the lease, which sometimes extended for as long as "three lives," but when the lease expired the landlord was free to set his own terms or to refuse to renew altogether. Customary tenants were both the largest and the most vulnerable group. Some customary tenants were also copyholders, which meant that they held their rights as tenants by virtue of a copy of the court roll. Their rights were thus documented. However, the claims of most customary tenants were based on immemorial custom rather than legal documentation. Although copyholders had some legal protection, it was seldom strong enough to prevent a determined landowner from evicting them. Save for squatters, undocumented customary tenants were in the worst position of all peasant landholders.[12]

Under the open-field system, all work had to be communally organized. The same crops had to be grown in adjacent selions at the same time and, after the harvest, the fields were thrown open for common pasture. Plowing, sowing and harvesting all had to be synchronized. Without such cooperation the system would have collapsed. This system proved viable as long as cultivation was primarily for subsistence. It ceased to be viable when profit-making displaced subsistence as the fundamental motive for agriculture. *The enclosure movement thus marks the beginning of capitalist agriculture in England.*

Because the enclosures facilitated the rationalization of agriculture, they sometimes benefited the peasants as well as landlords. Wherever peasants held widely scattered strips of land, it was to everybody's advantage to consolidate each person's holdings.[13] In general, before the Tudor period enclosures created few problems. Land was plentiful and people scarce even before the Black Death (1347) decimated Europe's population and threw thousands of acres onto an oversupplied market. However, as England began to recover from the Black Death, its population increased, while the supply of land remained more or less constant. At the same time, a money economy began to supplant the older subsistence economy, a development that was intensified by the influx of silver from the New World.

Although most peasants continued to practice subsistence farming, a number of more enterprising farmers began to lease large tracts of land in order to produce a cash crop for the growing commercial market. Concurrently, serfdom, with its requirement that the villein render personal service and a share of his crop to the lord, was disappearing. As the population increased and new tenants were added, manorial authorities preferred money payments to the older system of personal feudal obligations. In addition, manorial authorities often found that they had more unskilled labor than they needed. Money was becoming more important than people.[14]

When money was first accepted in payment, rent was calculated on the basis of the estimated value of the peasant's commuted services. However, as the value of land increased, this arrangement proved extremely disadvantageous to the landlords, whose money rents were fixed at a constant amount. As long as prices remained stable, landlords could count on a dependable income. However, prices began to rise sharply in the early part of the sixteenth century and landlords found themselves with fixed incomes and rising costs, a condition not unknown in our own inflationary times. The landlords found themselves under pressure to realize a greater return from their land, either by raising rents or by replacing unprofitable subsistence tenants with more profitable agricultural enterprises or entrepreneurs. Because the enclosures had such terrible social consequences, much of the anti-enclosure literature has with justice stressed the greed of the land-owners. However, the landlords were not altogether free agents. They were compelled to abandon uneconomic traditional methods of agriculture in order to increase their frequently declining incomes.[15]

From the landlord's point of view, the enclosures and such related measures as "engrossing" were a happy solution to the problem of finding additional revenue. (Engrossing was the accumulation in the hands of a single person of agricultural holdings that had formerly served to maintain more than one family.) Since enclosed land was better suited to cash farming than the old strip system, such land almost always increased in value. Not infrequently, land was enclosed for purposes of speculation. Perhaps the most questionable use to which enclosed land was put was its conversion into private parks for the enjoyment of the landowners. After enclosure, some common land was emptied of people and stocked with animals for the hunt.[16] The hunt animals were preserved for the pleasure of the lords and were protected from hungry, poaching peasants by game laws that became progressively more stringent.[17]

In Tudor times the most profitable enclosures normally involved the conversion of arable land to pasture. Wool was a cash crop in heavy demand both in England and the Low Countries. Sheep-raising also had an important modern advantage: it was cost-effective. Instead of dozens of tenants eking out their subsistence by traditional methods and paying the lord a paltry rental fixed generations before, a single shepherd was engaged to tend a large flock of sheep whose wool yielded a handsome return in the marketplace. There was also money to be made in dairy farming to supply the growing urban population with milk, butter, and cheese. Here again, a far smaller labor force yielded a far greater return than did the older system.[18]

Landlords could also secure a greater return from the land through planting better-yielding crops and the employment of new, more efficient agricultural methods. Although Henry VII's policies favored the production of wool rather than grain, after 1500 a general rise in prices encouraged the raising of grain for the market.[19] The landlord thus had a double incentive for enclosing common fields: there was profit in the conversion of arable land to pasture and in the consolidation of small holdings for the more efficient production of grain.

As land came to be regarded as a source of monetary gain, investment and speculation in real estate also became important. After enclosure it was often possible to increase rents as much as 200 percent, thereby greatly enhancing the value of the land itself.[20] Rich merchants joined established landowners in purchasing land. Rising rents also made the leasing of land to a few large cash farmers more attractive than to a whole community of small subsistence cultivators.[21] This led to the practice of "racking" the rent of small cultivators, that is, increasing the rent exorbitantly. Among the related usages of the verb "to rack" is to torture and to inflict pain. The rack rents had their intended effect. A large number of small holders were driven off the land because they were unable to pay the higher rents.

According to R. H. Tawney, the appropriation of the commons for sheepraising proceeded in several stages.[22] At first there were encroachments on the rights of customary tenants through deliberate overstocking of common pasture by the lord of the manor or his large tenant farmers. Such overstocking tended to edge out small cultivators. The second stage involved the normalization of the new arrangements through actual enclosure. Even where there were legal restraints against enclosure, some lords erected hedges in order to stake out their claims, leaving it to the tenants to stop them if they could.

After a field had been enclosed, it was difficult for tenants to undo the landlord's action. Undocumented tenancy, which was the most prevalent condition, gave the tenants few, if any, legal rights. Nor did the fact that one man stood to gain while many stood to lose carry weight before the law. In contrast to earlier times, in the Tudor period the landlord's claim to the land was increasingly regarded as absolute and immemorial custom, the basis of the peasant's claim, of no account. Legally, the landlord was reckoned as a majority of one.[23]

The one small group whose rights were strong enough to stand against an enclosing landlord were those tenants who possessed a documented freehold. Hence, when a landlord decided to enclose, he would usually begin by buying them out. It was then possible to evict the other tenants, tear down their house and set the dispossessed peasants adrift. Peasants whose ancestors had worked the land for centuries were transformed by a single action into units of a homeless and landless mass, often lacking any means of support whatsoever. It does not take much imagination to understand the social catastrophe that befell thousands of families who were wholly unprepared for any way of life save that which they and their ancestors had known.

Although there was much profit in enclosing, initially there was also considerable opposition. Around 1460 John Rous, a priest of Warwick, petitioned to Parliament concerning the depopulation caused by the enclosures.[24] He later offered a detailed account of the depopulation in his own county, citing sixty-two townships, manors and parishes that had been partly or wholly depopulated.[25]

Sir Thomas More is perhaps the best-known critic of the enclosures of the Tudor period. In an oft-cited passage from *Utopia* (1516), More depicted a peasant addressing a Cardinal on the subject of the enclosures. The peasant says:

> ...my lorde...your shepe that were wont to be so meke and tame, and so smal eaters, now as I heare saye, be become so great devowerers and so wylde, that they eate up, and swallow down the very men themselves. They consume, destroye, and devoure whole fields, howses, and cities. For looke in what partes of the realme dothe growe the fynest and therfore dearest woll, there noblemen, yea and certeyn abbottes, holy men no doubt, not contenting them selfes with the yearly revenues and profytes, that were wont to grow to theyr forefathers and predecessors of the land...yea much noying the weale publique, leave no grounde for tillage, thei inclose al into pastures; they throw doune houses they pluck down tounes, and leave nothing standynge, but only the church to be made a shephowse...
>
> Therefore that one covetous and insatiable cormaraunte and very plage of his native contrey maye compasse aboute and inclose many thousand akers of ground together with one pale or hedge, the husbandmen be thrust owte of their owne, or els either by fraud, or by violent oppression they be put besydes it, or by wronges and injuries thei be so weried, that they be compelled to sell all: by one means therfor or by other...they needs departe awaye, poor selye wretched soules, men, women, husbands, wives, fatherlesse children, widowes, wofull mothers, with their yonge babes ...Away they trudge, I say, out of their knowen and accustomed houses, fyndynge no place to rest in. All their householdestuff...being sodainly thrust oute, they be con-

strayned to sell for a thing of nought. And when they have wandered abrode tyll they be spent, what else can they doo but steale, and then justly pardy be hanged, or els go beggyng. And yet then also they be cast in prison as vagabondes, because they go aboute and worke not: whom no man wyl set a worke, though thei never so willingly profre themselves thereto. For one Shephearde or Herdsman is ynoughe to eate up that ground with cattel, to the occupiynge whereof about husbandrye many hands were requisite...

Having described the effects of the enclosures on the dispossessed, More proceeds to describe how the new wealth is spent:

...to this wretched beggerye and miserable povertie is joyned great wantonnes, importunate superfluitie and excessive riot. For not only gentle mennes servauntes, but also handicrafe men: yea and almost the ploughmen of the countrey, with al other sortes of people, use muche straunge and proude newefanglenes in their apparell, and to much prodigalle riotte and sumptuous fare at their table. Nowe bawdes, queines, whoores, harlottes, strumpettes, brothelhouses, stewes and yet another stewes, wynetavernes, ale houses and tiplinge houses, with so many noughtie, lewde and unlawful games as dyce, cardes, tables, tennis, boules...

As early as 1516 More commented on the cruel juxtaposition of surplus people and surplus wealth that is so characteristic of the modern period. We have already noted a particularly unpleasant example of that juxtaposition in the occasional practice of enclosing land and evicting its tenants in order to create parks for the pleasure of the landowners. For More, the only appropriate remedy for both the wasteful poverty and the wasteful wealth would have been to bring the enclosures to an end:

Caste out these pernicyous abominations, make a lawe that they, which plucked down fermes and townes of husbandrie shal reedifie them, or else yelde and uprender the possession thereof to such as wil...Suffer not these riche men to bie up al, to ingrosse and forestalle, and with their monopolie to kepe the market alone as please them.[26]

The scene described by More is one in which greedy landlords have dispossessed large numbers of peasant families, who now find themselves uprooted and destitute. Deprived of their customary moorings and means of subsistence, compelled to sell at distress prices the few possessions they were able to carry with them, yet ill prepared for any kind of life other than that which they and their ancestors had known, the evicted peasants were driven to beg, steal, or join the proliferating companies of vagabonds that appeared in England at the time of the Tudor enclosures. More's description can be summed up in the bitter observation that was current in his time: "Sheep eat men." Perhaps the most depressing aspect of More's description of the way many of the evicted peasants were compelled to maintain themselves is how closely it resembles the way in which a goodly number of the American poor are compelled to maintain themselves in our own time.

Whereas the condition of the dispossessed peasants became increasingly precarious, the profits derived from the conversion of arable land to pasture created a new monied class as well as a host of people ready to supply their wants. More depicts entire communities of honest Englishmen as reduced to bitter poverty while a privileged few enjoy useless luxury and the distractions of the bawdy and the gaming house. There is little ambiguity in More's indignation.

Nevertheless, in spite of the basic accuracy of More's account, from the perspective of the last quarter of the twentieth century, it would appear that More has in effect described some of the extremely painful, but perhaps unavoidable, social costs of the rudimentary "takeoff" period in which England's old feudal society was beginning to give way to an incipient capitalist economy. In the old economic order land was regarded as the shared resource of the entire community. In the new order land came to be regarded as the private property of the individual possessor. Moreover, those English landowners who abandoned the production of food for the production of wool for foreign markets were taking one of the first steps in creating the worldwide division of labor which in our time makes it possible for the United States to supply the rest of the world with food, computers and commercial aircraft while Japan has become a worldwide supplier of automobiles, electronics, and photographic equipment. Once the decision to begin the process of the rationalization of England's economy achieved a consensus, the tradition-bound peasants were destined to lose their share in the commons. Those peasants who were committed to subsistence farming stood in the way of "progress" and were brutally swept away in the transformation. They had become an economically and socially redundant class and suffered the bitter consequences of their superfluity. Although the methods employed in their removal were relatively mild in comparison with what was to follow, it was the fate of the dispossessed English peasants to be perhaps the earliest surplus population targeted for elimination by those with decision-making power within their own community. Moreover, even if the decision to rationalize the economy had not been taken, as long as England's population continued to increase, sooner or later a large number of peasants were fated to be driven off the land. In a subsistence economy with a growing population, either some people leave the land in every generation or the land is eventually subdivided beyond the point at which it can sustain small cultivators, as happened in Ireland, parts of Germany, and Poland at a later time.

If the opposition of men like Sir Thomas More and Cardinal Wolsey to the enclosures contained little ambiguity, the attitude of the Tudor monarchs was more complicated. Although the Tudors encouraged the commercial development of their country, they were inclined to oppose enclosures that led to wholesale depopulation. Their opposition was reflected in the anti-enclosure legislation of the period. Their ambivalence was reflected in the ineffectiveness of the same legislation.

The first anti-enclosure legislation was the Depopulation Act of 1489 "agaynst pullying down of Tounes"; the last Tudor law against depopulation was enacted in 1597.[27] Tawney has commented that the most fundamental change that took place in the Tudor period was that the command of money became more important than the command of men.[28] Nevertheless, those favoring retention of the traditional economic and social arrangements of the old order continued to exercise a measure of power until 1660, the beginning of the Restoration period. The Stuart kings, James I and Charles I, both attempted, albeit with considerable difficulty to limit the enclosures. In particular, Charles I appears to have acted with determination in attempting to limit the enclosures and to punish landlords who were responsible for depopulation, but, in general, the Stuarts proved as ineffective as the Tudors. Both the Tudors and the Stuarts were compelled to rely for the administration of their anti-enclosure measures on the very class who had most to gain from the enclosures.[29]

Some opponents of the enclosures argued that landed peasants were the backbone of the nation and that a depopulated country-side would constitute a serious military hazard. There were, for example, far fewer enclosures in the North Country adjacent to the Scottish border than in the Midlands. In the border area military considerations outweighed the lure of economic gain even for the landlords.[30] There was also considerable fear of dynastic and religious strife during the Tudor period. Henry VIII was especially reluctant to add an embittered, famished, and dispossessed peasantry to the number of his discontented subjects.[31]

Ironically, peace and the establishment of a relatively stable central government had a negative effect on the well-being of England's peasants. With the centralization of the government under the Tudors and the union of England and Scotland under James I, the era of the private feudal wars came to an end. It was no longer necessary for individual lords to maintain larger contingents of peasants than could be justified on strictly economic grounds. The advent of civic tranquillity hastened the destruction of the peasant's world.

3
THE ENCLOSURE MOVEMENT IN ENGLAND AND ITS SOCIAL CONSEQUENCES
The Age of Enlightenment

THE SECOND and most important period of enclosures began about 1760 and ended around 1840, an era more or less corresponding to the reign of George III (1760-1820). Between 1700 and 1760 there were a total of 208 acts enclosing 318,000 acres. Between 1761 and 1844, there were 3883 acts enclosing 5,630,000 acres. From 1700 on the total acreage enclosed came to about 7,000,000 acres.[1] In terms of both the number of enclosures and the number of acres enclosed, this period can be considered the enclosure period par excellence. Hundreds of thousands, if not millions, of people were affected.

After the Restoration of 1660, the situation of the peasants changed for the worse. The power of royalty was effectively curbed by the landowning and commercial classes that favored enclosure. There were no further parliamentary commissions seeking to prevent depopulation, nor were punitive measures taken against enclosers. As noted, by causing rents to rise, the enclosures increased the value of the land. Since the level of rents was taken as an index of national prosperity, the enclosures were seen as benefiting the nation as a whole in spite of the eviction of the peasants and the depopulation of the villages.[2] Moreover, scientific progress in agriculture tended to parallel progress in other fields. Since the newer farming methods were best employed on large consolidated landholdings, the enclosures were seen as fostering agricultural progress. The subdivided strips of the old system were too narrow to permit farmers to employ the new methods as long as their neighbors insisted, as many did, on retaining both traditional crops and traditional methods. When, for example, roots such as turnips were introduced as field crops, it became necessary to prevent the cattle of neighboring landholders from grazing where the roots had been planted. This required employment of uniform agricultural methods in all holdings. Underground drainage also required the kind of uniformity that only consolidation made possible.[3] In addition, it was difficult for subsistence farmers to survive economically. Thus, enclosure came to be regarded as identical with agricultural progress and, as such, was actively encouraged by the state.

From a political perspective, the most striking difference between the Georgian and Tudor periods was the disappearance of effective opposition to the enclosures within both the state and the Established Church. As we have seen, the Tudors and the Stuarts had mixed feelings about the enclosures. In the earlier period, the traditional belief that human beings are a greater national resource than money and official distaste for the disruptions caused by rural depopulation pulled the state in the direction of hostility to the enclosures; a desire to encourage British predominance in finance and commerce pushed the state in the opposite direction.

This ambivalence did not survive after the Restoration. The leaders of the Anglican Church became advocates rather than opponents of the enclosures. By increasing the value of the land, the enclosures increased the value of tithes, a principal source of income for the clergy.[4] According to Tate, the Anglican clergy of the period concentrated "on securing for themselves as large as possible a share of the proceeds."[5] The Established Church thus came to identify itself almost entirely with the dominant class.

No figure comparable in stature to Sir Thomas More arose to protest against the effects of enclosing and engrossing between

1660 and 1800. With some notable exceptions such as Oliver Goldsmith's poem *The Deserted Village* (1770), writers of the period were not greatly concerned with the peasant's loss of status. Instead, a new and ironic element enters the picture in the form of Enlightenment rationality. Some of the most influential writers of the period begin to argue that there is an inherent rationality to mass poverty and the precarious economic condition of both the industrial and the agricultural worker.

Those who believed in rationality, system, method and progress had little use for the old system of subsistence agriculture. They regarded it as permitting an overly independent peasantry to enjoy an excess of unproductive leisure. The observations of John Billingsley are characteristic:

> Besides, moral effects of an injurious tendency accrue to the cottager, from a reliance on imaginary benefits of stocking a common. The possession of a cow or two, with a hog, and a few geese naturally exalts the peasant, in his own conception, above his brethren in the same rank of society...he acquires a habit of indolence. Quarter, half, and occasionally whole days are imperceptibly lost. Day labour becomes disgusting; the aversion increases by indulgence; and at length the sale of a half-fed calf, or hog, furnishes the means of adding intemperance to idleness.[6]

If the commons were regarded as retrograde and morally evil, the harsher conditions facing the evicted peasants after the enclosures were seen as a positive good. In 1794 J. Bishton offered his views on some of the salutory effects the shift from subsistence farming to wage labor was destined to have: "...the labourer will work every day of the year, their children will be put out to labour early...that subordination of the lower ranks of society which in the present times is so much wanted, would thereby be considered secured."[7]

Even the aesthetics of the Georgian period, with its sense of order, symmetry and cool rationality, predisposed society to look with favor upon the contrast between enclosed and consolidated fields on the one hand and the older system's haphazardly scattered, narrow peasant holdings on the other.[8] There were also powerful social pressures during the Napoleonic wars tending to favor greater agricultural efficiency and productivity. (Let us recall that this was a period during which the number of enclosures and the acreage enclosed reached an all-time high.) England's population was increasing rapidly, and a series of bad harvests drove up grain prices to near-famine levels. In order to guarantee the country's food supply, it was necessary to bring more land under cultivation and to increase the productivity of the land already in use.

In 1793 the semiofficial Board of Agriculture was founded and Arthur Young was appointed its Secretary. Young was generally regarded as England's most important agricultural writer. An ardent exponent of agricultural improvement, Young originally regarded the enclosures as indispensable to farming progress. Initially, he believed that the more the landlords pressed the farmers, the more the farmers who rented their land would press their hired laborers. The end result would be a more efficient and productive agriculture.[9] Later in his career, Young had second thoughts about the merits of the enclosures. His change of heart came about when he realized that indigent cottagers and even squatters who had been able to retain a small piece of land made herculean efforts to avoid becoming dependent on poor relief. This was not the case with workers who had been rendered wholly landless. When members of the latter group became unemployed, they had neither the psychological nor the economic resources to avoid welfare dependency.[10]

Although the enclosures were not a central concern of Thomas Robert Malthus, a contemporary of Young, his thought was extremely influential in facilitating the subordination of traditional political, social, and ethical values to the exigencies of the absolutely impersonal, value-free workings of a self-regulating money economy. By so doing, Malthus helped to discredit one of the most telling objections against the enclosures, namely, their destructive and uprooting effect on the lives of hundreds of thousands of English men and women. Although it was not his intention, Malthus' writings provided the intellectual underpinnings for an attitude of "reasoned insensibility" on the part of members of the upper class toward the victims of mass poverty at a time when the greatest number of enclosures in English history were taking place.[11]

As is well known, Malthus argued that population, when unchecked, increases geometrically, whereas the food supply increases only arithmetically. Inevitably, the balance between population and subsistence would be restored either by such man-made checks on the growth of population as "moral restraint" or by "some species of misery." What is less well known is that Malthus saw the imbalance between population growth and resource availability as an expression of God's perfect wisdom and rationality. Malthus set his bleak drama of scarcity, deprivation, and overpopulation within the context of God's all-wise providence in the last two chapters (18 and 19) of his *Essay on the Principle of Population* (1798), where he argued Providence ordained "that population should increase much faster than food." Malthus conceded this arrangement "produces much evil," but he cautioned that if we ". . . consider man as he really is, inert, sluggish and averse from labour unless compelled by necessity . . . we may pronounce with certainty that the world would not have been peopled but for the superiority of the 'power' of population to the means of subsistence."[12] For Malthus, mankind's original sin is "torpor." Were men not goaded by necessity to overcome their natural inertia, they would never have emerged from the "savage state."[13] In his wisdom and goodness, God has inflicted the goad of necessity and scarcity upon humanity.

Malthus, incidentally, was unambiguous in his division of mankind into the categories of the elect, the fortunate few whom Providence has favored, and those whom Providence has rightly cast away for all eternity: "Nothing can appear more consonant to our own reason than that those beings which come out of the world in lovely and beautiful forms should be crowned with immortality."[14] A very different fate awaits those whom Providence has rejected: ". . . those which come out misshapen, those whose minds are not suited to a purer and a happier state of existence, should perish and be condemned to mix again with their original clay. Eternal condemnation may be considered as a species of punishment."[15]

It would be a mistake to oversimplify Malthus' position and to depict him as a man without compassion. In his personal life, he was a highly intelligent and compassionate man who attempted to comprehend his own revolutionary world in its grim complexity.[16] Nevertheless, Malthus did agree with the Calvinist position and anticipated the Social Darwinist view that those who survive are either divinely elected or naturally selected. He also concurred in the bleak corollary of that essentially double predestinarian position, namely, in the nature of things a large proportion of mankind is rightly and irrevocably condemned. He opposed use of public funds for poor relief and was one of the first to advocate cutting adrift those without resources to feed themselves, although he did not object to private charity. Malthus argued that a policy of public relief for the indigent only accentuates their problems by causing them to multiply without overcoming their poverty. He held that as the dependent poor increase they would take an ever greater share of the community's resources without contributing anything in return. This would eventually lead to general scarcity and misery.

Consistent with his opposition to poor relief, Malthus held that it is wrong for a man to marry and procreate unless he has the means to support a family. True to the principles of political economy of his day, Malthus argued that no one ought to interfere with an indigent who chooses to marry, even though such a marriage would be "clearly an immoral act." According to Malthus, society need not punish the married indigent because nature will. In the light of twentieth century experience, Malthus' reflections on the subject have a sinister ring Malthus himself could hardly have anticipated:

> When nature will govern and punish for us, it is a very miserable ambition to wish to snatch the rod from her hand and draw upon ourselves the odium of executioner. To the punishment of nature he should be left, the punishment of want... All parish assistance should be denied him; and he should be left to the uncertain support of private charity.

> He should know that the laws of nature, which are the laws of God, had doomed him and his family to suffer for disobeying their repeated admonitions... [17]

Malthus thus argued that the dependent poor ought to be left to their own devices, a strategy which, if followed, would bring about both their riddance and the greater security from want of those who survive. That he did not flinch from following the logic of his position to its bitter conclusion is evident in the following incredibly harsh passage from the revised Sixth Edition of his *Essay on the Principle of Population* (1826). Referring to famine as a check on population, Malthus wrote:

> ...we should facilitate, instead of foolishly and vainly endeavoring to impede, the operations of nature in producing this mortality; and if we dread the frequent visitation of the horrid form of famine, we should sedulously encourage the other forms of destruction which we compel nature to use. Instead of recommending cleanliness to the poor, we should encourage contrary habits. In our towns we should make the streets narrower, crowd more people into houses, and count on the return of the plague. In the country, we should build our villages near stagnant pools, and particularly encourage settlement in all marshy and unwholesome situations. But above all, we should reprobate specific remedies for ravaging diseases; and those benevolent but much mistaken men, who thought they were doing a service to mankind by projecting schemes for the total extirpation of particular disorders. [18]

It would be comforting to think that such ideas no longer enjoy much support. Unfortunately, recent political experience has demonstrated that the tradition of harsh indifference to the fate of the poor has influential advocates in our own time. In effect, Malthus counseled that everything be done to increase the mortality rate of the indigent short of outright murder. At this point in his career, he clearly welcomed mortality as a "solution" to the problem of population redundancy. The next step was obvious. There are cleaner, more cost-effective ways to induce mortality on a large scale than by subjecting a target population to the random hazards of a pestilential and polluted environment while withholding medical treatment. Still, under proper conditions even Malthus' transitional methods of "solving" the problem of the dependent poor could yield a deadly harvest. As we shall see, a strategy for dealing with the dependent poor similar to Malthus' proposal was deliberately utilized by his intellectual disciples within the British government during the Irish famine of 1846 to 1848. While Malthus cannot be held responsible for the behavior of Britain's leaders during the Irish famine, their policies were consistent with his ideas concerning the treament of the poor.[19]

Malthus' thought anticipated Social Darwinism's fundamental conviction that "the survival of the fittest" is the universal law of nature. Both Malthus and the Social Darwinists naturalized all political values. Such thinking, which has lost none of its influence in our times, constitutes a radical rejection of the traditional conception of public life in the western world. Historically, the political sphere was understood to be a joint effort on the part of men to shield themselves from the ravages of nature. Just as a new human settlement begins with clearing the wilderness and creating a humanized space that is essentially a thing of artifice, so too political institutions are artificial creations designed to structure the conduct of human beings for the good of the community rather than permit unbridled instinct and unrestrained egoism to reign supreme.[20]

It is therefore to politics rather than metaphysics or theology that we must look for the distinction between fact and value and between "is" and "ought." Humanity transcends factuality whenever it creates a community whose purpose is to enable its members collectively to mitigate the hazards of nature. Rooted in nature, every human community is super-natural in its use of artifice to defend its members against the destructive side of nature. To naturalize political thinking, as did Malthus and the Social Darwinists (and they were by no means alone), is to deny the very purpose of the political order. It is also to take the first steps toward the dissolution of communities in which men and women are bound together by shared obligation and to transform these communities into aggregates of disconnected, isolated individuals, each of whom seeks to maximize his own gain at the expense of all others.

Nor is it surprising that the downgrading of political values that we find in Malthus and the Social Darwinists took place in a period of bourgeois supremacy. Historically, the bourgeoisie's distinctive sphere of activity has been trade and commerce. During the nineteenth century, members of the bourgeoisie were newcomers to the responsibilities of political leadership in most countries. In many countries the exclusion of the bourgeoisie from politics expressed itself in a national division of labor in which the commercial and professional classes have been members of ethnic and religious minorities rather than the dominant majority. This has been the case with the Jews in many Western countries, the ethnic Chinese in Southeast Asia, the Armenians in Turkey, and the Indians and Pakistanis in parts of Africa.

It is possible to view the enclosure movement as a social process involving the progressive subordination of political to economic values in the first world power to enter upon the path of modernization. The subordination of political values can also be seen as yet another aspect of the progressive rationalization of society. It is reason that dethrones politics by first desacralizing and then naturalizing political values. The reduction of human relations to morally neutral calculations of profit and loss, such as accompanies a universal money economy, represents an advance in rationality over a society in which bonds of loyalty and tradition limit the unimpeded harnessing of human energies and talents. By reducing men to craving biological units perpetually in competition with and potentially the mortal enemy of each other, naturalized social and political thought gives paradoxical expression to this advance in rationality.

Let us recall that in addition to being a reflection on the problem of population, Malthus' *Essay* is also a theodicy, that is, an attempt to demonstrate the inherent rationality of the ways of the absolutely omnipotent Creator. Malthus was a believing Christian and a priest of the Church of England. He was also responsible for formulating one of the most influential legitimating ideologies for a sociopolitical system in which the inherited ethical values of the Judaeo-Christian tradition gave way to ever more precise, value-neutral calculations of profit and loss. By seeing resource scarcity, superfluous human fecundity, and the universal struggle for existence as expressions of divine providence, Malthus was in effect arguing for the essential rationality of a social order in which the values of the marketplace were inexorably displacing traditional religious, social and political values. Admittedly, Malthus himself did not look with favor on such effects of the enclosures as the conversion of arable land to pasture for the raising of beef, which he regarded as an uneconomic source of food, or of horses for the pleasure of the rich. He regarded land used for amusement and luxurious diversion as a needless waste of scarce resources.[21] Nevertheless, the effect of Malthusianism and Social Darwinism, its intellectual offspring, has been to offer a rationale for measures which contributed materially to the modernization of English agriculture and commerce while reducing to a minimum concern for the extraordinary social dislocations attending those transformations. In a later age Social Darwinism was to be used as a legitimating ideology for state-sponsored mass murder on a scale never before witnessed in human history, both by the Turks in World War I and the Germans during World War II.[22] In Malthus' era the originating kernel of Social Darwinism was employed for the relatively mild purpose of buttressing the claim that there is an inherent rationality to a system resulting in the consolidation of landholdings in the hands of a small number of owners and the eviction of large numbers of former de facto possessors.

When the enclosures are studied, there is often a tendency to stress the greed of the landowning class as a principal motive for what took place. We have, however, already noted that something far more consequential than greed was involved in the extraordinary increase in the number of enclosures in the Georgian period, namely, the spirit of Enlightenment rationality. This is not without a measure of irony as the manifest aims of the Enlightenment included the liberation of men from fear, superstition, and the dead hand of the past.

In spite of its promise of human liberation, in the economic sphere the Enlightenment tended to express itself in a spirit of dehumanized functional rationality. I stress the word "dehumanized." The most rational market is one in which buyers and sellers are wholly unknown to each other. Only in the context of complete anonymity can all considerations other than price be excluded. When one compares modern anonymous markets such as the world's stock and commodity exchanges with the oriental bazaar with its elaborate bargaining rituals and face-to-face encounters between buyer and seller, one can discern the degree to which the rational markets of modern times have been so to speak "dehumanized."

As we have seen, the enclosures became increasingly attractive to property owners as the old subsistence economy was displaced by the new money economy. This was part of a larger cultural transition involving the reduction of quality to quantity in both science and society, one aspect of which was the valuation of all aspects of human existence in terms of the common numerical standard we call money. Unfortunately, the reduction of quality to quantity was accompanied by a tendency to eliminate concern for the well-being of those persons who stood in the way of economic "progress." Undoubtedly, Sir Thomas More's indignation at the early progress of the enclosures was partly due to his inability to make the transition from quality to quantity in social relations. More was a man of traditional values which he was not prepared to abandon even when his life was at stake.

An important aspect of the Enlightenment was the cultural and intellectual effort aimed at what Weber has characterized as the "disenchantment of the world." In their essay on the Enlightenment, Max Horkheimer and Theodore Adorno have observed that this "disenchantment" involved the "total extirpation of animism," the practical consequence of which is that nothing whatsoever is regarded as possessing any inherent power capable of resisting humanly defined intentions.[23] Thus, "disenchantment" fosters calculation and rational control. Such calculation is an expression of a spirit of "dissolvent rationality" capable of reducing all things without exception to a single, abstract, universally quantifiable standard. In the world of commerce, this reduction facilitates the ascription of a monetary value to all things. It also facilitates the impersonal value-free treatment of every element in the process of production, distribution, and exchange as a commodity, that is, an object available for sale in the marketplace. Moreover, "disenchanting" rationality not only sought to eliminate the political and social traditions that impeded the universal quantification of the human world, it also attempted with considerable success to eliminate the people and the institutions that were resistant to the reduction of goods, services and institutions to monetary calculation. In the case of the English peasants, this meant wholesale eviction; in the case of the Irish at the time of the great famine, it meant deliberately letting one million people die. We observe the seeds of this dark side of the Enlightenment at work in the Georgian enclosures. As we shall see, before it runs its deadly course, this shadow side will assume the shape of mass terror, total domination, and genocide.

It may be asked: Whose rationality do we speak of when we identify the spirit of reason as at work in the enclosures? The enclosures were, of course, rational for the landlords, but were they rational for the dispossessed? Regrettably, what was rational for the losers was of no consequence. The Enlightenment did not value highly the kind of theoretical rationality which esteemed knowledge for its own sake as did, for example, Aristotle. Francis Bacon expressed the Enlightenment's preference for instrumental rationality when he identified knowledge with power and denigrated the kind of knowledge that is sought for its own sake: "...knowledge that tendeth but to satisfaction is but as a courtesan which is for pleasure and not for fruit and generation."[24]

The Enlightenment was interested in the "fruit" and "generation" of knowledge, not the unproductive "pleasure" it could offer the contemplative intelligence. The rationality of the Enlightenment was not an end to be gained but a value-free instrument to be used. The peasants had no voice in the choice of ends within their community. Those who did saw traditional agrarian rights as an obstacle to the objectives they had elected. For the landowners the proper use of reason involved eliminating a human impediment rather than heeding the interests of those who stood, however feebly, in their way. As we have emphasized, those English peasants who were incapable of adapting to the agricultural revolution were doomed to be swept away by it. And, they were the forerunners of millions of other peasants who were destined to find themselves in a similar predicament in the generations that followed. What might have been rational to England's peasants would only have mattered if they had had the power to enforce their will or if there had been an impartial agency capable of adjudicating the claims of both tenants and landlords. Ideally, the state ought to have fulfilled that function, but there is little evidence of state impartiality at the time. Lacking both power of their own and access to the power of the state, what was rational for the peasants was largely irrelevant. *Reason had become the handmaiden of power.*

Lest I be misunderstood, I want to stress that these observations are set forth neither as a defense of a world governed by "dissolvent rationality" nor as an expression of a romantic yearning to return to a pretechnological world. It is my conviction that the progressive rationalization of the world's economy is our destiny; a destiny which cannot be altered, save through self-defeating, suicidal, nuclear war. We can, and I believe we should, change the way we respond to the technological world. Until now, those who have effectively controlled our productive resources have been more interested in the gain to be derived from "progress" than in the loss suffered by those who, like England's peasants, were rendered redundant in the process.

According to Max Weber, a fully rationalized money economy presupposes "the struggle of man against man."[25] We have seen this struggle at work in the destruction of England's peasant class in the enclosures. If Weber's observation is valid, we must conclude that behind the seemingly bloodless and unemotional veneer of rational accounting and marketing we find not peace but the perpetual war of all against all, albeit in sublimated guise, which Thomas Hobbes saw as the condition of man in the state of nature.

In an expanding economy, such as the United States enjoyed during much of the nineteenth century, the destructive aspects of the universal competitiveness of bourgeois society is not as evident as it is in a static or declining economy. The mutual hostility that is intrinsic to a system in which all the actors are compelled to maximize their gains at each other's expense becomes obvious in a zero-sum or declining economy. If the enclosures were not an expression of the war of all against all, they were certainly an example of undisguised class warfare. In the protracted conflict, the peasant landholders were the defeated class. Yet, we can never forget that their bitter defeat was a paradoxical expression of the triumph of instrumental reason in human affairs. In an automated, computerized, high-technology civilization, one won-ers what the human costs of reason's future triumphs may be.

4
THE FATE OF THE
DEFEATED PEASANTS

IN THE PROTRACTED STRUGGLE between England's peasants and landowners, the victory of the landowners was total. When the conflict was over, the peasants ceased to exist as a class within English society. As a result of the modernization of English agriculture, the defeated class was in large measure transformed into the dependent poor.

There were important differences between the social consequences of the enclosures in the Tudor and the Georgian periods. As noted, in the Tudor period the enclosures usually involved the conversion of the land from the production of grain to sheepraising. In the Georgian period, the purpose of the enclosures was more likely to be to facilitate efficient cultivation. When arable land was converted to pasture, the need for labor decreased sharply; where land was consolidated for the sake of efficient cultivation, there was usually a smaller decrease in the size of the labor force. At times, the number of laborers in the village even increased.[1] Nevertheless, as a result of the enclosures in the eighteenth and nineteenth centuries, an agricultural labor force consisting of relatively independent small landholders was replaced by a propertyless, agricultural proletariat. The Georgian enclosures thus had a greater impact on the quality than on the quantity of farm labor.

Although accurate statistics are not available with which to measure the social impact of the earlier enclosures, we know that some evicted peasants found work as wage laborers on the land they and their ancestors had cultivated as de facto possessors. Some became squatters. Others sought, usually with little success, to find a place for themselves in villages where the old open-field system remained intact. Still others drifted into the towns.[2]

As early as the accession of Henry VII (1457), the enclosures had resulted in wholesale evictions, which in turn had caused hundreds of villages to be deserted and to decay.[3] Depopulation of the villages was accompanied by large-scale unemployment. Where arable fields were converted to pasture, both the cottagers and the younger sons of more fortunate peasants found themselves permanently without work. Before conversion they had been able to hire out as seasonal laborers whenever the manor needed help. Now their work was no longer needed. For the first time, there was an oversupply of agricultural workers, and the sixteenth-century village had little need for nonagricultural workers. Many of the unemployed had no choice but to leave their native villages to seek work elsewhere. As Tawney has observed, although poverty was hardly new, the phenomenon of large numbers of willing, able-bodied men who could find no work was without precedent.[4]

The initial response of the authorities to the novel experience of large-scale unemployment was to blame the victims, a response which has by no means disappeared in our time. Before the enclosures, the causes of poverty were normally personal rather than structural. No able-bodied man with dependable work habits had reason to fear long-term unemployment. Although hunger was widespread in famine years, the causes of want were natural rather than social.[5]

The situation changed radically as a result of the enclosures of the Tudor period. As peasants were evicted wholesale, there was a serious increase in vagrancy. Some evicted peasants attempted to settle in communities in which the open-field system was still intact to find that they could usually remain in the new villages only as squatters on the wasteland. Other dispossessed peasants gravitated to the towns and to London, where they were usually barred from practicing or acquiring a craft by the monopolistic

practices of the guilds. Some of the dispossessed joined the bands
of vagabonds and gypsies, who had become a serious social
problem on the roads and in the countryside. Still others, lacking
any alternative, turned to theft, crime, and prostitution in order
to survive. The magnitude of the problem can be seen in the fact
that in 1688 it was estimated there were no fewer than 60,000
vagrant families in England or approximately 300,000 people.[6]
At the time the population of England and Wales was about
5,500,000.

The state could not ignore the thousands who had been set adrift
but it was uncertain as to what to do with them. In the Middle
Ages the poor had been cared for by religious institutions, but
in the sixteenth century care of the poor was increasingly regarded
as a political rather than a strictly religious affair. The Poor Laws
enacted in response to the growing numbers of dependent
indigents were both welfare and police measures. As is the case
to this day, the poor had to be fed; they also had to be controlled.[7]

The question of how to deal with the poor elicited a number
of conflicting proposals. One proposal of particular interest in
the light of subsequent events is Robert Cushman's argument that
"England is overstocked and those who can find no work in the
mother country ought to attempt to create a new life for themselves on the other side of the Atlantic."[8] Cushman wrote in the
seventeenth century. He saw the problem of coping with the poor
as getting progressively worse. He wrote: "There is such pressing
and oppressing in town and country about farms, trades, traffic,
so as a man can hardly anywhere set up a trade but he shall pull
down two of his neighbors. . . ."[9] By the seventeenth century land
was no longer abundant, nor were people few, but there was a
realm across the sea where the old conditions of abundant land
and sparse population could be expected to prevail almost indefinitely. As long as they did, emigration from the Old World to
the New would provide an outlet for the redundant people of the
British Isles and, at a later time, the rest of Europe.

In Cushman's time emigration could provide a solution only
for a very small number of the very adventurous. Nevertheless,
a growing and potentially troublesome surplus population had

arisen and had to be controlled. In 1517, the Privy Council demanded that all of London's poor be required to register as a means of controlling vagrancy. Those legally entitled to beg were to be given badges. Those who did not qualify were to be compelled to return to their home villages where, presumably, the parish would sustain them.[10] When these initial measures against vagrancy proved ineffective, new measures were tried. In 1530 magistrates were ordered by royal proclamation to cause illegal vagrants to be whipped. The magistrates were further admonished to leave aside "vain pity."[11] In the 1530–1531 session of Parliament, gypsies were ordered to leave England within sixteen days of the proclamation of the statute. The expulsion order, which also proved ineffective, was in response to complaints concerning gypsy bands that were alleged to have been engaged in crime and vagrancy as they moved about the country.[12] As noted, the number of gypsies was sometimes augmented by dispossessed peasants. In addition, the authorities were often incapable of distinguishing between peasants who had taken to the road and genuine gypsies.

As the wholesale evictions continued in rural areas, the situation grew progressively worse. In the 1549–1550 session of Parliament, a statute was enacted for the placing of indigent children over five in servitude without parental consent. In 1572 Parliament passed "An Acte for the Punishment of Vagabondes and for the Relief of the Poore and the Impotent." This statute provided for the incarceration of illegal beggars over fourteen and for the whipping and ear-branding of those convicted as vagabonds unless someone took them in as servants. Second offenders were to be regarded as felons and third offenders sentenced to death. The statute also called upon Justices of the Peace to register and provide for the maintenance of those unable to work.[13] Later Poor Laws included the provision that able-bodied recipients of poor relief were to be compelled to work at whatever tasks the parish might assign them in exchange for their maintenance. In the 1572 Act no such provision was made for compulsory work for the able-bodied poor.

The most important acts in the Tudor and Stuart period for

the setting of long-term policy for poor relief were the Act of 1601 (43 Eliz, c2) and the Law of Settlement of 1662 (13 and 14 Ch II, c12). The Act of Elizabeth made it compulsory for each parish to provide for the poor by levying a rate on all occupiers of property within its boundaries. Unpaid "overseers of the poor" were to be appointed who would be responsible for levying and collecting the rate. Their duties also included setting to work children whose parents could not maintain them, care of the aged and infirm, and providing work for the able-bodied poor. It was also to be the duty of the parish to erect houses for the poor in which more than one family could be placed. Once used as habitations for the poor, such houses could not be used for any other purpose.[14]

The Law of Settlement of 1662 empowered the parish overseers to return indigent newcomers within forty days of their arrival to their place of settlement. This could be their place of birth or a place in which they had "gained a settlement" by a three year period of residence. The effect of the Law of Settlement was to limit the mobility of workers seeking employment outside their own parish. It led eventually to considerable exploitation of the poor. Some parishes tried to evade the responsibility of maintaining the poor by smuggling them into a neighboring parish where they would be entitled to collect poor relief if they were able to remain for more than forty days.[15]

From the perspective of our own century, the petty dumping activities of seventeenth- and eighteenth-century English parishes anticipate modern dumping activities in which public authorities have sought to rid themselves of groups of ever greater size that, for one reason or another, have been deemed unwanted or superfluous. Dumping by local officials through subsidized emigration was a relatively frequent occurrence in nineteenth-century Europe. It has reached unprecedented dimensions in the twentieth century.

As the principle developed that paupers could be removed to their place of settlement (that is, the community in which they were legally entitled to parish support when in need), economically marginal wage laborers found themselves at an enormous disadvantage. Those who chose to remain in their own parish usually had to rest content with declining employment opportunities. Those who ventured to a new location risked the possibility of what amounted to summary deportation to their place of settlement in hard times. Until 1795 a worker could only settle in another parish if invited to do so or if his own parish gave him a certificate guaranteeing that he would not become a charge on the new community.[16] Since the cost of returning an indigent pauper and his family fell upon the parish in which he was entitled to relief, some parishes refused to issue certificates, thereby preventing their unemployed from seeking work elsewhere even when as many as two thirds of a parish's labor force was idle.[17] Some employers encouraged laborers to come to their village, but, once settled, the workers were refused certificates with which to go elsewhere, thereby compelling them to accept prevailing wages and work conditions. Since the employers as a class exercised control over both the administration of parish relief and the community's business, they were able unilaterally to determine working conditions to their own advantage.[18] Thus, the effect of the Laws of Settlement and its subsequent amendments was to weaken the hand of the workers and to strengthen the hand of the landowners and employers.

As the size of the wage-earning proletariat increased, so too did the number of unemployed. As it did, the question of the conditions under which the able-bodied unemployed were to be given relief also became urgent. Poor relief was divided into outdoor and indoor support. Basically, outdoor relief was assistance given by the parish to an impoverished family in its own place of residence. Indoor relief was assistance given to paupers who resided in the poorhouse. As poor relief evolved, authorities found relief could best be dispensed to certain categories of people within the poorhouse. These included the aged, the physically infirm, orphans and abandoned children, the mentally incompetent, and mothers who had either been abandoned or whose children were illegitimate. In the eighteenth century, such women constituted a large proportion of the poorhouse inmates.[19]

One of the most hotly debated issues among students of the

English system of poor relief continues to be the treatment of the poor in these residences. There is little disagreement that there were disgraceful abuses. There is also little disagreement that a certain Christian spirit originally motivated the whole system of alms-giving and often acted as a break against the worst abuses. There is debate on the subject of the overall condition of the poor in the houses.[20] We need not enter that debate. Nevertheless, even under the best of circumstances the poorhouses were special precincts in which those deemed superfluous, whether because of want of means, age, or other incapacity, were officially segregated. Moreover, the dependent poor lost their normal civic rights and, when confined to the poorhouse, were wholly under the control of the overseers.[21]

Admittedly, there were usually limits to the kind of control overseers could exercise. However, with the advent of the Age of Reason, intolerable abuses became far more prevalent than in an earlier, more traditional era. The evolution of the poorhouse itself as a distinctive institution with its own specialized personnel was an expression of the tendency toward the specialization of function that characterizes the modern period.[22] In the subsistence economy of the feudal period, there was little need for specialized institutions to house the indigent or the infirm. With the disappearance of the ancient economy and the extended family, large numbers of people were left without a viable place in the new economy or protecting kin willing to look after them in time of need.

The phenomenon of the able-bodied unemployed worker was also a by-product of the same specialization of function. In the seventeenth and eighteenth centuries, many people were puzzled by unemployment and the question of how it came about received a wide variety of answers. In the old subsistence economy unemployment had usually been the result of idleness and vice. It was difficult for people whose perceptions had been formed by the old order to understand the new phenomenon of structural unemployment in which large numbers of men and women are periodically thrown upon a labor market in which there is simply no demand for their services. A certain inability to comprehend the structural character of modern unemployment persists to this day among an influential segment of the American public.

When a pauper entered the poorhouse, his family normally entered with him. As noted, destitute widows with small children were also confined. In addition, the poorhouse was often the only recourse available to unwed mothers. Thus, there were normally a large number of pauper children among the inmates. Over the years innumerable schemes were put forth for the employment of poorhouse inmates, and, inevitably, child labor played an important part in them. Provision was made for apprenticing pauper children as early as the Act of 1601. Unfortunately, this frequently led to vicious abuse of the children. Parish officers were eager to be relieved of the expense of maintaining their young charges and were often unconcerned with the character or the morals of the masters to whom the children were bound. There was widespread exploitation of indigent children, a situation that grew much worse with the coming of the Industrial Revolution. According to John and Barbara Hammond, child labor was considered normal in pre-industrial England, but such labor was always an integral part of the overall life of the family.[23] By contrast, the factory system of the industrial age was originally based on the regimented and impersonal employment of large numbers of children. The earliest mills, such as the water-powered spinning mills, used "cartloads" of pauper children who were supplied to the factories by the workhouse authorities.[24]

The children were miserably housed and fed. The Hammonds cite the testimony before the Parliamentary Committee on the State of Children in Manufactories (1816) of John Moss, who had been in charge of the workhouse at Preston. Moss testified that he had been a master in a cotton mill in Lancashire from February 1814 to March 1815, where the regular working hours, including Saturdays, began at 5 A.M. and lasted until 8 P.M., with half hour breaks for breakfast and lunch; 150 pauper children six years old and older worked in this particular mill. There was also cleanup work on Sundays. The employers did not deny his charges, but insisted that arrangements had been made for the religious life of the children. They further pointed out with some pride that "only" six children had died during the period in which Moss had been employed.[25] Even worse conditions were to be found in the mines, where pauper children were used as beasts of burden to push or draw trucks from the miners to the foot of the mine shaft. Other children worked as trappers, that is, they sat in pitch dark holes for twelve hours opening and closing the doors that directed the draughts of air through the mines. The children were generally from five to eight years of age. Similar work was done by women and girls at an earlier period.[26]

Children were also used as chimney sweeps, especially in the Georgian period. Because of the style of Georgian houses, chimneys in fashionable houses tended to be exceptionally narrow. The task of sweeping could only be done by very young, naked children. The work itself was extremely hazardous. The incidence of cancer, lung disease and disgusting scabrous skin conditions was high. There were about 400 masters and 1000 chimney sweeps in London. Conditions were so bad that a society was formed in 1803 to develop a machine to do the work in place of the children. The masters rejected the idea of using machines, which they would have had to operate themselves. Chimney sweeps were generally castoffs whom nobody wanted, the "refuse" of society, to use Jeremy Bentham's term. In most cases the boys were apprenticed by parish authorities to the master sweeps, but children were sometimes sold by their parents for a few guineas. Pauper children who refused the work assigned to them could be denied parish relief and even sent to prison.[27]

Until the reforms of 1767 known as Hanway's Act, pauper children, especially infants, were considered expendable. Their high mortality rate was welcomed because it reduced the cost of poor relief. The more infants died, the fewer would have to be supported by the parish. The death rate was especially high among infants born in the workhouses.

Acting out of religious and humanitarian motives, the reformer Jonas Hanway sought successfully to reduce the infant mortality rate in London's poorhouses. He was responsible for the Parliamentary Act of 1761 (2 George III,c.22) that required the parish clerk to record (1) the names of all pauper children under four years of age, (2) the names of the nurses who attended them, and (3) the date of their death or discharge. When the records were compiled, they revealed that the death rate of pauper infants was between 60 and 70 percent! Hanway then introduced another bill, the Act of 1767 (7 George III,c.39), which required the parishes of London to provide maintenance for pauper children outside the workhouse until they reached the age of six. According to one authority, Hanway's Act resulted in "a deficit of 2100 burials a year" with a predictable increase in parish expenses.[28] Apparently the viability of the unwanted infants proved inconvenient to the parishes responsible for their support.

In the early years of the eighteenth century, the belief was widespread that the unemployed could find work if they really wanted to. Hence, relief was only dispensed to able-bodied workmen within an institution where they could be compelled to work. That institution was, of course, the workhouse. According to the Poor Relief Act of 1722 (9 George I,c.7) several parishes could unite for the purpose of acquiring a building to be used as a workhouse. The Act also empowered the parishes to hire someone to manage the institution. Able-bodied paupers who refused to enter the workhouse could be barred from eligibility for relief. This feature of the poor relief system was known as the "workhouse test." It was based on the assumption that only those with no other recourse would be in straits so desperate as to submit to confinement for themselves and their families.

The workhouse test became especially important in connection with the Poor Law Reform of 1834. For several decades before the 1834 Act, the indoor relief requirement (namely, that able-bodied paupers be given relief only in the workhouse) had been relaxed. It was reinstated in 1834. Sir Edwin Chadwick was the person most responsible for the 1834 Report of the Poor Law Commission, perhaps the most influential single document of its kind published in nineteenth century England. Chadwick saw the workhouse test as a simple yet absolutely certain way of restricting the distribution of poor relief to the truly destitute. By making the conditions under which relief was given as degrading as possible, the very act of applying for poor relief became undoubted proof of need.[29]

Chadwick's approach to poverty was based upon philosopher Jeremy Bentham's principle of "less eligibility."[30] Chadwick, who had been Bentham's disciple and former literary secretary, defined the principle as requiring: ". . . that the condition of the person relieved at the public expense must be made less eligible on the whole than the person living on the fruits of his own labor."[31]

By requiring that relief be dispensed to the able-bodied unemployed only in the workhouse, the fundamental purpose of the less-eligibility principle was assured. Moreover, once the pauper was confined to the workhouse, the less-eligibility principle became a means of rationalizing harsh and abusive treatment for him and his family. In 1821 Robert Lowe, the superintendent of a workhouse near Nottingham, wrote a letter to his friend, the Reverend J. T. Becher, in which he described his method of managing his workhouse. It was a ". . . system of forcing able-bodied paupers to provide for themselves through the terror of a well-disciplined workhouse."[32]

The terror inflicted on Lowe's inmates was not the old-fashioned terror of the dungeon or the torture chamber but a new and modern form of terror, an antiseptic, depersonalized, and absolutely rigid regimen which began the moment the inmates arose and continued until they went to sleep. Clean beds, good food, and hygienic surroundings were combined with separation of the sexes, thereby breaking up families and facilitating the strictest control and discipline.[33] Lowe's regimen, and others like it, proved far harsher to men and women used to the laxer routines of country life than the more emotional and sporadic abuse to which inmates of less rationalized institutions had been subjected. Where the system was employed workhouses became so intolerable that the number of applicants for poor relief decreased sharply.[34] In addition to the rationalized terror of a depersonalized regimen, there were, as we shall see, a plenitude of examples of older forms of terror, all being expressions of the less eligibility principle, a governing principle in the distribution of relief to this day.

One method used to keep able-bodied inmates of the workhouse employed, especially after 1795, was the Roundsmen system, in which dependent paupers were sent around the parish to inquire whether any householder had work.[35] When work was available, wages rates were set by the parish and paid partly by the employer and partly by the parish.Children ten years old and older were often put on the rounds.[36] In some parishes laborers were auctioned off to farmers who bid two or three pence a day, a very low wage, for their services. The difference between the wage paid by the employer and the subsistence needs of the laborer was made up by the parish. Farmers often found it more profitable to employ workhouse inmates than their normal help.[37]

There were also attempts to turn workhouses into profit-making, capitalist ventures by transforming them into "Houses of Industry." As the economy was rationalized, even the opportunities for profit in mass poverty did not go unnoticed. One of the earliest such ventures was initiated in Bristol in 1696. It was followed by many others. At Bristol the paupers were set to work preparing wool, flax, and hemp, as well as spinning, weaving, and shoemaking.[38] There were also a number of workhouses devoted to agriculture and, as the textile industry developed in the eighteenth century, factories were often set up in the workhouses. However, workhouse enterprises seldom proved economically viable.

The Act of 1722, which empowered parish authorities to hire paid administrators for the poorhouses, was one of the first steps toward rationalizing the control of a surplus population. Initially, a number of parishes took bids from contractors who sought franchises to manage the poorhouses in return for a fixed annual sum. The contract normally went to the lowest bidder. This relieved parish authorities of an unpleasant burden and quickly led to predictable abuses. Because of uncertainty about economic conditions, it was seldom possible for contractors accurately to estimate the number of people who would seek relief during the term of the contract. It was in the contractor's interest to keep as many paupers as possible out of the workhouse, no matter how needy they might be, and to spend as little as possible on those who had to be admitted. It was also in his interest to extract as much work as possible from workhouse inmates. Some speculators even attempted to expand the scope of their ventures by offering their services to a number of parishes within a twenty or thirty-mile radius. The brutality of the system requires little elaboration. The negative reaction to the system, which turned the workhouse into what was called by contemporaries a "House of Terror," was so great that in 1782 yet another parliamentary act (22 George III,c.83), known as Gilbert's Act, was passed, repealing the requirement that able-bodied paupers be confined in the workhouse in order to be eligible for relief. Outdoor relief was once again sanctioned for them.[39]

Although the capitalist potentialities of managing the poor and the infirm for profit were first grasped by petty speculators, they were envisaged on a much grander scale by Jeremy Bentham. He proposed the establishment of 250 "Houses of Industry," ten and two-thirds miles apart, each of which would hold 2000 inmates to be run by a profit-making Joint-Stock Corporation. Bentham believed that the system of large establishments would make possible economies of scale in building, management and supply. The enterprise would be managed by a National Charity Company which would receive a charter empowering its directors to purchase real estate and to raise capital through a stock offering. It would also have the power to apprehend beggars and vagrants and confine them within the institution. Able-bodied paupers would be denied outside relief. Bentham was convinced that the venture would yield a profit, repay its investors in twenty years, and eliminate the poor rates entirely. He proposed that the institution be managed along rational, systematic, bureaucratic lines. For example, the principle of "Segregation and Aggregation" would govern the way the various classes of paupers would be housed within the establishment:

> Next to every class from which any inconvenience is to be apprehended, station a class unsusceptible of that inconvenience. Examples: 1. next to raving lunatics or persons of profligate conversation, place the deaf and dumb ...2. Next to prostitutes, and other loose women, place

the aged women. 3. Within the abodes of the blind, place melancholy and silent lunatics, or the shockingly deformed...[40]

The buildings themselves were to be circular so that all quarters could be observed and controlled from a central inspection lodge. Bentham characteristically called the design "Panopticon." Undoubtedly Bentham would have appreciated the potentialities of closed-circuit television for surveillance. Practically every inmate, including the blind, would be given work appropriate to his or her capacities. The inmates would be paid on a piecework basis in order to work off the value of the relief received. As was the custom at the time, child labor was integral to the project. Bentham was convinced that proper management could overcome the shortcomings of poor relief as it had been hitherto administered. He became so taken with his own proposals that he thought in terms of training pauper children to assume positions of responsibility within the institution as they grew to maturity.[41] Although he held that the principle of less eligibility would guarantee that only the "refuse" of society would seek relief, he did see his "pauper kingdom," as it has been called, as a new type of society that would eventually coexist alongside the larger society of private enterprise.[42]

Bentham prided himself on the logic and rationality of his thought. His proposals for the relief of the poor were part of his overall conception of a centralized government for England to be administered by a salaried cadre of bureaucratic functionaries working in specialized departments responsible for such public services as the police, prisons, hospital, education, and poor relief.[43] In contrast to Adam Smith, who believed in the self-regulation of the marketplace, Bentham believed in centralized direction and strictly regimented control. While he was willing to permit a policy of laissez faire in industry and commerce, he believed that criminals, lunatics, and the impoverished could not be expected to manage their own affairs. Although well-intentioned, Bentham's Panopticon proposal possessed a manipulative and a totalitarian quality which prevented its adoption by a society only partially rationalized.

In spite of the totalitarian cast to Bentham's ideas, there is justice in the comment of Sidney and Beatrice Webb: "When all its defects are duly noted, the scheme emerges as a remarkable forecast of the twentieth-century machinery of government in the highly evolved State."[44]

As has been the case with so much of our story, in the light of twentieth century experience there is a sinister aspect to Bentham's thought that he himself could not have anticipated. Bentham saw in the phenomenon of surplus people an opportunity to transform a mass liability into a profit-making asset. His plan was based upon rigid, depersonalized control in which each individual's capacity to yield a net gain for the institution was to be precisely calculated. As Bentham's thoughts concerning his "pauper kingdom" matured, he came to envisage the institution as a permanent community rather than a temporary refuge. For Bentham mass indigence had not only become an opportunity for capitalist investment, it had also become the basis for an alternative form of society.

The Webbs have pointed out that Bentham's proposal for the management of government and public services by rationalized administration anticipated twentieth century government. However, Bentham's proposal to create a corporation profiting from the labor of surplus people also anticipated, albeit unknowingly, a far more murderous twentieth-century corporate venture, the I. G. Farben factories at Auschwitz, which employed thousands of death-camp inmates as slave labor for the manufacture of synthetic rubber during World War II.[45] The decision to erect a very extensive industrial installation adjacent to the death camp at Auschwitz was made by the highest echelons of one of the world's largest petrochemical cartels. Moveover, the corporate decision was not based on an ideological interest in implementing the "Final Solution" but on what were perceived to be the profit-making potentialities of employing people who were regarded as wholly superfluous to, and therefore wholly expendable by, German society. Furthermore, Bentham's principle of less eligibility involved resort to psychological and at times physical terror, both to discourage the able-bodied from entering the workhouse and to exact from them the greatest compliance when they did. The corporate executives of the I. G. Farben also used a combination of psychological and physical terror, albeit in a far more vicious form, to exact compliance from the inmates of their institution. The threat implied by the never-ceasing smoke from the nearby crematoria added a dimension of terror to the twentieth-century profit-making venture in the employment of surplus people that the threat of merely being cast adrift did not have for the inmates of the nineteenth-century institution.

Admittedly, Bentham's proposals were motivated by a desire to find a rational solution to a tragic social problem, whereas the corporate directors of I. G. Farben were motivated by no such concern. Nevertheless, looking backward from the grim vantage point of the twentieth century, one can discern a continuity between Bentham's proposals for the profitable utilization of those whom he identified as society's "refuse" and the infinitely more vicious attempt by I. G. Farben to profit from the labor of what was regarded as their society's refuse. Although Bentham's Panopticon scheme was never adopted, through his disciple Edwin Chadwick, Bentham probably had a greater influence on the most important single formulation of poor-relief policy of the nineteenth century, the 1834 Poor Law Reform, than any English thinker save his friend Thomas Robert Malthus.[46]

According to Beatrice and Sidney Webb, the rapid increase in the number of indigent persons in the last decade of the eighteenth century and the first decade of the nineteenth century was actually welcomed by British ruling circles. Their attitude was spelled out by Patrick Colquhoun:

> Without a large proportion of poverty, there could be no riches, since riches are the offspring of labour, while labour can result only from a state of poverty...Poverty is therefore a most necessary and indispensable ingredient in society, without which nations and communities could not live in a state of civilisation.[47]

One wonders whether such views have regained a certain respectability in contemporary America.

The period to which we refer witnessed a greater increase in population and in the number of enclosures and wholesale evictions than any other in English history. The Napoleonic wars resulted in a heightened demand for both military personnel and home front laborers. However, when peace came, England was faced with an unprecedented level of unemployment. In addition, since 1795 English poor relief had been complicated by the Speenhamland system which obliged the parish to pay the difference between a laborer's earnings and his family subsistence requirements. Like the contemporary practice of distributing food stamps, Speenhamland was an income supplement scheme. The system attempted to provide a "safety net" for the English poor. Although benevolent in motivation, the actual consequences of the system were devastating. Since employers were assured that the difference between a worker's wages and his subsistence needs would be met by the parish, it was in their interest to pay the lowest possible wages. Workers could not refuse available work on penalty of being denied poor relief altogether. The result was the pauperization of large segments of the English working class.[48]

The system became especially unmanageable as a consequence of the postwar unemployment. Parishes were burdened with ever-increasing poor rates, while rate payers found their obligations difficult to meet because of the hard times. Inevitably, parishes were tempted to reduce payments to the poor, both for the sake of economy and to discourage workers from applying for assistance. There was also a difference between what was generally regarded as an acceptable minimum allowance during wartime prosperity and during the postwar depression. Just as today, the rising cost of maintaining the poor was considered a serious obstacle to economic recovery. Not surprisingly, Malthus' ideas concerning the destructive effects of poor relief were looked upon with increasing favor.[49]

In the fall of 1830, there was a widespread rural insurrection in the southeast of England, a prominent feature of which was the destruction of barns and threshing machinery. After the enclosures, threshing was one of the few types of work providing agricultural workers with a viable living. The introduction of labor-saving machinery threatened the last remaining opportunity for agricultural workers to maintain themselves decently. Their condition had reached a level of despair that required only a spark to set the fires of rebellion ablaze.[50]

The Speenhamland system was a major cause of resentment. Most agricultural workers received a portion of their income in the form of supplementary parish relief. This meant that they were kept continually in a state of degrading dependency. The Roundsmen system of auctioning off unemployed workers exacerbated an already difficult situation. Paupers were often brought to the auctions chained like animals to the carts by iron collars. In addition, the reduction of the supplementary subsistence allowances paid to workers by the parishes under the Speenhamland system was a cause of much anger and resentment. In those locations in which the insurrection was strongest, the poor were convinced that they had a right to parish assistance. Much of the anger of the rebels stemmed from resentment that what they regarded as their "parish pay," their supplementary allowance, was either reduced or terminated altogether by economy-minded parish authorities.[51]

In the aftermath of the failed rebellion, the entire subject of poor relief was reexamined. In 1832 a Royal Commission was appointed to investigate the whole question of poor-law reform. Among the commission's leading members were Edwin Chadwick and the political economist Nassau Senior, whose approach to poor relief can with justice be called cold-blooded. In March 1834 the commission published its famous report.[52] Among the commission's recommendations was that, save for special cases such as medical disability, outdoor relief be terminated and all assistance to able-bodied persons and their families be given inside "well-regulated workhouses." This requirement was, in effect, the workhouse test to which we have referred.

As noted, once admitted to the workhouse, the inmate and his family were separated according to age and sex, dressed in prison-like uniforms, and denied unsupervised contact with the outside world. In accordance with the less-eligibility principle, the diet, routine, and surroundings of the workhouse were designed to intensify the unpleasantness of the institution. Chadwick wrote that the system was designed to make the workhouse

> . . . an uninviting place of wholesome restraint, preventing any of its inmates from going out or receiving visitors without a written order to that effect from one of the Overseers: disallowing beer and tobacco, and finding them work according to their ability; thus making the parish fund the last resource of a pauper, and rendering the person who administers the relief the hardest taskmaster and the worst paymaster that the idle and the dissolute can apply to.[53]

Although there was some attempt to keep the aged, the sick, the insane, and the able-bodied poor in specialized institutions, this proved infeasible. All such institutions served one fundamental purpose. They were "dumping heaps" for the destitute, isolating them from contact with normal society. As a result, the General Mixed Workhouse came to be the predominant form of public shelter for every category of the dependent poor. The placing of the aged and children together with prostitutes and the insane had predictably demoralizing results.[54]

In actual practice, it was impossible to abolish outdoor relief because of the sheer magnitude of the indigent population. At the end of 1839, there were 98,000 paupers in workhouses and 560,000 receiving outdoor relief. England then had a population of about 16,000,000.[55]

Poor relief itself aroused dire fear among the poor. In the case of outdoor relief, the poor were often given part of their allowance in kind rather than money. However, in 1835 an Assistant Poor Law Commissioner reported that in parts of England the poor refused to accept food offered to them, believing it had been poisoned in order to kill them off. They also believed that when the children in a pauper family exceeded three in number the excess was to be killed off, and all young children and women under eighteen were to be sterilized.[56]

The worst fears of the poor appeared to be confirmed by the appearance of a number of works originally written for private circulation advocating the extermination of superfluous pauper infants. The most notorious work was a pamphlet known as

"Marcus on Populousness." It was widely believed that the author was a member of the Poor Law Commission, although this was emphatically denied.[57]

The actual authorship of this and similar works that appeared around 1838 has never been ascertained. It is equally possible that they were written by Malthusians or by anti-Malthusians who sought to discredit the work of the Poor Law Commission. Nevertheless, neither these writings nor the fears of the poor that they were to be sterilized and poisoned can be dismissed as simple paranoia. The poor could not fail to understand their own superfluity or the options available to the state in dealing with them. At the time there was, as noted before, a good deal of discussion of how to solve the problem of England's redundant population. The Sixth Edition of Malthus' *Essay* contained the passage cited in Chapter 3 in which Malthus advocated placing the dependent poor in conditions that were deliberately calculated to kill them. In an age in which the fate of masses of men and women was decided on the basis of economic calculation, it did not take an overly active imagination to perceive that the least costly way to "solve" the problem of surplus people was to eliminate them altogether.

Given the principle of less benefit and the intensified economizing spirit with which poor relief was administered after 1834, it was inevitable that the abuse of the poor would reach a point of public scandal. That point was reached in the Andover affair of 1845.[58] Inmates of the workhouse at Andover, Hampshire, were given the task of crushing the bones of recently dead animals to be used as manure. It was discovered that some of the inmates were eating the rotting gristle and marrow of the bones to supplement their deficient rations. The Andover case was the most dramatic, but by no means the only, instance in which workhouse inmates were alleged to have been outrageously abused. A Select Committee of Parliament was appointed to investigate the case. Among its findings were the following:

> 4. That from the evidence taken before the Committee, the Committee believe, that from the formation of the Union until last Autumn, the general Dietary of the Workhouse was, in quantity at least, too low, and more particularly that

the allowances of bread insufficient; and they find that this dietary was often diminished by the dishonesty of the Master. Some of the inmates of the Workhouse were in the habit of eating raw potatoes and grain and refuse food which had been thrown to the hogs and fowls.

5. That it was also proved that instances occurred in which inmates of the Workhouse, employed in Bone-crushing, ate the gristle and marrow of the bones which they were set to break.

6. That...by a very irregular and improper practice, the produce of the labour of the paupers in bone-crushing at the Workhouse is stated to have been disposed of among the Guardians, by the Chairman putting up the same at a sort of mock auction in the Board-room.[59]

The Andover scandals resulted in the dissolution of the Poor Law Commission and some attempts to ameliorate the conditions of workhouse inmates, such as permitting married couples over sixty years of age to occupy a separate bedroom in the workhouse. According to the Webbs, conditions in the workhouses improved gradually. To Chadwick's disgust and England's credit, the harshest provisions of the New Poor Law were gradually abandoned in practice if not in law.[60]

The actual horror of the workhouses has been well documented both in literature and in social history. Instead of reviewing the horror in full detail, it will serve our purpose to cite George Lansbury's account of his first visit to a workhouse. Lansbury (1859-1940) was Leader of the British Labour Party (1931-1935) and a Member of Parliament (1910-1912 and 1922-1940):

My first visit to a workhouse was a memorable one. Going down a narrow lane, ringing the bell, waiting while an official with a not too pleasant face looked through a grating to see who was there, and hearing his unpleasant voice—of course, he did not know me—made it easy for me to understand why the poor dreaded and hated these places, and made me in a flash realise how all these prison or bastille sort of surroundings were organised for the purpose of making self-respecting, decent people endure any suffering rather than enter. It was not necessary to write up the words "abandon hope all ye who enter here." Officials, receiving ward, hard forms, whitewashed walls, keys dangling at the waist of those who spoke to you, huge books for name, history, etc., searching, and then being stripped and bathed in a communal tub, and the final crowning indignity of being dressed in clothes which had been worn by lots of other people, hideous to look at, ill-fitting and coarse — everything possible was done to inflict mental and moral degradation. The place was clean: brass knobs and floors were polished, but of goodwill, kindliness, there was none. There is a little improvement in the ordinary workhouses of today, but not much. Most of them are still quite inhuman, though infirmaries, hospitals, and schools are all vastly improved. But 30 years ago the mixed workhouse at Poplar was for me Dante's *Inferno.* Sick and aged, mentally deficient, lunatics, babies and children, able-bodied and tramps all herded together in one huge range of buildings. Officers, both men and women, looked upon these people as a nuisance and treated them accordingly... The paupers, as they were officially styled, were allowed out once a month and could be visited once a month. Able-bodied men were put to stone-breaking and oakum-picking. No effort was made to find work for men or women.[61]

Lansbury knew the workhouse from firsthand experience. He served as a guardian in one institution in 1892. His description is a graphic account of what happened to the descendants of the English peasants who had been cast out of their ancient way of life and who were unable to adjust to the new world of modernization.

The poor called the workhouses "Bastilles." The Webbs described them as "gaols without guilt." The workhouse has also been called "the gaol as well as the goal of poverty." The workhouses were, in effect, small-sized concentration camps. They fulfilled the basic function of all concentration camps, namely, to provide an institution of incarceration for people whom society wished to eliminate either temporarily or permanently without necessarily killing them, most of whom had committed no crime and could not be confined through the normal workings of the criminal code. Put differently, in contrast to normal prisons, concentration camps tend to be extra-legal institutions of incarceration for the guiltless but unwanted. It was to such institutions that those peasants who could not recover from their defeat at the hands of the landowners were condemned.

5
THE SAFETY VALVE OF EMIGRATION

WE HAVE SEEN that as early as the seventeenth century emigration had been proposed as a way of solving the problem of Britain's growing number of paupers. However, it was not until the end of the Napoleonic wars that serious consideration was given to emigration as a solution to what was for the first time called Britain's redundant or surplus population. There had been some emigration in the eighteenth century from the British Isles to America. For example, 43,720 people left from five Irish ports to settle in America between 1769 and 1774.[1] Between 1763 and 1775 about 25,000 Scots emigrated to America, but the principal source of emigrants to the New World from Great Britain during the eighteenth century was Ulster. It is estimated that approximately 225,000 Ulstermen came to North America between 1717 and 1775, the vast majority emigrating to what is now the United States.[2] Canada first became a goal of British emigrants after the American War of Independence. The first sizable group of non-French immigrants to Canada were the Loyalists who left the United States after the war.

The end of the Napoleonic wars was followed by a severe economic crisis. About 300,000 demobilized soldiers and sailors were thrown on the labor market at a time when war-related industries were being dismantled. At the same time the enclosures and evictions continued without letup. Unemployment reached unprecedented levels. Wages fell both in the country and the city, causing poor rates, the rates property holders were required to pay for the maintenance of the destitute, to rise to as much as 50 percent of the rents.[3] Malthus' grim prediction about population outrunning subsistence appeared to be confirmed by the course of events.

With both unemployment and the poor rates rising, the problem of what to do with the poor assumed a new urgency. In 1814 the same Patrick Colquhoun who in 1803 had written about the social benefits of mass poverty pointed out that the far-flung British colonies offered the country a superb resource for "the beneficial employment of a redundant population."[4] There was little initial response. There was, however, a great deal of pamphlet literature on both the Poor Laws and overpopulation, but much of it was Malthusian in tone, stressing the harm done by poor relief.[5] The question of emigration was taken up by Malthus himself in the Fifth Edition of his *Essay* (1817). Malthus did not see emigration as a long-term solution to Britain's population problem but he did see it as the most viable means of alleviating the unprecedented unemployment problems facing Great Britain as a result of the sudden demobilization of manpower and industry after twelve years of war.[6]

In the same year Robert Torrens and W. G. Hayter placed papers on the subject of government-assisted emigration before the Select Committee of the House of Commons on the Poor Laws. Both advocated the adoption of official programs by means of which able-bodied men on poor relief would be assisted in settling in the British colonies overseas. W. G. Hayter argued that such a program would cost no more than keeping a family in the workhouse for a year.[7] Robert Torrens proposed that the program be made compulsory and that any person on poor relief who refused to emigrate be denied poor relief.[8] Hayter opposed compulsory emigration, arguing that the government would not lack voluntary participants and that compulsory emigration would be too arbitrary an act of the state. Although there was considerable interest in the proposals, no action was taken. Nevertheless, from a historical perspective, Torrens' proposal was one of the first to advance the idea that the state ought to adopt what amounted to a program of compulsory emigration of its economically redundant population. Because of the abundance of overseas land available to the British government, the proposal was relatively mild. Nevertheless, it was a deliberate plan for the systematic, involuntary uprooting of a group of citizens from their native land by their own government.

Until 1819 the Colonial Office was skeptical about government-assisted pauper emigration. There had been several small efforts to aid emigrants from Scotland and Ulster to settle in Canada between 1815 and 1819 but the purpose was to increase the population of Britain's North American colony and limit the population growth of the United States. It was feared that an underpopulated Canada might eventually be taken over by the United States.[9] However, in 1819 a combination of an exceptionally poor harvest the previous year, high unemployment, and a precipitous decline in wages, especially among Scottish weavers, led to widespread despair, civic disturbances, and finally the so-called Peterloo massacres.[10]

After 1819–1820 fear of working-class disturbances led the Colonal Office to consider subsidized emigration. Parliament voted £59,000 for a program of assisted emigration to the Cape Colony in what is now South Africa. When the program was announced, about 80,000 people applied and 3500 actually emigrated. The emigrants found settlement far more difficult than they had anticipated and the program was only marginally successful.[11] The following year, a more modest program was initiated to assist some impoverished Scottish weavers from the Glasgow area to settle in Canada.[12] Both the South African and Canadian projects were initiated in response to the civic disturbances that accompanied the economic depression. Only after civic disorders had dramatized the destabilizing potentialities of a surplus population did the government act even on a small scale.

The most important advocate of emigration as a solution to the problem of population superfluity in this period was Robert John Wilmot Horton, who served as Parliamentary Under-Secretary in the Colonial Office from 1818 to 1828.[13] Horton became interested in emigration as a result of his official concern for the defense of Britain's North American colonies. He had also taken the trouble to read the political economists and had became convinced that redundant labor, though a "curse of the mother country," could become the "blessing of the colonies." He argued that every unemployed laborer was superfluous and a tax on the community. He estimated that the superfluous population of the British Isles approached 2,000,000 out of a total of 10,000,000. He conceded that population redundancy was a relative phenomenon depending on the relation between available work and the size of the labor force. He envisaged a time when Britain might support a much larger population but argued emigration would provide immediate relief. He also argued elimination of the surplus labor would cause wages to rise. As the labor force shrank, the laws of supply and demand would make it possible for many paupers to find work at good wages. Thus, there would be a 'multiplier' effect in emigration and it would not be necessary to get rid of every pauper in order to eliminate pauperism.[14]

Although Horton agreed with Malthus that emigration would provide a temporary solution to a situation stemming from the postwar economic crisis, he did not agree with Malthus that no matter what happened population would eventually outrun society's food resources. If the standard of living rose, Horton argued, people would be likely to have fewer children.[15] Malthus had argued the reverse. In actual practice, Horton rather than Malthus appears to have been vindicated by the subsequent course of events.

Horton also believed that as long as there were more workers than jobs, it would be possible for employers to take advantage of the situation and lower wages to subsistence levels in the knowledge that there would always be desperate people willing to take whatever work was available. He therefore opposed repeal of the Corn Laws and lowering of taxes, arguing that manufacturers would not pass on the savings but would use the opportunity to lower wages and increase profits.[16]

Horton could envisage only one solution: large-scale emigration. He therefore proposed that £12,000,000 be appropriated for the purpose of transporting 1,000,000 paupers to the British colonies overseas.[17] Horton's proposals were radical and the scale he suggested approached that of the mass population transfers of the twentieth century.

Horton was primarily interested in assisting the emigration of agricultural workers rather than artisans. Some of his more important writing on the subject dates from 1822, when a severe drop in food prices caused great distress among rural workers.[18] From Horton's point of view there were simply too many of them in England and too few in North America.

While Horton was attempting to secure government support for his emigration project, a number of English parishes had their own small-scale schemes for pauper emigration. To illustrate: several parishes in Cumberland sent their paupers off to North America, with only £3 each. The parishes wanted to get rid of the paupers in such a way that they would be unable to return home.[19] There was a characteristic callousness to some of the British people-dumping schemes that anticipate in a small way Fidel Castro's boast during the Cuban refugee crisis of 1980 that he had got rid of over 100,000 of Cuba's "scum" and dumped them on America's shores. A Scottish journal declared that "Emigration is considered a riddance of diseased population."[20] One English lady wrote approvingly of dumping undesirables in America:

> In 1830 the parish of Corsley, Wiltshire, shipped off at its own cost sixty-six of the least desirable of its inhabitants, about half being adults and half children...The emigrants consisted of several families of the very class one would wish to remove, men of suspected bad habits who brought up their children to wickedness, whilst there were several poachers among them, and other reputed bad characters.[21]

Horton was not interested in mean and petty dumping schemes. He was seriously interested in solving a critical social problem which, he believed, would only get worse if ignored. His chance to set his ideas before the public came in 1826 and 1827 when the House of Commons appointed Select Committees to consider the question of emigration. The topic had been discussed in the Poor Law Committees of 1817 and 1819, but the Select Committees of 1826 and 1827 were the first to consider the topic by itself. Horton was chairman of both the 1826 and 1827 committees.[22]

Several committee members possessed large estates in Ireland. This aroused the suspicion that the committees were interested in securing public funds for the purpose of removing evicted peasants from Ireland. The suspicion seemed to be confirmed by the suggestion of E. G. Stanley, a committee member who owned property in Ireland, that emigration would be a useful means of gradually removing Ireland's numerous evicted peasants. Actually, there was no special stress on Ireland in the work of the committees.

Nevertheless, there was an element of violence in Stanley's proposal, as well as in many of the other schemes for Irish emigration. Most owners of large estates in Ireland were absentee landlords whose title to the land was originally based upon naked conquest. Having conquered the land and extracted rents from the conquered population in one age, the English landowners set about evicting the peasant descendants of the defeated population in another. Finally, in the nineteenth century they began to float proposals for eliminating through emigration whatever portion of the native population was no longer useful to them. Although the proposals called for state-assisted emigration rather than deportation, many of the Irish suspected the British government would welcome any program or event likely to reduce the population of their native land. This is hardly surprising in view of the widespread fear among England's own poor that the food offered to them by parish authorities had been deliberately poisoned to reduce their number. At the time of the famine, Irish suspicions concerning English intentions seemed to be confirmed by the way Irish distress was handled by the British government. We shall return to this subject.

A large number of witnesses from both the British Isles and the colonies appeared before the Select Committees, including Malthus. Malthus' view on population had been especially influential in creating sentiment in favor of emigration, which was seen as a principal means of preventing England's population from outstripping its resources. Yet, Malthus himself was not wholeheartedly in favor of emigration. As we have noted, he saw emigration as useful in certain limited situations, but, in the long run, he regarded it as a palliative incapable of preventing a population crisis.

The Scottish landlords who testified before the committees were skeptical about emigration. They acknowledged Scotland had a problem of population redundancy. Nevertheless, they argued, every departing Scot would be replaced by an even less fortunate Irishman. In effect, the Scottish lords preferred their own kind in the slums of Glasgow.

One of the strongest opponents of Horton's proposal for pauper emigration was William Cobbett, perhaps the most important journalistic defender of the rights of agrarian workers of the period. Cobbett argued that the poor had as much right to live in England as anyone else. He asked why a farm worker, who produced more than he consumed, should be forced to leave the country while someone who lived off tithes or taxes, consuming more than he produced, could stay. He did, however, believe members of the middle class might want to emigrate before they were ruined by excessive taxation. Cobbett urged those who intended to emigrate to go directly to the United States, which was better suited to receive immigrants than the British colonies.[23]

It was Horton's earnest hope that his plan for mass emigration would ultimately be adopted by Parliament. Nothing of the sort took place. Whereas many of Britain's leaders saw some merit in large-scale emigration and were prepared occasionally to assist small groups of emigrants, they were unwilling to adopt Horton's ambitious plan. Horton was convinced that only an uncompromising solution would work. The leaders were unprepared to go along. Nevertheless, they did take Horton seriously, and had there not been some changes in the upper echelons of government Horton might have gotten more of what he sought.[24]

With or without government assistance, almost 10,000,000 people emigrated from the British Isles from 1815 to 1900.[25] Even though this figure includes emigrants from Ireland, it is an emigration statistic of unprecedented magnitude in the history of humanity. Never before did so many people voluntarily undertake to uproot themselves from their native land. Moreover, these figures do not begin to suggest the full magnitude of the uprooting process caused by the agricultural and industrial revolutions. Many more millions left the countryside for urban habitations within England that proved to be among the most dreary, unsanitary, and degrading shelters in which free human beings have ever dwelt. The condition of the English working class in the early stages of the industrial revolution has been the subject of numerous official reports, book-length studies, and works of fiction. It is not necessary to review the literature for our purposes. However, the extraordinary scope of the uprooting process resulting in both mass emigration and debilitating urbanization must be kept in mind when the question of the social consequences of the enclosures and the overall rationalization of British society is explored. When we turn to authors such as Karl Marx, Friedrich Engels, R. H. Tawney, John and Barbara Hammond, Karl Polanyi, E. P. Thompson and Eric Hobsbawm, we are impressed with the tragic and devastating social consequences for the working people of what the economic historian Carlo Cippola has identified as one of the "deep breaches in the historical process."[26]

It is Cippola's opinion that the two most radical breaches in the continuity of human experience were the agricultural revolution that began between the ninth and the seventh centuries B.C. and the industrial revolution that began in Great Britain in the eighteenth century. According to Cippola, "With each one of these two Revolutions, a 'new story' begins: a new story dramatically and completely alien to the previous one. Continuity is broken between the cave-man and the builders of pyramids, just as all continuity is broken between the ancient ploughman and the modern operator of a nuclear station."[27]

Cippola stresses the discontinuity between the industrial revolution and the culture preceding. It is my opinion that a radical discontinuity in values and consciousness occurred before the industrial revolution and facilitated its development. The industrial revolution was part of a larger revolution in consciousness, the revolution of rationality, an early manifestation of which was the shift from subsistence to cash agriculture. That is why we have focused our attention on the transformations in land tenure at the beginning of the English agricultural revolution. Nevertheless, whether one takes the agricultural or the industrial revolution as the starting point of what Karl Polanyi called the "great transformation," the question of the long-range social consequences of the revolution continues to be a matter of debate. The elder Arnold Toynbee's description of the industrial revolution can be taken as representative of the pessimistic view. According to Toynbee, the industrial revolution was

> a period as disastrous and as terrible as any through which a nation ever passed; disastrous and terrible, because side by side with a great increase of wealth was seen an enormous increase in pauperism; and production on a vast scale, the result of free competition, led to a rapid alienation of classes and the degradation of a large body of producers."[28]

There is, however, another body of opinion that stresses the economic growth that the English agricultural and industrial revolutions made possible. According to the English economist R. M. Hartwell, before the industrial revolution the social product was distributed by command, whereas afterwards distribution was more directly determined by the marketplace. Hartwell argues that the latter method made it possible to relate distribution to productivity. As a result, wages tended to rise as labor productivity increased. Labor was also able to organize in defense of its interests for the first time.[29] Hartwell conceded that those rendered workless by the industrial revolution were extremely numerous. Nevertheless, he holds that the factories created far more jobs than were lost by the elimination of inefficient producers. Moreover, Malthus' fear that a growing population would prove catastrophic to England was refuted by the extraordinary increase in productivity made possible by the industrial revolution. According to Hartwell, England's extraordinary material during the nineteenth century was a direct consequence of the operation of a free and, hence, rational market economy:

> If one views the industrial revolution as the outcome, institutionally, of an increasingly efficient market (i.e., of a market in which economic behavior, rational, maximizing behavior, could operate with expectations of reward and punishment according to the successful prediction of market trends and responses), then factors making for efficiency of the market were of paramount importance for the industrial revolution. Those changes which enabled economic

behavior, whether by consumers or producers, to be satisfied and rewarded, and hence encouraged, gave the market system its ongoing impetus. As consumers maximised satisfaction and producers maximised profit, incentives to work and produce were sustained and reinforced. As custom and command ceased to determine economic decision-making, and as the market increasingly determined such decisions, rationality permeated the whole of social life in a mutually reinforcing process of change.[30]

G. E. Mingay has offered a judgment on the transformations of English agriculture that is similar to Hartwell's: "The reorganisation of scattered holdings into more compact blocks, the more soundly constructed and enlarged farm buildings, and the gradual consolidation of small farms into larger units made for more efficiency and provided the basic framework within which improved techniques could be exploited more successfully."[31]

Whether one agrees with those who stress the negative consequences of reason's revolution or those who stress its achievements, there is general agreement that the historical transformation was extraordinarily costly in human terms and that, short of an unprecedented demographic catastrophe, the process appears to be irreversible. There is, however, one question seldom considered by either group: What if overseas emigration had not been available to England and, at a later time, to the rest of Europe as a means of moderating the monumental sufferings? Of course, a counterfactual hypothetical question seldom yields a satisfactory answer. Nevertheless, the question is important because, allowing for local variation, the revolution that first began in England has become a worldwide phenomenon at a time when there remain few, if any, relatively empty territories to which those people currently displaced by the revolution can emigrate. At present, large numbers of migrant workers from Turkey, Yugoslavia, southern Italy, and Spain have found work as *Gastarbeiter* in the countries of northern Europe, thereby relieving the endemic problem of unemployment and overpopulation at home. In addition, the United States has become the goal of hundreds of thousands of economically distressed persons from the Caribbean, Mexico, and Central America. Still, sooner or later these migratory movements are likely to be terminated. Emigration will then no longer serve as a safety valve for the dislocating effects of the modernization process.

The closing of the safety valve is already evident in West Germany, where fifteen leading professors have recently signed a manifesto deploring: "...the undermining of the German people through the presence of several million foreigners and their families, the deGermanization of our language, our culture and our national character."[32]

West Germany's economic boom is over. At this writing unemployment has reached a postwar high of 8.2 percent for Germans and 12 percent for foreign workers, the *Gastarbeiter*. There is widespread public sentiment for the departure of the 4,650,000 foreigners who work in West Germany. The largest single contingent of these workers are 1,500,000 Turks. They are also the object of the greatest animosity. They tend to have more difficulty learning German than other foreigners and their children normally do not do well in school. If they remain in Germany, they are likely to form a permanent undercaste. Their situation is further complicated by the fact that most are not Christian. At the end of World War II, it appeared that the National Socialists had succeeded in creating a homogenous German ethnic community, a *Volksgemeinschaft*, by exterminating the Jews. However, the labor requirements of an overheated industrial economy soon led to the recruitment for German industry and commerce of a larger contingent of foreigners than were ever before domiciled in Germany. With the advent of hard times, hate scribblings were once again found on the walls. The message used to be *"Juden Raus."* Today it is *"Out with the Turks."*

It would, however, be a mistake to assume that what is happening in West Germany is an expression of a distinctively German lack of tolerance. On the contrary, the more one studies responses to the phenomenon of rising unemployment throughout the world, the more one is likely to be convinced that ethnic and religious tolerance falls as unemployment rises. Clearly, migration has its limits as a solution to the problem of surplus people.

When we turn to the current situation in the United States, especially the condition of what has been called the American "underclass," we may gain some idea of what nineteenth-century England might have been like without the safety valve of emigration. Although the United States has been the destination par excellence of other nation's surplus populations, there does not appear to be any place to which its own increasingly massive surplus population can migrate. Perhaps that is one of the reasons why some American science enthusiasts have proposed schemes for space colonies.

America now possesses an underclass numbering millions of persons who are superfluous to the normal functioning of its economic system. In recent years, the United States has experienced a steady rise not only in normal crime but, far more alarming, in crimes involving gratuitous viciousness. These include rape, vandalism, excessive violence, often with homicide, in minor disputes between strangers, as well as cases of armed robbery and mugging wherein victims have been murdered even though they were willing to surrender their valuables. Among the most vicious examples have been crimes in which individuals have been pushed in front of oncoming subway trains by total strangers in New York City. When apprehended, the perpetrators seldom express any sense of remorse or regret.

Many of the crimes are drug related. Both the sale and the habitual use of drugs can be seen as expressions of rejection of a work-oriented society by those who either derive no benefit from that society or who are incapable of conforming to its disciplines. Because of the high cost of the habit, drug use frequently can be maintained only by criminal activity, thereby placing further strain on the texture of normal society.

The problem of the American underclass remains one of the most potentially explosive issues facing all Americans. Millions of men and women have found it impossible, more often than not through no fault of their own, to find a place for themselves in contemporary technological civilization. The rewards of that civilization are a source of anger, frustration, envy, and criminal temptation for those who are barred from attaining them. Moreover, the penalties for deviance from society's norms do little to deter those whose lives have neither goal nor hope. The presence of this underclass affects the quality of life of all Americans, as can be seen in the pervasive sense of fear and threat among the general population, as well as the widespread purchase of guns as a defense against enemies who, though unseen and unknown, are thought to be likely to strike at any time.

In spite of the steady rise in crime, until now most members of the underclass have been more or less pacified by the availability of welfare payments, inexpensive or free medical services, and food stamps. At present, a monumental cutback in such pacification measures is being undertaken by the federal government. The full effect of the cuts has yet to be felt, and there is no assurance that present reductions will be the last. It is not difficult to imagine the destabilizing consequences of a situation in which people who have proved incapable of creating a viable place for themselves find that they can no longer meet their subsistence requirements. Crime will then appear to an ever-growing proportion of the population to be the only remaining survival strategy. That process is already under way. As we have seen, the earliest motive for poor relief in England was not charity but concern for public order. Should present trends continue in the United States or should an economic depression render it even more difficult for the government to allocate scarce resources to the indigent, the problem of coping with the underclass will become a police matter pure and simple. Again, it is not difficult to imagine the grim consequences of such a scenario. We shall return to this issue.

Nor are members of the underclass the only Americans without full-time employment who have been pacified by government financial assistance. For example, in 1979 there were approximately 9,700,000 persons enrolled in American colleges and universities, many of whom received indirect subsidies in the form of low-cost student loans guaranteed by the federal government and tax-supported tuition rates that did not cover the true cost of a university education. As of this writing, the current administration is attempting stringently to reduce the number of such loans, although it is by no means certain that the administration has taken into account the full social costs of the proposed economies. One of the most important non-learning functions of the American system of higher education has been to provide a very large sector of otherwise unemployable middle-class men and women with a respectable and useful environment in which to await their turn to enter the labor market. The system also provides an environment to which people can turn in later life. In any event, the problem of population redundancy in the United States would be far more dangerous if a large number of the middle class youth who currently attend colleges and universities were suddenly to be thrown upon an overly saturated job market.

Although the availability of the American continent for mass settlement enabled Europe to avoid some of the worst social consequences of the agrarian and industrial revolutions, the United States may in time be compelled to endure the full, albeit delayed, impact of those revolutions. During the nineteenth century there were frequent complaints by Americans that Europe was dumping its problem people on America's shores.[33] In actuality, the descendants of those who were allegedly dumped by the Europeans have not been the major source of America's current problems. While the workless include white Anglo-Saxon Protestants from Appalachia, Hispanics and blacks constitute the majority of those in dire straits. Because blacks and Hispanics are culturally and ethnically distinct from the American mainstream, it is unlikely that the harshness of their treatment, insofar as they are members of the underclass, will be mitigated by any bonds of community and compassion felt by those who control the nation's resources. On the contrary, one of the most dismal lessons of English history is that, with the onset of modernization, the bonds of community were radically attenuated even where peasant and lord shared a common origin, or at least came from families who had lived and worked together for centuries, spoken the same language, and worshipped in the same parish. There is, as we have stressed, an abstract and depersonalizing element in functional rationality, the practical effect of which has been to attenuate whatever bonds between persons could not be defined in economic and contractual terms. That the enclosures were largely responsible for the disappearance of any bond of community between persons in rural England is the opinion of W. E. Tate, who writes:

> Enclosure had much to do with making the English village a class society of clearly demarked possessors and dispossessed... It may well be due to enclosure that the village nowadays is the abode of an assembly of disconnected individuals and classes, rather than that of a well-knit and finely graded community, with class distinction it is true, but these much more blurred than they became in later times and often still remain.[34]

We have seen the grim practical consequences of this attenuation of community in a land in which, as was the case in the Scottish enclosures, the laird and peasants were actually members of the same clan. In America no such bond exists. The underclass and those responsible for policing them are largely separated by differences of race, religion, culture, and class. In a time of crisis, the absence of community would in all likelihood facilitate the imposition of harsh measures against the underclass with little or no psychological resistance on the part of the police. This is already evident in the mistrust, hostility, and downright brutality that so frequently characterize the relations of the police and the underclass.

Thus, the story of population redundancy, beginning with the enclosures and continuing with the treatment of the indigent and redundant in England from the period of the Tudors onward, is part of a story yet to reach its final dénouement. By both opening up new sources of wealth for the British landowners and making possible a vastly enlarged food supply, the enclosures facilitated the huge increase in population that created the human foundation of Britain as a world economic and imperial power. Nevertheless, there was, as we have seen, a terrible night side to this unquestioned means of improving agricultural productivity. The enclosures created the beginnings of a problem that continues to hang like an ever-enlarging sword of Damocles over civilization as we know it, the intractable problem of population redundancy, a population made redundant less by its size or by resource scarcity than by technological efficiency and surplus productivity. Had it not been for the safety valve of emigration, in all likelihood the history of Great Britain in the nineteenth century would have been far bloodier than it was. Nor did the safety valve function only for those lacking the capacity to integrate themselves into the new civilization. Thousands of men with skills appropriate to an industrializing society found use for their skills only because Britain's colonizing and imperial ventures absorbed their talents. Imperialism and emigration prevented these people from experiencing the bitter downward social mobility that might have been their lot had they been forced to remain bottled up in an England devoid of population outlets.

6
THE IRISH FAMINE

FEW DEMOGRAPHIC CATASTROPHES in modern times have been as devastating as that which the Irish people endured in the years from 1846 to 1848. Out of a population conservatively estimated at 9,000,000, Ireland lost approximately 2,500,000 people, half of whom emigrated and half perished as a result of the famine and famine-induced causes.[1]

To this day, debate continues concerning the extent to which the famine was a natural or a man-made catastrophe. There was, however, an undeniable man-made component to the tragedy, the introduction of the potato as the basic food of the Irish peasantry. The potato had been introduced in Europe from North America by the early explorers who returned from their voyages of discovery with such unknown plants as maize and the potato. Although not a native plant, the potato was more suited to northern Europe's climate and soil conditions than was grain. An acre planted with the potato could yield four to six times as much food as an acre planted with grain. In addition, potato cultivation required far less effort, as well as fewer and simpler farm implements, than the cultivation of grain. According to historian William L. Langer, the quantum leap in food supply made possible by the potato materially contributed to Europe's "initial population explosion."[2]

The potato reached Ireland about 1600 and soon became the staple food of that nation's peasantry. In addition to being plentiful, cheap, and easy to cultivate, the potato was nutritionally very satisfactory. When combined with milk or milk products it served as an all-purpose diet for both children and adults. It was also used to feed hogs, cattle, and fowl.

Unfortunately, reliance on a single crop contained the seeds of disaster. When the potato crop failed, there were no cheap substitutes. Given Ireland's primitive subsistence economy, peasants had no money with which to import other foods in an emergency. The situation was further complicated by the fact that as time passed the potato-cultivating peasants lost the complex skills required for the cultivation and preparation of grain and meat. Survival became wholly dependent upon the success or failure of the potato crop.[3]

The exploding population was a further complicating factor. In 1700 Ireland's population was approximately 2,500,000. Fifty years later it was 3,000,000 and in 1800 it reached 5,250,000. In 1841 the official census placed the population at 8,175,124, but many authorities believed the actual population to have been one-third higher.[4] Ireland was the most densely populated country in Europe. It also had the highest rate of population increase. The population of England and Wales was also increasingly rapidly, but between 1779 and 1841, the English increase was at most 88 percent whereas Ireland's was 172 percent.[5]

Ireland was a conquered nation and was treated as such. England prevented the country from developing an industrial base that might have provided employment for the population. Moreover, jobs in government administration were reserved almost exclusively for Protestants in an overwhelmingly Roman Catholic country. Protestants were favored and Catholics distrusted by the British government. Over the years Ireland's Roman Catholic landowners had been systematically deprived of their property. In spite of the fact that most people were Roman Catholic, the Established Church was the Anglican Church of Ireland. Until the Tithe Commutation Act of 1838, the occupiers of the land, that is, the desperately impoverished peasants, were obliged to pay the tithe to the Church of Ireland. After 1838 the tithe became the obligation of the owner rather than the occupier of the land. However, the practical effect of the Act was merely to change the tithe from a direct to an indirect tax on an unwilling and hard-pressed population. To make matters worse, the Established Church favored a policy of using the military to enforce the collection of the tithe when necessary.[6]

Many of the English landowners never visited their Irish estates. Rents in Ireland were as much as 80 percent higher than in England. During the eighteenth century the "middleman system" developed, in which landowners rented out large tracts at a fixed sum to single individuals who were free to subdivide and sublet the land as they pleased. The landowners were guaranteed an assured income without being burdened with the day-to-day management of property. The middlemen were free to extract whatever the market would bear from the subtenants, the vast majority of whom were tenants "at will" who could be evicted at any time by the landlord or the middleman. Unlike English tenants, evicted Irish peasants had no legal recourse.[7] The system discouraged peasants from noticeably improving their holdings. Since improvements on the property belonged to the landlord, peasants who made improvements ran the risk of being evicted and replaced by someone willing to pay a higher rent.

There is a sense in which landlords treated their Irish properties like slum properties. Slum conditions usually develop when a district becomes overcrowded and single-family units are subdivided. Moreover, because of the competition for space, the landlord has little reason to improve the property no matter what health hazards develop. Something of this sort happened in Ireland. As Ireland's population grew, there was no alternative to subdivision. Without land the peasants were doomed to starve to death. The cities provided no employment opportunities. For twenty weeks of the year, the peasants were engaged in preparing, tending, harvesting, and storing the potato crop; for thirty weeks there was absolutely no work. In 1835 it was estimated that 2,385,000 people were unemployed thirty weeks of the year.[8] The more resourceful peasants emigrated, but in spite of emigration the population grew more rapidly than anywhere else in Europe. As a result, the size of the individual peasant holding became smaller in each generation. Not surprisingly, rents rose and the condition of the peasants became ever more desperate.

Only the potato saved the situation. A small family could live for a year from the produce of one acre. According to the 1841 census, 45 percent of the holdings was under five acres. However, plots of less than one acre were not counted, and it is estimated there were several hundred thousand such plots.[9] Unfortunately, the situation fed on itself. Early marriage was the rule, the girls often marrying at sixteen and the boys at seventeen. Since there was little hope of accumulating capital, there was no reason to delay marriage. As long as there was no crop failure, peasant families could normally meet their minimum requirements for food, clothing, and shelter without too much difficulty. The basic food was easily attainable, although there was usually a period of hunger every winter after one year's potato crop had been consumed and the next year's crop had yet to be harvested. A cabin could be erected by a couple in a few days with available materials. Save for a stool and a stove, peasant dwellings had little if any furniture. By cutting turf and using it for fuel, peasants were able to heat their dwellings.

With food and shelter easily available, married women proved remarkably fertile. Until 1838 Irish peasants could look forward to no protection in their old age. Children were, in effect, the peasant's only form of old-age protection.[10] Yet, as the children came in great numbers, they placed an ever greater strain on the land. It does not take much imagination to see that a Malthusian catastrophe was in the making. As long as the potato crop did not fail, Ireland's population could continue its spectacular growth. Nevertheless, sooner or later population would exceed the limits of the food supply, either through an increase of people or crop failure. It was, as we know, the potato that failed.

From time to time the potato failed in some parts of Ireland.[11] These failures led to frequent prophecies of disaster, but, as people are wont to do, the Irish continued in their accustomed ways. In reality, they had little alternative save emigration, a solution that a sedentary agrarian population initially rejected. However, in 1845 potato blight became general throughout Ireland. The blight had originated in North America during the previous year and affected wide areas of northern Europe, but only in Ireland did the bulk of the population depend on a single crop for its food supply. Without the potato or outside relief, a goodly portion of the Irish nation was doomed to starve to death or succumb to the diseases that would surely attack their famine-ridden bodies. When the seriousness of the situation was first realized in the summer and fall of 1845, a number of futile measures were suggested by the English government. These included suggestions concerning how to treat the rotted potatoes so as to make them edible and the decision of Sir Robert Peel, the English Prime Minister, to import £100,000 of Indian corn or maize from America.[12] It was not Peel's intention to supply Ireland with the food she needed but to use the sale and distribution of small amounts of maize to keep prices from getting out of hand. There were many difficulties with the maize scheme that need not detain us. The fundamental difficulty was that an estimated 4,000,000 people would have to be fed in May, June, and July of 1846 until the new potato crop was ready.[13] The maize could not feed more than the smallest fraction of the population.

There was something of a consensus among England's leaders concerning how the crisis was to be met: it was to be met by free enterprise operating strictly according to the laws of supply and demand. Under the influence of many of the same political economists and their disciples who had formulated the Poor Law Reform of 1834, the British government's commitment to laissez faire came close to being an inflexible religious dogma. Neither Sir Robert Peel nor his successor Lord John Russell believed the government ought to disturb the marketplace. Given the commitment to laissez faire, Peel's decision to purchase maize to stabilize prices represented an intelligent attempt to balance two conflicting imperatives, relief for a starving population and the conviction the government ought not to interfere with commerce. The trouble with reliance on laissez faire was that the overwhelming majority of Ireland's peasants hardly ever saw money and had next to none. The peasants did not farm for the market but to eat and pay the rent. To the extent the British government adhered to a laissez faire policy, it was in effect condemning the peasants to death.

To the commitment to laissez faire was joined the conviction that the right of private property was absolute. Belief in the unconditioned character of private property had been fundamental to the English enclosure movement. In Ireland it was to operate to make even worse a situation already catastrophic. When the failure of the potato crop became known, many landlords were eager to get rid of tenants whom they knew would be unable to pay the rent. In addition, the same market forces operated on the proprietors of Irish property as in England. There was money to be made by eliminating uneconomical subsistence producers and replacing them with farmers or sheepraisers who could produce a cash crop. There was, however, an important difference between the two countries legally united by the fiction of the "Act of Union" (January 1, 1801). In England, at worst eviction resulted in throwing evicted peasants on poor relief. In Ireland eviction could be tantamount to a death sentence.

During the famine years large numbers of peasants were unable to pay rent and were subject to immediate eviction. Merciless evictions were one of the worst aspects of the famine years. Starving, impoverished peasants were turned out of their holdings and their cabins immediately torn down. The lucky ones found shelter as squatters in nearby ditches. The unlucky ones were driven from the ditches by troops or local police. Instead of declaring a moratorium on debts or offering some kind of disaster relief, the English government employed its troops to drive away famine-stricken families.

One especially vicious eviction took place at the beginning of the famine crisis in March 1846 in the village of Ballinglass. The landlord, a Mrs. Garrard, wanted to get rid of her tenants so that she might use her land for grazing. The tenants, numbering 61 families and about 300 persons, were not behind in their rent payments, but as tenants "at will" they had no power to restrain the landlord.[14] The motive for the evictions was similar to that of the English enclosures in which arable land had been converted to pasture. The evictions, however, were carried out with a violence which mirrored the status of the Irish as a conquered people. As the evicted tenants were driven from their homes, the well-kept cabins were torn down and the families driven away. No neighbor was permitted to take them in, and when in desperation the people sought to find shelter in holes in the ground and in ditches, they were driven away by the troops.

An even worse case of eviction took place in the third winter of the crisis on December 19, 1847. The inhabitants of three villages on the estate of a landowner named Walshe were forced out of their homes with the aid of British troops. As was customary, their houses were torn down. The evicted families then attempted to put up tents and shacks, but these too were torn down. When, on "a night of high wind and storm," the wretches begged to be permitted to remain through Christmas, they were driven away. Finally, a Poor Law Inspector set up a "feeding station" for more than three hundred of the survivors. Many were too sick to leave their shelters and crawl to the station. The majority of those who reached the station were sick, naked, and starving.[15] As often happened, the troops were disgusted with the work assigned to them.

When Lord Londonderry, an Ulster landowner of great substance, heard of the Ballinglass evictions, he investigated personally and reported to the House of Lords on March 30, 1846, that he was "grieved" to learn the reports were true.[16] Londonderry's distress at the evictions was not shared by Lord Brougham. In an address to the House of Lords on March 23, 1846, he claimed eviction as the absolute right of the landlord. Should he choose to exercise this right, tenants ought to be shown by the authorities they had no power to resist. According to Lord Brougham, without the landlord's "sacred right" to do as he pleased with his property, "property would be valueless and capital would no longer be invested in cultivation of land..."[17]

By the middle of October 1846, the worst fears concerning the potato crop were realized. When first harvested the crop appeared to be perfectly healthy, but within a few days a very large part had rotted. Ireland's peasants were suddenly faced with the prospect of starvation. Moreover, relief was complicated by the mass unemployment which perennially plagued Ireland. Almost 2,500,000 people were normally unemployed between the previous year's harvest and the next year's planting. Even in good times these people had no hope of finding work.

As we have seen, the government's basic response was to look to the unfettered marketplace to solve the problem. Even Peel's scheme for importing Indian corn was based upon the idea that the marketplace was the fundamental resource for coping with the crisis. The purpose of the Indian corn scheme was to curb the worst excesses of a famine-inflated market.[18]

It is, however, worth noting that the government's commitment to free trade was not so firm as to conflict with the interests of England's landowning classes. One of the most bitter political conflicts of the period concerned the question of the repeal of the Corn Laws. The Corn Laws had a long history. At different times the government had attempted to protect England's agriculture through its control of the import and export of grain. After the Napoleonic wars the government sought to subject foreign grain to a sliding scale of import duties in order to keep the price of food produced in England artificially high. With the growth of the population and industrial urbanization, protection of English agriculture was seen as an unfair burden on the working class. The Corn Laws were also opposed by an influential segment of the middle class, especially factory owners, who saw protection as artificially raising their labor costs.[19]

When famine conditions began to prevail in Ireland, there was agitation to repeal the Corn Laws so that food could be imported cheaply. The Prime Minister, Sir Robert Peel, understood the contradiction between a policy of providing money for famine relief while maintaining high import duties on the food to be purchased. Peel, a Tory, became convinced that the Corn Laws had to be repealed. This made his position difficult within his own party. He resigned, but the opposition Whigs were unable to form a government. Peel was then asked by Queen Victoria to resume office. He did, and succeeded in effecting the repeal of the Corn Laws only to become hated by his own party. His situation thereupon became untenable. On June 29, 1846, he resigned a second and last time. Under the pressure of the famine in Ireland and urban agitation for cheaper food in England, the landowners finally lost most of the price protection they had historically enjoyed. There was, however, no comparable hesitation concerning the Irish. They were to pay whatever price market conditions demanded for their food.

Under Peel's administration there were some attempts to relieve conditions in Ireland, such as the purchase of Indian corn. The principal burden of Peel's plan was to fall on the Irish landlords. There was also a plan for employing the destitute on public works projects and the establishment of "fever hospitals" to care for those who had fallen ill.[20] The aid, however, was strictly limited to persons whose need was the result of the potato blight, and there was no provision for aiding the habitually needy. The distinction between the habitually needy and those affected by the famine was useless. Since several million were normally unemployed most of the year and most peasants were endangered by the crop failure, it was impossible to distinguish potato-related from ordinary distress. Furthermore, in earlier crises, reliance on the charity of the landlords had proved futile. Many of the estates were overly large, uneconomical, and debt-ridden. To inherit an Irish estate often meant inheriting responsibility for the debts of one's ancestors.[21]

Without going into detail, it suffices to say that none of Peel's proposals proved effective; but Peel at least was committed to doing what he could for Irish relief. When he resigned, the Whig government of Lord John Russell, grandfather of philosopher Bertrand Russell, proved more committed to free trade than to effective Irish relief. Russell's government was also more congenial to Sir Charles Edward Trevelyan, the Assistant Secretary of the Treasury, a title that did not reveal the full scope of his authority. He was in fact the permanent head of the Treasury and, as such, the ultimate arbiter of any and all money spent on Irish relief. We shall shortly consider Trevelyan's conduct of his office during the crisis. At present, we note that he was an unswerving believer in laissez faire. His commitment to laissez faire was shared by Sir Charles Wood, the Chancellor of the Exchequer in the new government, Trevelyan's superior in the Cabinet, and later the first Viscount Halifax. Both Trevelyan and Wood detested the Irish, a sentiment widely shared in England at the time.[22]

Had there been a successful crop in 1846, there still would have been disease and other aftereffects of the previous year's potato failure. Unfortunately, as Trevelyan was in the process of winding down the meager public assistance dispensed for the previous year, it became apparent the potato crop was ruined once more. If anything, the failure of the 1846 crop was far worse than the previous year's. Moreover, the people were now at the end of their resources. They faced a second winter of famine, but with the government of England in the hands of Lord John Russell. Unlike Peel, Russell had no plans for importing food or involving the English government in any but the most minimal expense on behalf of the Irish. The burden of relief was again thrown onto local sources which were even less able to be of effective help than they were before.[23] Nevertheless, the second crop failure had no effect on policy in London. Trevelyan was determined that no further food be purchased. Three thousand tons of Indian corn remained in government warehouses. Trevelyan gave permission to distribute this food in small quantities in extreme emergencies, but only to relief committees that had the means to pay for it. In addition, by August 8, 1846, the public works projects were terminated in accordance with Trevelyan's policies. However, the general misery was so great that a month later, Lord Bessborough, then Lord Lieutenant of Ireland, ordered that all unfinished public works be restarted.[24]

In London the government decided to initiate a new public works program but one calculated to throw almost the entire cost on the Irish property owners. This was embodied in the Labour Rate Act, which provided that the cost of public works was to be met in the district in which the works were carried out. The expenses were to be paid by all rate payers, that is, those whose property was assessed for the support of the poor. Save for a contribution of £50,000, no money would be forthcoming from the government. The government would, however, advance money at 3.5 percent interest payable over a period of ten years.[25] Since no money had to be paid immediately and the cost fell on all the rate payers in the district, no man felt that he would be especially taxed. Hence, the scheme encouraged a certain irresponsibility. In a short time proposals for L1,500,000 worth of projects were forwarded to the Board of Public Works. The Board was helpless to initiate the measures because of lack of funds. However, as the situation grew desperate and money was advanced by the Treasury, the number of people employed on public works rose spectacularly. In September 1846 there were 30,135; by the end of December there were almost 500,000.[26]

In 1846 the shortage of food was general throughout Europe, and prices rose sharply. Trevelyan welcomed the increase as helping to limit consumption, as if the famine had not done enough to limit consumption.[27] Earlier Sir Randolph Routh, Chairman of the Relief Commission for Ireland and the head of the commissariat department of the British army, had reprimanded a government official for weakening and distributing food to starving people against policy.[28] Now, as Routh began to perceive the extreme need, he pleaded with Trevelyan to send modest amounts of food for the inhabitants of Ireland's west coast, who were in especially desperate straits. Trevelyan responded by rebuking Routh and warning him that any government food purchases would raise prices all over Europe.[29]

When Trevelyan finally relented and placed an order for Indian corn in September 1846, it was too late. There was no food to be had. Moreover, when the public works were started, people began to drop dead at work from hunger. Children were also dropping dead in the workhouses. By October bands of starved, crazed men and women in rags or half naked were roaming the highways in a desperate search for a means to stay alive.

By March 1847 there were 734,000 people employed on public works. The projects were often badly administered make-work schemes. Initially only men were to be employed, but it was difficult to refuse women and children in the face of the overwhelming need. Nor did employment on public works always prevent death by starvation. Wages were extremely low to start with, in part because of the less eligibility principle.[30] With the sharp rise in food prices, wages did not always provide for a minimum diet. The program was hastily conceived and often badly administered. Not only were there bureaucratic delays in initiating projects, but there were frequent delays in paying wages. For those who were used to spending the winter in their cabins warmed by a turf fire, outdoor work in the bitter cold without adequate clothing was an additional hardship. There was also violence, insubordination, and general disorder at many of the works projects, problems that were hardly surprising in view of the conditions.

In spite of their shortcomings, the projects were all that stood between the families of the 734,000 people employed on public works and starvation. Yet, at the beginning of March 1847 Trevelyan decided enough had been done for Ireland and ordered 20 percent of all those on public works to be dismissed by March 20th. By the end of June only 28,000 were still employed on public works! At the same time, the government consented to the establishment of soup kitchens. In place of work, soup kitchens, administered and paid for by local poorhouse authorities, were to constitute Ireland's "safety net."[31]

Ireland had experienced famine and cholera. As the public works were being shut down, it was to endure an epidemic of typhus and "relapsing fever," a related disease. The number of people stricken ran into tens of thousands. Although the exact number of the afflicted will never be known, it is estimated that as many people died of typhus as died of starvation. Typhus was also a principal cause of fatalities among those seeking to flee Ireland by emigration. Moreover, the sick who entered a poorhouse or a hospital had a far worse chance of survival than those who were treated at home.[32]

The same terrible story can be told of the potato failure of 1848. In this year Ireland endured its second complete crop failure, but the situation was complicated by the termination of public works projects, the continuing typhus epidemic, and the determination by Trevelyan and Wood to allocate no further Treasury funds for Ireland. The situation was further aggravated by cruel mass evictions. In the Kilrush district, for an instance, 7000 families were thrown out of their homes in a six-month period. Their cabins were immediately torn down as the inhabitants were cast out.[33] Thousands of such evictions took place all over Ireland in the worst part of winter. Nor did the misery subside in 1849. It took years for the country to begin to recover.

As indicated earlier, the senior official in charge of the relief program was Sir Charles Edward Trevelyan. Trevelyan can best be described as an incorruptible high-level bureaucrat who was prepared to go to any length to do what he regarded as right, even when the consequences involved the death of hundreds of thousands of helpless human beings. He was also an enthusiastic advocate of those measures that foster what we today would consider modernization. Anthony Trollope used him as the basis for the character Sir Gregory Hardlines in his novel *The Three Clerks,* where he is described as a "Civil Service Pharisee."[34] Both in the novel and in reality, Trevelyan is credited with the modernization of the British civil service. Before his reforms, appointment and promotion had more to do with connections than competence. It was he who rationalized the British bureaucracy to the extent possible in his time.[35] We in the twentieth century have learned that a competent bureaucrat, skilled in the repression of feeling and incorruptibly committed to the performance of his official duties, is often capable of doing extraordinary harm to masses of human beings with an undisturbed conscience. Trevelyan was such a man. His brother-in-law, Thomas Babington Macaulay, the great historian, described Trevelyan at the time of his marriage: "His mind is full of schemes of moral and political improvement, and his zeal boils over in his talk. His topics, even in courtship, are steam navigation, the education of the natives, the equalization of sugar duties, the substitution of the Roman for the Arabic alphabet in Oriental languages."[36]

Convinced of his own rightness and a stickler for rules, Trevelyan possessed a distaste for the Irish and their ways so strong that he could write to Colonel Harry Jones, Chairman of the Board of Public Works for Ireland, concerning them: "The greatest evil we have to face is not the physical evil of the famine, but the moral evil of the selfish, perverse and turbulent character of the people."[37]

Apart from the fact that Trevelyan's background was Cornish and Protestant, his enthusiasm for his own world of scientific and industrial progress left him with little sympathy for a premodern, agrarian, and Roman Catholic people who were with good cause bitterly hostile to their British conquerors.

Trevelyan was reluctant to become involved in any program to relieve Irish distress. As we have seen, he believed in the ability of the marketplace to solve the problems created by the food shortage. In October 1846 the magistrates of Cork petitioned that the government's food store be opened because people were starving and even those with jobs could not afford the price of food. The Cork petition was followed by over fifty others within a period of three days. Trevelyan decided that government depots would not be opened save in the western part of Ireland. Even there, Trevelyan ruled that the stores would be opened only after private traders proved unable to supply food in sufficient amounts. There was to be no interference with the marketplace.

On October 18, 1846, Routh wrote to the relief committees in the western part of Ireland telling them not to expect that food from government stores would be sold cheaply. He warned the committees not to stop traders from realizing their full profits from the situation. At the time, people were starving to death. When the Marquess of Sligo complained against the government's refusal to open its stores to the hungry people, Routh responded that in times of scarcity "...high price is the only criterion by which consumption can be economized."[38]

One of the ironies of the crisis is that Ireland exported grain in fairly large quantities during the famine years, some of it to supply the distilleries of England and Scotland. For a balanced picture we must also note that far more grain was imported than exported. However, in September 1846 Routh appealed to Trevelyan to ban the export of grain from Ireland so that the food produced within the country would be available to feed the people. Trevelyan refused.[39] But, when angry crowds gathered to protest the export of food, money was available to send British troops to control the crowds. In some locations the encounters led to fatalities.[40] In December 1846 conditions became so bad in the neighborhood of Skibbereen that two Protestant clergymen from the district journeyed to London to implore Trevelyan to send immediate assistance. They told him that without government aid the people of the district would die of hunger. Not only did Trevelyan refuse, but he wrote to Routh warning him not to open the food depots. Trevelyan concluded his letter to Routh: "We attach the highest public importance to the strict observance of our pledge not to send orders [for food] abroad, which would come into competition with our merchants and upset all their calculations."[41]

At the very moment Trevelyan wrote to Routh, Skibbereen was a district inhabited by hundreds of ragged, emaciated, living corpses. More than 200 people had already died. One eyewitness, Nicholas Cummins, a magistrate of Cork, was so horrified by what he had seen at Skibbereen that he wrote a letter to *The Times* describing conditions there. The letter was published the day after Christmas 1846. Finally, on January 8, 1847, Trevelyan wrote to Routh giving him permission to establish "effective relief" for Skibbereen. However, Trevelyan still refused to allow funds from the British Treasury to be used. Instead, he urged Routh to get the local relief committees to finance aid. This was impossible because of the crop failure. In spite of Trevelyan's verbal change of heart, his actual policy did not change. Nothing was done for Skibbereen.[42]

The free-enterprise system did operate in Skibbereen. While people dropped dead and rats ate their unburied corpses, food was available in the shops, as was the case in most of Ireland. Nevertheless, without money and without the potato, their staple food, the peasants perished for want of a way to acquire the available food.

Trevelyan supported the view that by selling expensive grain Ireland's merchants could earn the money with which to buy cheap substitutes for the potato. His calculations were unrealistic. There was simply no market system available in Ireland for the purchase and distribution of food for mass consumption. Some food was imported for the luxury but not the mass market. Moreover, even if such a system had been in place, the vast majority of the peasants were strangers to a money economy. It would, however, be an error to regard Trevelyan's attitudes as unique and to hold him responsible for the tragedy. It is highly unlikely that a person holding radically different views could have enjoyed the confidence of the Prime Minister.

Although Trevelyan's attitudes were usually seconded by Routh, there were times when Routh, whose position exposed him directly to Ireland's travail, was not as able as Trevelyan to place his commitment to free trade above the sufferings of human beings. It was often easier for London bureaucrats, safely ensconced in their offices, to discount the human consequences of their policies than it was for British officials, both civilian and military, who were on duty in Ireland.

Although Trevelyan never went as far as Nassau Senior, the famous political economist and Chadwick's partner in formulating the Poor Law Reform of 1834, who expressed regret that the famine had killed only one million people, Trevelyan did express satisfaction at the large numbers who were forced to emigrate from Ireland because of the famine. Moreover, he regarded the mass deaths as the unanticipated way in which an "all-wise Providence" had solved the problem of Ireland's imbalance between population and food. He expressed this opinion in a letter to Lord Monteagle: "This [problem] being altogether beyond the power of man, the cure had been applied by the direct stroke of an all-wise Providence in a manner as unexpected and as unthought of as it is likely to be effectual."[43]

In 1848 the authorities observed that the emigrants included many of the more enterprising and energetic farmers. There was apprehension that their loss would seriously hamper the recovery of Irish agriculture. By contrast, Trevelyan was pleased with the emigration:

> I do not know how farms are to be consolidated if small farmers do not emigrate and by acting for the purpose of keeping them at home, we should be defeating our own object. We must not complain of what we really want to obtain. If small farms go, and then landlords are induced to sell portions of their estates to persons who will invest

capital, we shall at last arrive at something like a satisfactory settlement in this country.[44]

There was, of course, yet another way to clear Ireland of peasants and make way for "persons who will invest capital": do nothing during the famine and let the unwanted people die. As the crisis worsened, Trevelyan based his policy on the conviction that famine could best be dealt with by leaving matters to "the operation of natural causes."[45] Trevelyan was wholly supported in this policy by the Prime Minister, Lord John Russell, who in 1848 refused to consider the allocation of further public funds to assist Ireland. The consequence of letting nature take its course was mass starvation and death.

While Trevelyan would never have done anything to kill the Irish outright, as Hitler caused the Jews to be killed a century later, he was knowingly committed to a policy the effect of which was to condemn them to death. If this was not apparent to Trevelyan, it was to Twistleton, the Poor Law Commissioner for Ireland. Toward the end of 1848 Twistleton told Trevelyan it would be advisable to omit from the Irish Poor Law Commission's annual report any figures on how much was being spent on each pauper lest it be said the commission was "slowly murdering the peasantry by the scantiness of our relief." Trevelyan's refusal to commit British funds to Irish relief finally caused Twistleton to resign. Early in 1849 the threat of cholera was again added to the ravages of famine, and even *The Times,* which had steadfastly opposed any aid to Ireland for three years, finally came to the conclusion that exceptional aid had to be given. Charles Wood, the Chancellor of the Exchequer, remained opposed to giving Ireland either a loan or a grant no matter how desperate the situation. Wood was reported as confident the misery would run its course and land prices would fall to a level low enough to attract capitalists to invest.[46]

The government's response to the pressure for emergency aid was a "rate-in-aid" scheme of which the author was Trevelyan. The plan provided that those Irish Poor Relief Unions alleged to be most prosperous were to be compelled to contribute to the support of the distressed unions. The Treasury would immediately advance L50,000 to the distressed unions. They in turn were to be responsible for an additional poor relief levy of 6d in the pound to be paid by all unions. The Treasury's advance was a loan. The scheme created consternation among both Protestants in Ulster and Catholics throughout the country. Its effect was to throw the entire burden of Irish relief upon the Irish themselves after they had endured three years of demographic catastrophe. Although Ireland had been legally united with England since 1801, absolutely no English funds were be be expended. The Irish complained that the plan would be of no real help to the poorer unions but would add a ruinous burden on those unions that had escaped the worst consequences of the famine.[47]

The rate-in-aid scheme was more than Twistleton could take. He resigned, declaring that he considered himself to be an "unfit agent for a policy which must be one of extermination."[48] As the rate-in-aid scheme was being put into effect, a cholera epidemic broke out in Ireland, but this had no effect on British policy. At this point Lord Clarendon, the Lord Lieutenant of Ireland, wrote to the Prime Minister asking for assistance. Commenting on the indifference of the British Parliament to Irish suffering, Clarendon wrote: "... I don't think there is another legislature in Europe that would disregard such sufferings as now exist in the West of Ireland, or *coldly persist in a policy of extermination.*"[49] (italics added)

Agrarian peoples tend to be sedentary rather than nomadic. They love the ground from which they and their ancestors have drawn their sustenance for millennia. The bones of their hallowed dead are implanted within it. They can think of no worse life than that of the nomad and no worse fate than that of the exile. Only a catastrophe unmistakably demonstrating that all possibility of a viable existence in the homeland has been smashed beyond repair could persuade them to move on. And so it was with the Irish. Only utter hopelessness could have driven them from their native soil. It took the famine years to convince them that they had to leave. As a direct result of the famine in excess of 1,000,000 people left Ireland for the New World.[50] An even greater number left for England. Liverpool received the largest number. At the beginning of the famine years, Liverpool had a population of 250,000. By June 1, 1847, it had an additional 300,000 emigrants from Ireland.[51] Its population had more than doubled.

The most compelling reason for Irish emigration to England was the knowledge that as soon as an Irish emigrant set foot on English soil, because of the English Poor Laws, he or she would not be permitted to starve. The trip took a few hours and cost only a few shillings. Very often, money was given to emigrants by landlords or relief officials anxious to get rid of them. The price of the boat trip often meant the difference between life and death. There was another reason why the Irish reversed their age-old pattern and began to flee their native land. When famine-ridden tenants were unable to pay their rent, many of the landlords began to apply to the courts for judgments against the delinquent tenants instead of simply evicting them. Eviction left a peasant homeless but at least his family remained intact. When a landlord secured a judgment against a delinquent tenant, the defendant was thrown into prison and his wife and family were left on their own resources. In the best of times this would have been a terrible fate. In the famine years it was often a death sentence. Hence, as soon as it became known that delinquency proceedings had been initiated, the tenant and his family took whatever possessions they could carry and fled. The land was then cleared and the peasant's dwelling torn down, with the assurance the peasant would never return. In one district alone, County Mayo, there were more than 6000 applications to the courts for such judgments.[52] Again, we note that *instead of helping people to cope with a tragedy of unprecedented scope, the apparatus of government was used to get rid of the unwanted people.*

In England the Irish emigrants were met by almost universal hostility. They were especially hated by the working class, because the desperate Irish were willing to work under worse conditions and for less money than the English. The worst slum districts in England were inhabited by the Irish. Nor did the entrance of masses of ragged and starving Irish into England arouse compassion. Their appearance and their need had the opposite effect. A reaction not unknown elsewhere of blaming the victim for his misfortune became prevalent among people in every level of English society.[53]

The Irish were even less welcome after the typhus epidemic broke out. The emigrants carried the disease with them. In Liverpool alone 40,000 cases were reported, with 2589 deaths. Many of the fatalities were among those who were involved in relief activities on behalf of the Irish. Ragged, starving, and suspected of carrying a deadly disease, the Irish were a burden few English wanted to bear. In June 1847 Parliament passed a law enabling local authorities to return Irish paupers to Ireland, thereby denying to them the assurance that they would at least be fed if they succeeded in reaching England. Many were forcibly and even brutally expelled although the majority were permitted to remain.[54]

Emigration to North America was naturally more expensive, but it was surprisingly cheap because of the British government's policy of encouraging emigration from the British Isles to British North America. The government hoped both to deflect Irish emigration from England and Scotland and at the same time build up the population of Canada. Another reason why the rates were low was that ships carrying timber from Canada to Great Britain required some sort of ballast on the return trip. By 1845 there were 2000 ships involved in the timber trade. Many of these ships took a human cargo of emigrants as a paying ballast.[55]

Conditions aboard the ships were what one might expect where everything had been sacrificed to extreme economy. Before the Passenger Act of 1842 shipowners normally provided the passengers with water and fuel, the passengers providing their own food. After 1842 ships were required to provide passengers with adequate water and seven pounds of provisions, but it was easy for emigrant ships to cheat on water and provisions. During the famine it was not unusual for several hundred people to be crowded into a space that contained only forty or fewer bunks. Sanitary facilities were either woefully inadequate or nonexistent. Both government regulation and enforcement were minimal. As a result, it was possible for a poor emigrant to secure passage from Britain to Quebec for no more than three pounds.[56]

Conditions were materially better on American ships, which were subject to more stringent government regulations concerning safety, construction, and the competence of the crew. Passage on an American ship was also considerably more expensive. The cheapest tickets were about seven pounds, but, among other advantages, American ships were less likely to sink.[57] In addition, American immigration regulations were controlled by the states rather than the federal government. Without some capital and assurance that one would not become a public charge, it was difficult to be admitted to New York or Massachusetts, the two chief goals of the Irish emigrants.[58]

Normally, Irish emigrants traveled on British ships to Quebec, made their way to Montreal, and then crossed the American border. Their final destination was usually Boston or New York. Although the Irish were hardly welcomed in what was then an anti-Catholic, largely Anglo-Saxon Protestant America, almost none of the Irish wanted to remain under British rule in Canada. Their experience with English law and government had convinced them that they could never expect to receive fair treatment in a British territory. By contrast, the United States was a country far in advance of Canada in population, development, and promise. A sizable Irish contingent had already made its way to the United States, where the most important Irish community was located in Boston.

The emigration began in earnest in 1846. The first emigrants reached Canada in April. They were healthy and reasonably well-to-do. However, by the end of the summer, the character of the emigration had changed. Thousands of peasants with little more than the price of passage sought to escape what had become for them an accursed land. Thousands even took the hazardous and unprecedented step of making the North Atlantic journey in winter. This had never before been done by emigrants.[59]

Not all the emigrants completed the voyage. Just as today desperate Vietnamese "boat people" and Haitian refugees risk their lives on ships that are unseaworthy and untrustworthy, so too

Irish refugees took a similar risk during the famine period. The situation was made worse by speculators and ticket brokers who sold passage on unseaworthy or marginally seaworthy boats in excess of capacity. There was profit in human misery. Laws guaranteeing minimum safety were not enforced. There was also cheating and abuse of passengers by unscrupulous crews and dishonest provisioning merchants. Conditions on some ships were so intolerable that they became known as "coffin ships." On one such ship, the *Elizabeth and Sarah,* 42 out of the 276 emigrants died on the trip from Ireland to Quebec in the summer of 1846. In addition to having to endure intolerable overcrowding, the passengers were not given the minimum amount of food and water necessary for survival. Instead of dying of starvation at home, they perished and were buried at sea. This was also to be the fate of thousands of their countrymen.

Conditions deteriorated even further as the typhus epidemic spread over Ireland in 1847. When the St. Lawrence River, closed to traffic during the winter months, was opened in May 1847, there were 84 cases of typhus out of 241 passengers on the *Syria,* the first boat to arrive at the Canadian quarantine station, Grosse Isle. Nine passengers had died at sea and it was estimated that 25 other passengers would develop typhus during the quarantine period. The station was situated in the middle of the St. Lawrence about 30 miles from Quebec. The Grosse Isle quarantine hospital could only accommodate 200 persons. By July there were 2500 persons stricken with typhus on the island. Conditions were appalling. It was impossible to get doctors and nurses to care for the sick. Many of the doctors who responded initially died in the epidemic. There were almost no toilet facilities on an island that was intended to care for a few hundred people and now held thousands of sick, starving, and dying refugees.

As passenger ships disgorged their human cargo, the extent of the horror became fully manifest. The ships were ideal breeding grounds for disease. The experience of the *Virginius* was typical. It left Liverpool with 476 passengers: 158 died en route, 106 arrived with typhus. The quarantine station also became a breeder of disease. One ship, the *Agnes,* arrived with 427 passengers; two weeks later only 150 were alive. Over-crowding became so bad that the authorities were forced to release "healthy" immigrants. The epidemic then spread to Montreal and Quebec, which were wholly unprepared to house and care for the avalanche of sick and desperate refugees. It is estimated that of the 100,000 Irish emigrants who left England and Ireland in 1847, approximately 38,000 perished. Of these 20,000 died in Canada. No less than 5300 died on Grosse Isle; 14,706 died in Montreal and Quebec, and 1120 in New Brunswick. In addition 17,000 perished at sea. These figures do not include those who died in New York and Boston.[60] For all too many, emigration was no escape from death.

The health situation in the United States was far better than in Canada. Boats carrying epidemic-ridden passengers were turned away from American ports and compelled to disembark their passengers at Canadian ports. There were bitter scenes when passengers who had been at sea for seven weeks were turned away from what they hoped would be their final destination. The harsh-ness of the American action had the effect of discouraging captains of ships with typhus-ridden passengers from attempting to disembark them at non-Canadian ports. Nevertheless, it was impossible completely to control the disease among the immi-grants. Both New York and Boston experienced outbreaks of the disease, although not nearly on the scale of Montreal and Quebec.[61]

We shall not discuss the fate of the Irish in the United States in detail. Because of their agrarian background and the suddenness with which they were uprooted and thrown into an urban and capitalist environment, the Irish were at first unprepared for the revolution that had occurred in their lives. In this the story of the Irish anticipates that of many citizens of contemporary under-developed nations. The Irish had been forcibly thrust into the modern world by a demographic catastrophe that was intensified by the government in power in their homeland. They had a native intelligence which had never been directed to the problems of a modern capitalist society. Their failure to develop a capitalist mentality may have been due at least in part to restraints placed by the English upon the development in Ireland of enterprises that might have competed with the newer industries in England. In any event, in the famine years, the peasants were simply incapable of comprehending what had happened to them. When knowledge of the first crop failure became general, the people naively expected the British government would take effective action. It was utterly beyond their comprehension that the government would discern in the famine a welcome opportunity to get rid of them. They understood an ancestral way of life measured according to the rhythms of the land and the seasons. They had no understanding of political economy or of the investment potentialities inherent in their elimination. Nor did they understand that Jeremy Bentham's Utilitarian philosophy, with its principle of the greatest good for the greatest number, could be used by bureaucrats and political economists to justify the sacrifice of their lives to the "greater good" of the agricultural improvement of Ireland.

In the New World they had no choice but initially to take the most menial jobs at the very bottom of the economic ladder. Paradoxically, the very traditionalism which had endangered their existence in the food crisis in Ireland saved them in the New World from disintegrating into a horde of anomic, dislocated and isolated individuals. Their Church was the mainstay of their traditionalism. It was their ultimate source of stability as they attempted to enter a world whose values were so foreign to their custom and their ancient wisdom. The Roman Catholic Church was the repository of the spiritual and cultural values of the mainstream of Western civilization. As such, it was the educator of this uprooted people at every level of development and competence as they attempted to enter the modern bourgeois capitalist world.

The fate of the Irish illustrates as dramatically as any lesson from history the costs involved in the transition from the premodern to the modern world. Shortly after the end of the famine period, the London *Economist* commented on the extraordinary size of the Irish emigration:

> It is consequent on the breaking down of the system of society founded on small holdings and potato cultivation...

> The departure of the redundant part of the population of
> Ireland and Scotland is an indispensable preliminary to every
> kind of improvement...The revenue of Ireland has not
> suffered in any degree from the famine of 1846-47, or from
> the emigration that has since taken place. On the contrary,
> her net revenue amounted to £4,281,999, being about
> £184,000 greater than in 1843.[62]

The views of *The Economist* are no different from those of the
political economists and Trevelyan. They were undoubtedly
written by a cultivated journalist who looked with great satisfaction on the developing modern civilization that his nation had
done so much to bring into being. In all likelihood, like Jeremy
Bentham, he believed in the greatest good for the greatest number.
What furthered "improvement" was to be fostered. Those groups
and classes that stood in the way were to be sacrificed. And, so
they have been throughout the modern period.

Our journalist saw the "departure" of the "redundant part"
of the population of Ireland as "an indispensable preliminary to
every kind of improvement." But, note his language. He wrote
of the "departure" of the Irish, a word which represses knowledge of the tragically compulsive character of the emigration and
hides the fact that as many people died of starvation and disease
as emigrated.

As with so much of our story, the journalist's interpretation
of the events have a sinister meaning in the light of twentieth-
century experience. If the writer had wanted to employ a relatively neutral term with which accurately to describe the experience
of the Irish, he might have written "the *elimination* of the
redundant part of the population...is an indispensable
preliminary to every kind of improvement." His language would
still have repressed the fact that riddance of the Irish took the
form of mass death as well as mass emigration. Had he used
"elimination" instead of "departure," his fundamental point
would have been the same: riddance was the fate of those who
stood in the way of "improvement." Like England's peasants,
who also stood in the way, the Irish had to go.

It is also instructive to note the kind of evidence our journalist offered that Ireland was better off now that its redundant population had been eliminated. We are told Ireland's net revenue has increased and that in 1851 it was £184,000 greater than it had been eight years earlier. In an earlier age no country suffering so sudden and so extraordinary a decline in population would have been seen as having thereby improved itself. Nevertheless, it is entirely possible that the journalist was correct and by the "departure" of so large a portion of its population, Ireland had "improved" itself. But, if he is correct, we are left with questions at least as urgent for our age as they were for his. Perhaps the most important is whether so monumental a sacrifice of human beings, either through emigration or more tragic events, is the price nations must pay for entering the modern world. When our horror over Ireland's agony subsides, we are left with the thought that Ireland's travail anticipates in many ways the experience of so many of the peoples of the earth who have been thrust, often unwillingly, into the modern world. No two peoples or classes have had the same experience with the entrance to modernity, but few have avoided what sociologist Peter Berger has called "pyramids of sacrifice."[63] The death toll visited upon the Irish is not without a further lesson for our time. It seems as if few, if any, nations have a choice about entering the all-encompassing culture of modernity. The penalty of failing to enter may very well be the same as that endured by the Irish peasants. Unfortunately, there is no certainty that even those who succeed in adapting to the new civilization will be able to survive within it. The sacrifice of classes and whole peoples for the sake of "improvement" does not stop with admission to the culture of modernity.

Did the British government actively pursue a program of genocide during the famine years? If we ask what future Trevelyan had in mind for Ireland, we have only to turn to his own words. Trevelyan wanted Ireland cleared of its backward peasants and their small subsistence holdings. There was nothing exceptional in such an aim. We have seen that it was one to which the London *Economist* gave its approval. It was one the leaders of Britain had pursued for several centuries in the enclosure movement in their own country. If Britain's landowners were willing to eliminate their own peasants, Trevelyan and his associates were hardly likely to be more concerned about the fate of Irish peasants even when the human consequences of eliminating them proved far more tragic.

According to Cecil Woodham-Smith, the British government did not have a plan to destroy the Irish people. Woodham-Smith holds that the misfortunes occurred because Lord John Russell's government failed to foresee the consequences of its actions.[64] Although I am largely indebted to Woodham-Smith for my knowledge of the famine, it is my opinion that a government is as responsible for a genocidal policy when its officials knowingly accept mass death as a necessary cost of implementing their policies as when they pursue genocide as an end in itself. Moreover, genocide is seldom elected by a government as an end in itself. Genocide is always a means of eliminating a target population that challenges an economic, political, cultural, religious, or ideological value of the politically dominant group. Whether Trevelyan and his government planned mass death in Ireland is irrelevant. The famine could only be grasped as an "opportunity" to eliminate the Irish peasantry if the British government was prepared to accept mass death as part of the price of achieving that end. Had the government wanted to avoid mass death, its leaders would have elected other policies in the crisis. This they did not do.

Woodham-Smith points out that the British government was no less callous in its treatment of its own troops in the Crimea, where the British army was destroyed seven years later, than it was in Ireland.[65] Similarly, the British High Command under General Sir Douglas Haig was willing to accept 500,000 fatalities in a single battle in World War I, the Second Battle of the Somme.[66] The same indifference to the loss of life, someone else's life, is evident in those in command positions in all three instances. Nevertheless, there is a difference between regarding members of one's own armed forces as expendable in wartime and accepting the elimination of a large portion of the population of what was in fact a conquered nation in peacetime.

In addition to the modernization of Irish agriculture, there were other reasons why the British government wanted to alter the demographic balance between Ireland and England. Immediately before the famine, the population of Ireland was increasing at twice the rate of England's.[67] Since the Act of Union in 1801, there was no effective way to bar Irish immigrants from entering England. Because of their extreme poverty, the Irish were willing to work in the industrial towns of England, sometimes as strike-breakers, at lower wages than those British and Scottish workers would accept. The Irish were both a necessary component in the industrial expansion of England and a destabilizing element. One did not have to be a Malthusian to see that there was an upper limit to Irish immigration.

Ireland's population increase was also a potential military threat. As the most modern state in Europe, England had little reason to fear Ireland directly. Nevertheless, in any war England could be certain that Ireland's heart would be with England's enemies. While the Irish could not by themselves alter the power equation between Ireland and England, a time might come when Ireland's population, if unchecked, might approach England's in number and could be organized against England by a wartime enemy. The weaker and the less numerous the Irish were, the less likely they would ever become a serious threat to England's security. In this respect, some of England's apprehensions concerning the Irish were not unlike Turkey's concerning the Armenians at the beginning of the twentieth century. As we have seen, after the first massacre of more than 300,000 Armenians in a two-year period beginning in 1894, the Turks had little reason for confidence in the loyalty of the Christian Armenians, whose homeland straddled both sides of the frontier between Turkey and Czarist Russia. Although the behavior of the Armenians gave the Turks little warrant for action against them, they were perceived by the Turks as an objective danger. When in 1915 wartime conditions made possible resort to radical measures, the Turkish government instituted a program of genocide against them. Unlike the Turkish government, the British government did not inaugurate an active program of genocide against the Irish. It did, however, "let nature take its course." No other action was necessary. In motive and result, the British handling of the strangers on their border bore more than a little resemblance to the Turkish handling of the strangers on theirs.

There may also be parallels between the course of action taken by the British government toward the Irish during the famine and its conduct toward Europe's Jews during World War II. In 1939 the British government limited the immigration of Jews into Palestine to 15,000 a year for a period of five years, after which there was to be no further immigration without Arab consent. In order to implement this policy, the British navy was ordered to cause to return to Nazi-dominated Europe any and all boats carrying Jews seeking to escape extermination by entering the one community prepared unconditionally to accept them, the Jewish community of Palestine. Possessing accurate knowledge of the Nazi program of extermination, the British government nevertheless forced thousands of Jews to return to certain death in Europe.[68] Moreover, the British government, in concert with the American government, steadfastly refused to take any action, such as bombing the railroad approaches to the death camp at Auschwitz, that might have slowed down or impeded the extermination program. When a request for such bombing was made by Chaim Weizmann, who was later to become Israel's first President, the British lamely refused.[69] At the time, the American government not only had eyewitness reports of the extermination camp but aerial photographs of pinpoint accuracy showing lines of naked prisoners waiting their turn to enter the gas chambers. The British government was not directly involved in the murder of Jews during World War II. Nevertheless, its actions had the effect of materially diminishing the possibility that many Jews would escape the Nazi net.

In the nineteenth century, England was the most important beneficiary of Ireland's tragedy. The smaller the number of Irish peasants remaining in Ireland, the more advantageous would the military and economic situation be for England. In the twentieth century, the British government was a direct beneficiary of the Nazi extermination of the Jews. In World War II England controlled both India and the Suez Canal; it was clearly in its interest to placate Arab concerns. The smaller the number of Jews who survived the war, the less urgent would be Jewish pressure on Britain for immigration into Palestine and the creation of a Jewish state. Apart from the action of the British navy in turning back the Jews, all that was necessary for the British to eliminate yet another troublesome population was to let "nature," in the form of the SS, take its course. If the British government did not actively exterminate populations it deemed undesirable, over a period of several centuries it pursued policies that facilitated their elimination by one means or another.

7

THE UNMASTERED TRAUMA
The Elimination
of the European Jews

OF ALL THE population-elimination programs of modern times, none came as close to destroying the entire target population as the destruction of the European Jews. In attempting to understand the elimination of the Jews as a significant religious, cultural and demographic presence on the European continent, it will be necessary to consider theological as well as economic and political issues. As the full magnitude of what had been wrought by the government that exercised sovereign power on behalf of the German people from 1933 to 1945 became known, the scholarly attempt to understand what had taken place inevitably involved a search for historical antecedents. From the perspective of the Holocaust, all earlier manifestations of anti-Jewish hostility were seen in a new and more sinister light. It was not difficult for scholars to identify a thread of continuity between the religious defamation of Judaism in the Christian tradition, the policies of the Church toward the Jews in premodern times, the racist attacks on Jews in nineteenth- and twentieth-century Europe, and the so-called Final Solution itself.[1] In fairness to the Church, it must be stated at the outset that its historic position toward the Jews has been ambivalent rather than unremittingly hostile. Ever mindful of its Jewish roots, the Church saw itself as the "true Israel" and confidently expected that the Jewish community, called by St. Paul "Israel after the flesh" in contrast to "Israel after the spirit," would ultimately see the light and confess the lordship of Christ. Nevertheless, the continuity between Christian anti-Judaism and National Socialist anti-Semitism had been proclaimed by such leading perpetrators of the extermination process as Hitler, Himmler, and Streicher, all of whom insisted that in eliminating the Jews they were merely carrying to the appropriate practical conclusion attitudes and aspirations that had long been rooted in the very substance of Christian civilization.[2]

A number of Christian and Jewish scholars came to the conclusion that the National Socialists were not entirely mistaken in their understanding of the relation between the religious and cultural antecedents and the genocidal consequences.[3] Where the scholars took issue with the Nazis was in their sense of revulsion at the outcome. As the genocidal potentiality of religious hatred of the Jews came to be seen in a new light, there were serious attempts by Christian leaders to moderate their rhetoric concerning Jews and Judaism even when they were dealing with issues of abiding religious conflict.

Awareness of the genocidal potential of anti-Semitism also affected scholarly study of the Holocaust itself. Because of the objective innocence of the victims, Holocaust studies have tended to emphasize what was done to the Jews rather than those elements of conflict and competition between Jews and non-Jews that could have contributed to the tragedy. This tendency is even evident in Raul Hilberg's oft-quoted description of the evolution of anti-Jewish policies: "The missionaries of Christianity had said in effect: You have no right to live among us as Jews. The secular rulers who followed had proclaimed: You have no right to live among us. The German Nazis at last decreed: You have no right to live."[4]

Note the force of Hilberg's emphasis. In each of the stages, the Jews are depicted as the objects of the action of others rather than as parties to a conflict. Anti-Semitism is thus portrayed as something that happens to Jews rather than the outcome of a conflict between Jews and their adversaries. This interpretation is certainly understandable in view of the utter disparity between any conceivable Jewish failing and the fate visited upon almost every single Jewish man, woman, and child in wartime Europe.

Nevertheless, it may do more to obscure than to enhance our understanding of the Holocaust. It is my conviction that the Holocaust can be understood with least mystification if we do not ignore the abiding elements of conflict characterizing the relations between the Jews and their neighbors throughout the entire period of their domicile in the European Christian world. This view involves issues which must be handled with the greatest delicacy. Let me, therefore, first state what I do not mean: I do not in any sense want to suggest the Holocaust was a fate the victims deserved however remotely. Moreover, I reject as both false and malicious the thesis put forward by some psychohistorians that the Jews unconsciously elicited their terrible fate.[5] Group conflicts, such as those between Jews and Christians, are more likely to be a matter of inheritance than choice. Normally, the weaker party has every reason to avoid exacerbating the conflict wherever possible. Nevertheless, it is an unhappy fact that for almost two thousand years Jews and Christians have been involuntarily thrust into a situation in which by affirming their most sacred traditions each side negated the sacred traditions of the other.[6]

An overwhelmingly important expression of the conflict has been the persistence within Christianity of a tradition of virulent defamation of Jews and Judaism. Because the vilifications have been so extreme, often ascribing unremittingly satanic characteristics to Jews, and because the policies the vilifications have engendered have been so murderous, there has been a persistent tendency on the part of students of the Holocaust to interpret anti-Semitism as an expression of psychological disorder.[7] It should be obvious that those who so interpret anti-Semitism tend to reject or minimize the idea that Jews or Judaism have contributed anything to the antagonism. In the literature anti-Semites are described in terms taken from the vocabulary of mental illness such as "psychopathic," "paranoid," "obsessive," and "sadistic," whereas Jews are depicted as the neutral object of the anti-Semites' hostile and aggressive projections.

Apart from downplaying the conflict element in anti-Semitism, psychological interpretations of anti-Semitism contribute little or nothing to our understanding of one of the most important questions arising from the Holocaust: Given the fact that Christian Europe had the power to eliminate the Jews at almost any time in its history and did eliminate all the other non-Christian religions of the ancient world, why did the destruction of the European Jews occur in the twentieth century and not before?

In order to answer this question, it will be necessary to identify some of the conflicting interests, both material and nonmaterial, of Christians and Jews which ultimately led to so tragic a dénouement. In pursuing this investigation we may be assisted by the theory of cognitive dissonance elaborated by social psychologists Leon Festinger, Henry W. Reicken, Stanley Schachter, and others.[8] It should, of course, be understood that neither this nor any other theory can offer a complete explanation of what took place. In the words of Festinger, one of the original proponents of the theory: "This theory centers around the idea that if a person knows various things that are not psychologically consistent with each other, he will in a variety of ways try to make them consistent."[9]

Festinger defined a "dissonant relation" as one in which two items of information do not fit together psychologically. He held that these items of information "may be about behavior, feelings, opinions, things in the environment." According to Festinger, the word cognitive is employed to emphasize that the "theory deals with relations of information." A successful attempt to make dissonant items consistent with each other is called "dissonance reduction." Festinger and his colleagues found that the reduction of dissonance resembles hunger in that it is "a motivating state of affairs." It is, however, unlike hunger in that for most people in our society hunger can normally be assuaged by finding something to eat, whereas it is often difficult or impossible "to change behavior or opinions that are involved in dissonant relations."[10]

According to Festinger, the reason why cognitive dissonance is a "motivating state" is that all of us develop the expectation that certain patterns of behavior, opinions, values, and feelings go together and others do not. The intensity of discomfort produced by cognitive dissonance will depend upon the intensity of our emotional investment in the feelings, values or opinions we perceive to be threatened. For example, a child who has come to associate loving behavior with the presence of his mother is likely to experience a traumatic sense of disorientation if the mother were suddenly and inexplicably to behave in a cruel and sadistic manner. Confronted by the apparently inconsistent maternal behavior, the child may seek to reduce the dissonance between his expectations and the mother's actual behavior by explaining her conduct as a response to some real or imagined misdeed on his part. Even if objectively untrue, the child's self-accusation would enable him to retain a sense of trust in the all-important mother-child relationship.

When confronted by unanticipated, traumatic misfortune, a similar strategy has often been utilized by religious groups that believe a benevolent, all-powerful deity guides their destiny. Self-accusation and introjected guilt are dissonance-reducing strategies that permit a group to retain faith in the power and benevolence of its deity. We call the intellectual professionals who formulate such strategies on behalf of their religious communities theologians. Theology seeks to foster dissonance-reduction where significant items of information are perceived to be inconsistent with established beliefs, values, and collectively sanctioned modes of behavior.[11]

The dissonance-reducing function of theology is especially important in both Judaism and Christianity. Both religions make claims to accurate and exclusive knowledge of God's revealed will, which they assert to have been communicated at precise historical moments through the agency of certain prophets and holy persons. Regrettably, the traditions are not in agreement concerning either the content of the revelation or the circumstances under which the revelation is said to have been communicated. Each tradition thus finds itself in the position of disconfirming other to its rival.

The problem was made worse for Christianity by the fact that the person whom the Christian churches assert to be mankind's only hope for salvation was born into the Jewish community but was rejected by the majority of his own people. To the extent some Christians entertained the suspicion, however tentative, that the rival community might possess greater familiarity with the true circumstances of the Savior's earthly career than did the Church, a potential situation of cognitive dissonance might arise. In view of the fact that faith in Christ is a matter of ultimate concern to Christians, such a situation would inevitably call forth the most urgent dissonance-reducing strategies.

The defamation of the Jews in Christianity can be seen as one such strategy. Such defamation serves to discredit a potentially disconfirming item of information of enormous significance by discrediting its source. The emotional violence of anti-Jewish defamations can be seen as a function of the extent to which the potentially disconfirming information was perceived as threatening a value or an institution of overwhelming importance to the faithful. This helps to explain the bitter anti-Jewish animus of some of Christianity's most saintly personalities. The same genius, energy, and imagination which led them to initiate a universal religious civilization also impelled them to attack and discredit those whom they perceived to be challenging even by their silent unbelief, the very foundation on which Christian civilization was constructed, faith in Christ as the Savior of mankind.

Unfortunately, the intimate relationship of Judaism and Christianity vastly magnified the hazard of the weaker community. Had the Jews been completely alien to the Christian world, Jewish items of information concerning the Christian Savior would not have been perceived as potentially disconfirming. Such items would have elicited far less violent dissonance-reduction responses. For instance, the presence of a tribe of Buddhist traders from China in the heart of Europe during the Middle Ages would have elicited hostility and suspicion, but it is highly unlikely that such a tribe would have been perceived as the minions of the antichrist devoted to the destruction of Christendom, as were the Jews. In rejecting the Christian Savior, the Chinese could not have claimed the kind of historical familiarity with Jesus of Nazareth as did the Jews. No other rejection of Christian claims presented as serious a challenge as did that of Judaism and no other religion has been as abused by the best rather than the worst exemplars of a rival faith.

Total elimination of the disconfirming other has always been an ultimate theological aim of the Christian Church. The humane method of eliminating the disconfirming other is, of course, conversion. Over the centuries the Christian Church has had an active worldwide missionary program for precisely this purpose. Theologically stated, the ultimate goal of the Church is that all men and women eventually become one in Christ. From the perspective of social psychology, the unity of all men in Christ symbolizes an era in which cognitive conformity based upon shared religious faith will be the decisive test of membership in the human race. In fairness to the Church, it must be stated that the Synagogue has an analogous goal. Judaism looks forward to the day when all men will acknowledge and serve the God of Israel. Such a goal could, of course, only be realized were all men and women to abandon their own traditions and accept the faith of Israel. At present, the leading representatives of both Judaism and Christianity see the process whereby the truth of their faith will be universally affirmed as essentially peaceful. Nevertheless, there have been periods in which both traditions resorted to more forceful means of conversion, if not outright violence, in order to eliminate disconfirming others, and it is impossible to say that there will never again be such a time.

Thus, by virtue of the radical asymmetry between the Christian claim of Jesus as the Savior of mankind and the Jewish insistence on his human fallibility, the Jews were thrust into the most dangerous kind of religious and cultural conflict with an infinitely more powerful rival from the moment of the triumph of Christianity. Yet, as we have noted, the conflict did not lead to a systematic and unremitting program of genocide until the twentieth century. I should like to put forth a hypothesis: a principal reason for the survival of the Jews and Judaism in the Christian world in premodern times was that the harsh consequences of the religious conflict were moderated because the Jews played a necessary, albeit often resented and despised, role in Europe's precapitalist economy. Put differently, in the premodern period Jews were an economically complementary population. Some sociologists would say that, like the ethnic Chinese of Southeast Asia, the Ibos of Nigeria and the Armenians of the Ottoman empire, the Jews were an "elite minority" filling certain commercial and professional roles that were not being filled by the dominant majority.[12] With the rise of an urbanized middle class among the members of the dominant majorities of almost every European nation, the Jews ceased to play a complementary role and became highly visible competitors of members of an infinitely more powerful group.

Although some Jews engaged in agriculture in the early Middle Ages in Christian Europe and Jewish moneylenders occasionally gained possession of the real property of those members of the nobility who defaulted on their debts, Jews served primarily as agents of a money economy in a predominantly agrarian, subsistence economy. Whether Jews were merchants, traders, artisans, tax farmers, innkeepers, distillers of alcoholic spirits, or moneylenders, their occupations were oriented toward the marketplace at a time when most economic activity was directed towards subsistence. Of fateful importance was the fact that medieval and early modern Jewish economic activity did not include the establishment of any significant industrial production although there was an available supply of impoverished artisans in the ghettos who could have served as a labor pool.[13] The economic role of the Jews was primarily aimed at the exchange rather than the production of goods.

The situation of the Jews in western Europe tended to deteriorate as a capitalist economy replaced the subsistence economy of the feudal period. In the feudal period money was borrowed primarily for the purpose of consumption rather than production. Since consumption did not create new wealth, it was necessary to charge usurious interest rates to compensate for the risk. With the introduction of capitalist finance, money was more likely to be borrowed for production, that is, the creation of new wealth, rather than consumption, the expenditure of old wealth. Hence, the position of the creditor became less precarious. In addition, as we have seen, there was a progressive transformation of rents and other peasant obligations due the lord by the peasant from a share of the crop and personal services to money compensation. This in turn gave landowners access to their own source of funds and made them less dependent upon money-lenders. As an indigenous commercial class arose that was capable of filling the roles previously filled by Jews, Jews were forced into marginal enterprises such as peddling secondhand goods and pawnbroking. Eventually, the majority of the Jews found them-selves closed out and were forced, as often by financial compulsion as actual expulsion, to leave western Europe. From the beginning of the sixteenth century, there was a definite pattern of migration of Jews from western to eastern Europe. This was a movement from the regions of Europe that were more highly developed eco-nomically to those that were less developed. In the early Middle Ages, the majority of Europe's Jews lived in western and central Europe. For several centuries before World War II, the majority were domiciled in the economically backward regions of eastern Europe.[14] In 1825 it is estimated that there were 2,730,000 Jews in Europe, of whom 458,000 lived in western and central Europe and 2,272,000 in eastern and southeastern Europe. In 1900 1,328,500 Jews lived in western and central Europe and 7,362,000 in eastern and southeastern Europe. The largest number of Jews in Europe lived in Poland which had a Jewish popula-tion of approximately 3,250,000 immediately before World War II.[15]

The eastward migration was largely economic in origin. As long as western Europe lacked an indigenous commercial class capable of filling the same functions as the Jews, the Jews had a viable economic role. Eastern Europe served as a population magnet because it remained feudal and agrarian for several centuries longer than did the West. Eastern Europe offered Jews opportunities for earning a decent livelihood which they had lost in the West. Yet, implicit in the eastward population shift was the seed of its own destruction. Sooner or later, the economy of eastern Europe was to go through an economic development roughly comparable to that of the West, at least with regard to the shift from a subsistence to a money economy and the subsequent displacement of the Jews by the dominant majority. Unfortunately, the Jewish role in the economies of eastern Europe became precarious at a time of unprecedented increase in both the Jewish and general population, for which the economies of the region were unable to provide adequate work opportunities.

The transformation of the economies of eastern Europe controlled by Russia, the predominant power in the region, was accelerated by the land reforms beginning in 1846 in Poland and 1861 in Russia.[16] A process was initiated by which the serfs, who numbered 48,000,000, were emancipated from serfdom. The old bonds of mutual responsibility between peasant and lord were severed and the relationship put on a monetary basis. The majority of the peasants were both illiterate and among the least competent agriculturalists in Europe. In the new economic environment some peasants prospered and enlarged their holdings; most were not so fortunate and were proletarianized in a society with large-scale unemployment.[17] Even those peasant families in eastern Europe who retained their small holdings were subject to mounting pressures because of the growth of population. In the premodern period, the population was sufficiently stable so that adequate land could be found for the younger as well as the firstborn sons of the peasants. As the population began to explode, the old symmetry between population and land disappeared. At first thousands and then millions were threatened with the most disastrous form of economic and social degradation that could be visited on a peasant, loss of land. To avert this disaster, peasants in eastern Europe resorted to subdivision as the Irish had done.

Subdivision only worsened the situation. Subdivision brought reliance on the potato as the principal crop with which a peasant family could feed itself. As in Ireland, no other source of food could offer as much nourishment from so small an area of farmland. Also as in Ireland, there was a tendency to raise grain as a cash crop to pay for the land rent rather than for food.

Nevertheless, subdivision could not go on indefinitely. Agricultural units of ever-diminishing size could not meet the needs of an ever-increasing population. Unable to find work in the village, millions of landless peasants turned to the towns and cities in the hope of maintaining themselves. Some peasants found work, but the industrial base in eastern Europe was so meager that millions found themselves hopelessly without work in the ever-expanding urban centers.

While urbanization offered no solution to the problem of agrarian unemployment, it did offer a powerful impetus to the consolidation of small peasant landholdings. The cities created a vastly enlarged demand for agricultural products which could not be met by small peasant holdings. In its overall outline, the story of the modernization of eastern European agriculture is very much the same as elsewhere in the world. There was the same tendency toward the elimination of small holdings which we have seen in England in the enclosure movement and in Ireland as a result of the famine of 1846 to 1848. In Poland, the small holdings remained in peasant hands longer than in the West, but the movement toward consolidation was irreversible. There was no other way in which the growing urban population could be fed. Still, while consolidation enriched the larger and more enterprising farmers, it further disrupted the ancient social ecology of village life and greatly enlarged the number of dispossessed, landless peasants.

The destruction of the old economy had disastrous effects on Jewish life in the villages. The transition to a market economy replicated the conditions that had originally driven the Jews out of western Europe and into eastern Europe. As the larger farmers prospered, they began to displace Jews from their traditional economic roles. Under the goad of necessity, still other non-Jews divested themselves of the traditional distaste for trade and commerce and became direct competitors of the Jews. The statistics tell the story of the trend. In 1862 72 percent of the Jewish population of Warsaw was engaged in commerce; in 1897 the percentage had dropped to 62.[18] In 1914, 72 percent of the stores in the Polish villages were owned by Jews; in 1935 only 35 percent were in Jewish hands.[19] Only in the most economically retrograde regions of eastern Poland did the Jews continue to own the majority of village shops in the nineteen-thirties.[20] Nor were the petite bourgeoisie the only new competitors of the Jews. As both state policy and economic constraint forced the Jews out of the villages and into the cities, millions of Jews became a proletarian mass for the first time in their history. In 1781, the Jewish population of Warsaw was 3532, or 4.5 percent of the total; in 1882 it was 127,917, or 33.4 percent of the total, and in 1897, 219,141, or 33.9 percent of the total. In Lodz, an important manufacturing center, there were 2775 Jews in 1856, or 12.2 percent of the total; in 1910 Lodz had 166,628 Jews, or 40.7 percent of the total.[21] The Jews found themselves competing for scarce jobs with an equally desperate non-Jewish proletariat. At the same time, as we have seen, the Jewish population was experiencing an unprecedented explosion. In 1816 Jews constituted 8.7 percent of the population of Poland. By 1865 the proportion had risen to 13.5 percent and in 1897, in spite of massive emigration, 14 percent of the population was Jewish.[22]

Further deterioration of the Jewish situation, always exacerbated by religious conflict, was caused by the introduction of machinery into the processes of production. Jewish artisans were especially hard hit. In eastern Europe Jews traditionally worked as tailors, bookbinders, cigarmakers, watchsmiths, goldsmiths, and silversmiths. Before the machine these fields required little capital but some skill. With the introduction of machines, the need for skill diminished and the need for capital increased. Jewish employers often found that it made more economic sense to hire unskilled Polish workers rather than declassed Jewish artisans and petty merchants. Hopelessly undercapitalized, the majority of Jewish artisans and merchants became dependent upon wage labor, when they could find it, at a time when a Polish working class was available to perform the same tasks, often more economically.[23] Moreover, employment in heavy industry, one of the most promising sources of job creation, was largely barred to the Jews by state policy and worker resistance.[24]

Although it is always difficult to pinpoint a date as initiating a new historical trend, it is my conviction that 1881 can be seen as the watershed year for the fate of the Jewish communities of the Russian-dominated areas of eastern Europe. Because of the long-range impact of the fate of eastern European Jews on the Jews of western Europe, 1881 can be seen as a watershed year for them as well. On March 13, 1881 (new calendar), Czar Alexander II was assassinated by members of Narodnaya Volya, a revolutionary terrorist organization. Shortly thereafter, government circles began to blame the assassination on the Jews. On April 27, 1881, the first of a series of pogroms broke out in Elizavetgrad which continued until the summer of 1884. By the end of 1881, 215 Jewish communities in southern and southwestern Russia had been attacked. Although the violence appears mild by twentieth-century standards, there was considerable rapine, destruction of property, and loss of life. Thousands of Jewish houses were burned down by the mobs. More than 20,000 Jews lost their homes and at least 100,000 their livelihood.[25]

There was little doubt that influential circles within the government had actively encouraged the anti-Jewish outbreaks. While the attacks continued, the police did nothing until the violence threatened to get out of hand. When the government decided that the pogroms had lasted long enough, the security forces reacted strongly, even killing some of the rioters.[26] A second wave of pogroms, also government-instigated, took place between the years 1903 and 1906, beginning in Kishinev. There was a third wave between 1917 and 1921 during the Russian civil war.

In 1881 there were a number of government leaders who, while having no particular fondness for the Jews, strongly opposed state-instigated lawlessness. These included Count M. K. Reutern, Chairman of the Council of Ministers, and Dmitri Tolstoy, but their views did not prevail.[27] There was general approval of the pogroms among educated Russians, the terrorist Narodnaya Volya, and the authorities. The Czarist government regarded the pogroms as a useful outlet for the discontented masses and as a means of injuring a despised minority which it sought ultimately to eliminate. Narodnaya Volya welcomed the pogroms as a fore-taste of the political awakening of the masses that was expected eventually to lead to the overthrow of the Czarist regime.[28]

An important aspect of a state-instigated pogrom is its calculated denial of the normal protection of the law to the target population. This denial transforms the target population into a collection of outlaws whom members of the dominant majority are free to injure or kill at will. Although pogroms involve mob violence, they serve a rational purpose by putting the target population on notice that they are cast wholly outside the social contract. Even if for reasons of public order the government limits the period of active violence, it demonstrates its capacity to renew the violence at any time. Thus, the basic purpose of the pogrom, whether the Russian pogroms of 1881-1882, the anti-Armenian attacks in the Ottoman empire, or the Nazi *Kristallnacht,* is to provide the target group with the strongest possible motivation to leave the country.

The 1881-1882 pogroms had the desired effect: 1881 marks the beginning of the mass emigration of eastern European Jewry. Between 1871 and 1880 the average annual Jewish emigration from eastern Europe was 8000 to 10,000; between 1881 and 1900 the average was between 50,000 and 60,000 a year.[29] There was, incidentally, a high proportion of modernized Jews among the first emigrants.[30]

For those Jews who could not or would not interpret the pogroms correctly, the Czarist government offered an even more explicit indication of its intentions in what came to be known as the "May Laws" promulgated on May 13, 1882, which forbade Jews to settle in the rural villages and made it difficult for Jews living in the villages to remain there. Jews who left their village even for brief periods were prevented from returning. Itinerant Jews who moved from place to place looking for work were expelled from the villages as new settlers. The laws also prevented Jews from inheriting family property in another village; nor could a Jew help a family member who lived elsewhere to settle in his village. The number of Jews permitted to enter Russian universities was drastically reduced, as was the number of Jews permitted to enter professions such as law and medicine.

Stringent controls were placed on Jewish artisans. A Jew lost his status as an artisan if he used a machine in his craft. A pastry cook who served coffee with his pastry was reclassified as a merchant. Reclassification could be followed by expulsion from the village.[31] In 1887 Jews who had been living in the villages before 1882 were forbidden to move to another village.[32] The May Laws were made even more severe when provincial authorities widened their applicability by reclassifying larger towns as villages, and in 1891 the entire Jewish community of Moscow, numbering 20,000, was summarily expelled. The Jewish communities of St. Petersburg and Kharkov were also expelled. The effect of the May Laws was further to concentrate the Jews in the overcrowded and underemployed cities of what was known as the "Pale of Settlement."[33]

It is possible to discern a connection between the emancipation of the Russian serfs in 1861 and the Czarist government's anti-Jewish measures initiated in 1881. By laying the groundwork for the capitalist transformation of eastern European agriculture, emancipation created the conditions for the beginnings of a small but growing indigenous middle class. As this class developed, the Russian government, which had traditionally been hostile to the Jews, had even less reason to tolerate a minority that was seen as foreign to the nation's ethnic and the religious consensus.

The ultimate aim of Russian policy in the aftermath of the events of 1881 was the total elimination of the Jews. This was clearly understood by one of the leaders most responsible for the formulation of that policy, Konstantin Petrovich Pobedonostsev (1827-1904), a highly influential bureaucrat who served as "Supreme Prosecutor of the Holy Synod" from 1880 until his death. Pobedonostsev, a fanatic believer in Czarist absolutism, pursued a policy of unmitigated Russification of all non-Russian minorities.[34] He strongly supported the May Laws and all other measures designed to bring about the removal of the Jews from Russia. He was also hostile to the Armenians, who, although Christian, were not members of the Russian Orthodox Church.[35] Pobedonostsev favored the transformation of Czarist Russia into a homogenous, centralized theocracy in which the minorities would be integrated into a monolithic Russian Orthodox civilization. His program of homogenization and centralization arose from the same modernizing impulse as did the Young Turks'.

Historian James Billington's description of Pobedonostsev is strangely reminiscent of another modernizing bureaucrat we have met, Sir Charles Edward Trevelyan:

> Pobedonostsev...was a thoroughly prosaic lay figure, whose ideal was the gray efficiency and uniformity of the modern organization man. He was the prophet of duty, work, and order-shifting his bishops around periodically to prevent any distracting local attachments from impeding the smooth functioning of the ecclesiastical machine. He was unemotional, even cynical, about his methods. But they were generally effective and earn him a deserved place as one of the builders of the centralized bureaucratic state.[36]

As a figure of consequence in Jewish history, Pobedonostsev is perhaps best remembered for his own "solution" of the Jewish problem, which he is reported to have offered to a group of Jewish petitioners in 1898: "One third will die, one third will leave the country, and the last third will be completely assimilated within the surrounding population."[37]

Thus, decades before World War II Russian policymakers sought to achieve for their own country the very same goal with respect to the Jews as did the National Socialists. There was no difference concerning the end; there was, of course, an important difference between the means even a modernizing bureaucrat like Pobedonostsev was prepared to use before World War I and those the National Socialists would employ during World War II. Admittedly there were countercurrents of liberalism in Russia toward the end of the nineteenth and the beginning of the twentieth century, but the liberals were never more than a minority voice.

Nevertheless, while the Czarist program of pogroms and legal discrimination was neither as efficient nor as successful as Hitler's, it was one of the most effective state-sponsored programs of population elimination up to its time. It set in motion the mass emigration from eastern Europe of more than 4,000,000 Jews between 1881 and 1930. With the possible exception of the aftermath of the fall of Jerusalem to the Romans in 70 C.E., never before had so large a proportion of the Jewish people migrated from one country to another in so short a time. Undoubtedly economic hopelessness was as much a spur to emigration as state hostility. Nevertheless, the economic and political elements making for mass migration cannot be separated.

If we recognize that in fostering the departure of the Jews the leaders of Czarist Russia were pursuing a socio-political objective that was essentially identical with that of the Third Reich, although employing less radical and less systematic means, we shall also recognize that what is normally called the Holocaust can better be understood as the culmination of a historic movement that began in the last quarter of the nineteenth century and had as its objective the total elimination of the Jews from European civilization. With whatever insight hindsight can offer us, it would appear that the social, economic, and political forces set in motion by the accelerating process of modernization in Europe effectively sealed the fate of Europe's Jews several decades before the beginning of the twentieth century. At some level, this was understood intuitively by those emigrants who were fortunate enough to flee from the oncoming peril before the final blow. For those Jews who remained in Europe, only the hour and the manner of their elimination remained uncertain.

There is, incidentally, an eerie parallel between the beginnings of the process which led to the destruction of the European Jews and the one leading to the destruction of another "elite minority," the Armenians. The modern travail of the Armenians had its beginnings at almost the same moment as that of the Jews, namely, 1876, the year of the accession of Sultan Abdul Hamid to the throne of the Ottoman empire. The climax of the Armenian travail came sooner than did that of the Jews. Unfortunately, few Jews in the period between World Wars I and II were able to discern the sociological parallels between their situation and that of the Armenians or to draw the grim political conclusions from those parallels.

In western Europe the late eighteen-seventies can be seen as the launching period of the same ultimately genocidal movement. Bismarck's creation of a unified German empire in 1870 was followed by the crash of 1873 and the economic depression of 1873–1879. The financial disturbances created especially difficult conditions for the lower middle class. Unfortunately, even the resumption of an upward trend in the business cycle was of greater benefit to the owners, managers, and laborers in the large-scale financial and industrial enterprises than to artisans, small retail merchants, or rural laborers. Artisans, petty merchants, and rural workers tended to identify the new industrial capitalism with the Jews and to be equally resentful of Jewish industrialists, department store owners, bankers and peddlers, all of whom were perceived as threatening the small merchant.[38] It has been said that "anti-Semitism rose as the stock market fell."[39] In 1878 Germany's first overtly anti-Semitic political party, the lower-middle-class Christian Social Party, was founded by Adolf Stoecker, Court Chaplain to the Kaiser.[40] In 1879 Heinrich von Treitschke, one of Germany's leading historians, called for the transformation of Germany into a Lutheran *Kultur-Staat* and the elimination of Jewish influence.[41] In Austria in 1879 Georg von Schoenerer, the leader of the Pan-German movement, offered a political program with anti-Semitic elements, although he continued to work with Jews as late as 1882.[42] It is not without significance that Schoenerer was convinced of racial anti-Semitism by the student fraternities at the University of Vienna. In the Poland of the 1930s and the Germany of the Weimar Republic, a far larger proportion of university students participated in violently anti-Semitic activities than did the general population.[43] By 1885 the Pan-German societies had expelled their baptized Jewish members. The students saw their Jewish peers as potential competitors. Like the Young Turks who were being trained in the universities of western and central Europe in the same period, they had a modernizing bias toward homogenization and centralization. This was evident in their contempt for the multinational Hapsburg empire and their longing to unite German Austria with the rest of Germany in a single *Grossdeutschland*. While Jews tended mistakenly to identify rationality and modernity with pluralism, liberalism, and tolerance, by the beginning of the twentieth century their opposite numbers were increasingly identifying it with homogenization, standardization, and centralization.

While no single cause can explain a historical phenomenon, the first appearance of a modern, racist anti-Semitic movement in Europe can be related to several principal factors: (1) the insecurity and/or downward social mobility of the under-capitalized lower middle class in the takeoff period of large-scale industrial capitalism; (2) the sudden influx of large numbers of displaced east European Jews in the urban centers of Germany and Austria, especially the capital cities of Berlin and Vienna in 1881 and thereafter; and (3) the impulse to centralization, homogenization, and leveling that we find so frequently as a feature of modernization and bureaucratization.

In 1846, 3739 Jews lived in Vienna; 54 years later there were 176,000.[44] In 1852, 11,840 Jews lived in Berlin; in 1890 there were 108,044 or 5.02 percent of the city's population.[45] As eastern European Jews settled in cities like Berlin and Vienna in large numbers, the demand arose to restrict their immigration. Schoenerer, then a Pan-German member of Parliament, took the Chinese Exclusion Act passed by the United States Congress in 1882 as the model for his proposed legislation restricting the immigration of Russian Jews.[46] In 1887 he proposed that Jews be confined to ghettos and restricted as to profession.[47]

Moreover, as the eastern European Jews were migrating to Germany and Austria, Germany was experiencing the largest emigration in its history. Between 1871 and 1885, 1,678,202 people, approximately 3.5 percent of the entire population, migrated to the United States. The peak emigration of 250,000 occurred in the crucial year of 1881–1882. The majority of the emigrants were from the agrarian regions of northern and eastern Germany, regions that had experienced the greatest social destabilization as a result of the new industrial civilization.[48]

The phenomenon of the *Auswanderung,* or emigration, in nineteenth-century Germany was largely a lower-middle-class movement. Unlike the Irish, the very poor in Germany did not normally emigrate. Those who risked the overseas journey were generally artisans, small farmers, and small businessmen who had some capital with which to begin a new life overseas. The emigrants saw their prospects diminishing in Germany. They feared proletarianization were they to remain in a rapidly industrializing Germany and thereby exhaust their resources.[49] The members of the lower middle class who did remain in Germany constituted the class with most reason to be fearful of the consequences of capitalism with its inevitable bias in favor of large-scale enterprise. They were also the group most likely to be confronted by Jewish competition for available small business and professional opportunities. Barred from state employment, including the universities, the Jews had no alternative but to maximize their opportunities within the private sector.

Fear of socialism as well as proletarianization also added to lower-middle-class anti-Semitism, especially in the between-the-wars period of the twentieth century. The anti-Socialist attitudes of the German and Austrian lower middle class were not without an element of paradox. In general, the lower middle class understood that big business, whether it was the large-scale manufacturing firm, the big bank, or the department store, tended to undermine their economic and social standing. For example, the undercapitalized watchmaker could not compete with the assembly-line manufacturer, nor could the owner of a small retail store compete in price with the department store. In Germany, department stores, most of which were owned by Jews until the period of National Socialism, were a special object of lower-middle-class anger. In addition to promising to eliminate the Jews, before the seizure of power the National Socialists promised the lower middle class relief from the threat of large-scale enterprise; they were able to make good their promise about the Jews but not large-scale enterprise, which was indispensable to the power needs of a modern state preparing for war. In the takeoff period of industrial capitalism, the small businessman or artisan was often forced to choose between abandoning the dignity of his self-employed status and witnessing the steady erosion of his standard of living as he attempted unsuccessfully to compete against larger and better-financed enterprises.

There was thus an anticapitalist element in the perceptions of the lower middle class. However, it was impossible for the socialists to enlist their support, since Marxism could only promise the petite bourgeoisie the very fate they feared most, proletarianization.

Racial nationalism offered the lower middle class a political program which proved increasingly popular over the years. It legitimated hostility toward the hated Jewish competitor, while offering an ideological basis for community with the owners of large-scale enterprise and the managers of large-scale government, with whom they were inextricably related in any event. The middle class rejected the internationalism of a Marxism that proclaimed the coming triumph of the proletariat, the one class into whose ranks they did not wish to enter. The Social Darwinism inherent in racial nationalism offered the promise of wars of conquest against inferior peoples in which the declining fortunes of the lower middle class would be reversed as they shared in the spoils of a triumphant racial empire.

By contrast, if the petite bourgeoisie dreaded working-class affiliation, politically romantic sons and daughters of assimilated or assimilating members of the Jewish bourgeoisie saw such affiliation as offering both escape from Jewishness and entrance into the world of the indigenous majority. These sons and daughters of the Jewish bourgeoisie found it impossible to support established institutions in Germany, Austria, and, most especially, in Czarist Russia. Wealthy Jewish families could give their offspring superb educational and cultural opportunities but they could not rescue them from pariah status. The situation was, of course, worst in eastern Europe where the hostility of the government toward Jews was altogether without disguise. Older Jews withdrew into the consolations of private life. Others despaired of achieving any integration with the larger society and turned to Zionism. Those young Jews who did not abandon hope of integration but who despaired of doing so under current conditions tended to turn either to Jewish or to general socialist organizations. Moreover, the role of the Christian Church as the most important legitimating institution of the established order enhanced the attractiveness of antireligious Marxism to those young Jews who saw religion as ultimately responsible for their pariah status.

The adherence of a visible group of Jews to the cause of the left intensified the anti-Semitism of lower-middle-class racial nationalists. Not only were Jews hated competitors whose business activities threatened the petite bourgeoisie with reduction to proletarian status, but their sons and daughters sought the same result with their revolutionary activities. In the aftermath of the Russian Revolution, a very sizable group of the non-Jewish bourgeoisie came to see the Jews as enemies who threatened the very foundations of Christian civilization with their radicalism.[50] Ironically, the idealism of the Jewish radicals only intensified the resolve of important elements of non-Jewish society to get rid of them, yet when the left finally triumphed in Europe, its leaders were as interested in eliminating the Jews, at least as a distinctive group, as the right had been. Because of the unresolved conflicts of religious belief and the inexorable trajectory of modernization with its population dislocations and its economic competition, *the European Jewish situation was without hope of fortunate issue.*

It has been said that the one war in which the National Socialists were ultimately victorious was their war of extermination against the Jews. The program of genocide was implicit in one of the key terms they habitually used to express their ultimate political and social aspirations, *Volksgemeinschaft.* The term gave succinct expression to their yearning to create an ethnically and culturally homogenous community from which all dissonant others would be totally eliminated.

Ironically, while the emancipation of Europe's Jews appeared to offer them civic equality, as a leveling measure it did away with official recognition of very real differences in tradition, culture, and function between the varying elements of the population. It was only a question of time before voices were heard demanding the elimination of those whose differences could not be leveled. Moreover, in most countries it was only with the highly problematic triumph of bourgeois liberalism that Jewish emancipation was seriously considered. In the *Philosophy of Right,* Hegel identified bourgeois or "civil society" *(bürgerliche Gesellschaft)* as "the achievement of the modern world"[51] and the domain of universal egoism. By this Hegel meant that "individuals in their capacity as burghers in this state are private persons whose end is their own interest."[52] Put differently, in bourgeois society the private, self-aggrandizing interests of the individual (or individual corporation) take precedence over the well-being of the commonwealth. Community is exploded and society consists of a congery of self-regarding atoms whose interest in others is purely instrumental. When command of money became more important than command of men and English land-owners evicted their peasant tenants and depopulated the rural villages, they were exemplifying Hegel's view of civil society as the domain of universal egoism. If Hegel's characterization has merit, it can be said that the emancipation of the Jews, as well as the emancipation of Europe's peasants, occurred at a time when the realm of universal egoism was in the process of displacing traditional bonds of mutual dependence and responsibility. Only when a condition of universal otherhood displaced a society with some measure of brotherhood, however tenuous, were Jews permitted a status approaching political equality in western Europe. As every man became a stranger it was possible for the Jew to become a neighbor.

From this perspective National Socialism can be seen as a movement that sought to restore civic altruism, not on the basis of a religious or humanitarian ideal of human solidarity, but strictly on the basis of the myth of primal tribal unity. A few of the elements of its program that helped to shape its population policy are discussed here:

Racism or Neo-Tribalism: Racism was an attempt to establish a basis for community on the foundation of shared archaic roots. The exclusion of the alien was intrinsic to its very nature. Racism can be seen as a thoroughly modern response to the phenomenon of population superfluity and the fragmented affiliations of atomized bourgeois society. Racism was also an expression of the trend toward homogenization, centralization, and leveling that is a feature of modern bureaucratized society. Racism sought to establish an ideological basis for affiliation and community after all of the lesser units of community, such as the village, the Church, and even the nation, had proved unable to meet the challenge. Its message was simple and brutal: "Only those who share our roots can hunt with our pack. All the rest are prey, first the stranger within our midst and later on the others, for the world is neither big enough nor rich enough for all of us. Moreover, we know that our program requires the kind of political leadership that will not be deterred by legal and moral abstractions, such as common citizenship or taboos against murder of the innocent, from doing what has to be done."

The tribalism of National Socialism was the sociopolitical expression of its racism. It was, however, not a restoration of something old, save in the mythic imagination of some National Socialist ideologues. It was a neo-tribalism that could only arise in a modern, industrial mass society. Like most other large linguistic groups, the Germans had been a group of tribes often at war with each other. The National Socialists proposed to complete the work of tribal consolidation by creating a single Aryan neo-tribe. The National Socialist project was both elicited and made possible by such tools of modern technology as high finance, industry, bureaucracy, transportation, and wireless communication.

The call to a primal unity of origin and kinship was made all the more radical as a result of Germany's defeat in the most industrialized war in all history to date, World War I. Whatever divided the German tribes, they shared a common defeat. Two million lives had been lost on the battlefield, another million had been lost through home-front starvation caused by the Allied blockade, but to no avail. It was widely felt that only the most thoroughgoing internal cohesion would enable the nation to reverse the results of the lost war. Neo-tribalism was seen as a crucially important means to that end.

Lebensraum: In 1891, ten years after the beginning of the decisive Russian pogroms, Leo von Caprivi, the Chancellor of the German Reich, observed that "Germany must export goods or people."[53] Caprivi understood the classic dilemma of production and consumption that besets every modern technological society. Germany's ability to produce exceeded her capacity to consume. Without foreign markets, Germany would be faced with an unacceptable level of mass unemployment at home. Caprivi saw that domestic unemployment would have a destabilizing effect on German society and that the effect would by no means be limited to the working class.

In Caprivi's time, emigration was considered the normal, acceptable method of population elimination in Germany as well as elsewhere in Europe. It is estimated that 6,000,000 people emigrated from Germany in the nineteenth and early twentieth centuries.[54] For the period 1846–1932, we have the figure of 4,900,000 from Germany and 5,200,000 from Austria-Hungary.[55] Admittedly, the figure from Austria-Hungary includes a large number of non-Germans among whom were Hungarian and Galician Jews. Nevertheless, it is clear conditions propelled an extraordinarily large number of Europeans to uproot themselves willingly.

Even as a young man in Vienna, Hitler was keenly interested in the phenomenon of German emigration. According to historian Robert G. L. Waite, one of the books in Hitler's library whose marginal notes attest the young Hitler's strong interest was *Auswanderungs-Möglichkeiten in Argentinien* (Emigration Possibilities in Argentina).[56] In *Mein Kampf,* Hitler wrote of the need for land to the east to absorb Germany's population surplus.[57] He came to regard emigration to the New World as a poor solution to Germany's population problem, for such emigrants ceased to be a human resource for Germany. His program of seeking Lebensraum in the east was designed to solve that problem by providing an area adjacent to the Reich to which Germany's surplus population could migrate. The demographic strength of the migrants would thus be retained by their native land.

As a youthful reader of Karl May's German novels about the American Wild West, Hitler came to see the elimination of North America's native population by white European settlers as a model to be followed by Germany on the European continent. In his eyes the Slavs were destined to become Europe's Indians. They were to be uprooted, enslaved and, if necessary, annihilated to make way for Germany's surplus population. In his wartime *Tischrede,* his table talk, Hitler referred to the Russians as

"Indians" and advised German officers to read Karl May to learn how to deal with them.[58]

Many of the Nazi leaders, Hitler included, understood the urgency of the problem of population redundancy through their own personal experience. According to the German historian, Karl Dietrich Bracher, before the seizure of power in 1933, most members of the Nazi inner circles had been "petite bourgeoisie who had been for some time already engaged in the futile pursuit of a career."[59] Nowhere is this more evident than in the career of Hitler himself. Had he not succeeded in making a career out of politics, he might have spent his life as a shiftless outsider untrained for any normal vocation. Having escaped redundancy by the success of their political movement, the National Socialists were determined to bring the overseas *Auswanderung* to a halt and redirect the flow of people eastward.

Anti-Marxism: We have already noted the hostile reaction of the lower middle class to a political movement that promised them the very proletarian status they were trying desperately to avoid. There were other reasons as well why middle-class opposition to Marxism was an important element in the political success of National Socialism. With the exception of the rural South, the American view of private property comes closer than the European view to realizing the capitalist notion that land is an alienable commodity freely and impersonally available for purchase and sale. In parts of Europe, inherited real property still has something of an emotionally tinged, if not sacralized, aura about it. Socialist confiscation of property by the state is therefore felt to be profoundly offensive, not only because of human possessiveness but also because of the destruction of a family's link to its past and its ancestors.

The affront involved in Communist seizure of property was compounded by the fact that Marxism was seen by conservative Europeans as Jewish in origin and leadership, a view that was reinforced in Germany by the three successive left-wing regimes which succeeded the Bavarian royal house of Wittelsbach from November 7, 1918, to May 1, 1919, at the end of World War I. In Munich, the city that did more than any other to give birth to

National Socialism, and in the era in which Hitler first joined the minuscule party, a series of politically naive, left-wing Jewish leaders attempted ineffectually to bring about an enduring socialist revolution in Catholic, conservative Bavaria.[60] The brief episode ended in a right-wing bloodbath. Its effects were unfortunately enduring. Munich was a principal gathering place for White Russian refugees who brought with them *The Protocols of the Elders of Zion* with its myth of a Jewish conspiracy to rule the world. The book was speedily translated into German and English and then given worldwide dissemination.[61] When the White Russians depicted bolshevism as an assault by alien Jews on the very fabric of European Christian civilization and the very conspiracy to which the *Protocols* referred, the visibility of Jewish leadership in the short-lived Bavarian Republic and the even briefer Soviet Republics lent credibility to the accusations. Incidentally, Eugenio Cardinal Pacelli, who was to serve as Pope Pius XII during World War II, was the Papal Nuncio in Munich during this crucial period. He was harassed by troops of the Munich Soviet, and Munich's Michael Cardinal Faulhaber was detained by the left regime. One is tempted to speculate that Cardinal Pacelli's Munich experience helped to shape his wartime view that National Socialist Germany was Europe's bulwark against godless Bolshevism.[62] His experience may also help to explain his wartime silence on the extermination of Europe's Jews, a program concerning which the Pontiff had excellent information.

Identification of the Jews with Marxism did not prevent them from being accused by the National Socialists and other anti-Semites as being responsible for capitalism, a system which, as we have seen, the lower middle class had reason to fear and resent. At times, Jewish capitalists were depicted as being in league with Jewish communists to bring about world domination.[63] Such accusations, often coming from the same source, have been regarded by students of anti-Semitism as evidence of either irrationality or the manipulative insincerity of those who employed them. Undoubtedly, propagandists are more interested in manipulation than truth, yet there remains the question of why the propaganda was believed by so many people. The historic association of the Jews with money and the marketplace, as well as the mythic association of both Jews and the Devil with money and each other, undoubtedly reinforced the view that the Jews were responsible for inflicting the heartless, depersonalized world of money and universal otherhood on Christian Europe. In reality, Christian Europe required no Jews to inflict this world on itself.

If we recognize that both capitalism and communism are alternative expressions of the modernization process, the real intent of the accusations becomes apparent: they reflect resentment against modernization by those who perceived themselves to be its victims and who perceived the Jews to be both its carriers and its principal beneficiaries. In reality, no group was to pay more dearly for the modernization of Europe's economy and society than the Jews.

Genocide: Genocide was the almost inevitable consequence of the National Socialist program of anti-Semitism, Lebensraum, and Volksgemeinschaft as soon as wartime conditions gave the German government a free hand to employ whatever means it deemed necessary to achieve its objectives. The goal of Lebensraum, the creation of a vast German racial empire in the east, involved the merciless elimination of all indigenous population elements that could not be integrated into the new system. As we know, the harshest forms of elimination were reserved for the Jews.

The goal of creating a "racially pure" Volksgemeinschaft would have doomed the Jews even had there been no Lebensraum policy. Although neither Germany nor Austria was the goal of most eastern European Jewish emigrants, the Jews of eastern Europe constituted an immense reservoir of potential immigrants who might settle in Germany and Austria and compete with members of the indigenous population. This apprehension was given expression even before the twentieth century. Heinrich von Treitschke complained that "year after year there pours in from the inexhaustible Polish reservoir a host of ambitious pants-selling youngsters, whose children will some day control...the stock exchanges and the newspapers."[64] In spite of their foreignness, in some ways it was easier for eastern European Jews to adjust to German commercial and cultural life than it was for Slavs.

Eastern European Jews were literate and spoke a German dialect, Yiddish. Although Yiddish was regarded as a linguistic bastard by Germans, knowledge of Yiddish greatly facilitated the task of learning German. No other east European language was as close to Yiddish as German.

When the Germans invaded eastern Europe, they had a very simple and demonically successful way of creating their Volksgemeinschaft: namely, mass murder of Germany's Jews and those elements of the conquered population that might someday be tempted to migrate to Germany. This may explain why Himmler insisted on exterminating even those skilled Jewish laborers whom the Wehrmacht sought to keep working in Polish war industries. Thus, even when the war was lost, it was possible to achieve at least one crucial objective of National Socialism, creation of the Volksgemeinschaft.

With the doleful wisdom of hindsight, it is possible to see the doom of Europe's Jews becoming ever more certain in the between-the-wars period even before the National Socialist seizure of power. In the aftermath of World War I the problem of surplus people continued to worsen. As a result of the War, the Russian Revolution, the Spanish Civil War, and the tendency of modern regimes unilaterally to denationalize troublesome members of dissident political or national groups, millions of people had become apatrides, men and women without a country.[65] Unemployment, a problem few modern societies have been able to cope with, rose dramatically after 1929. Anti-Semitisni again rose as the stock market fell. In 1932, 6,000,000 people were unemployed in Germany alone.[66] In the United States, which had absorbed so great a proportion of Europe's surplus people before World War I, almost a quarter of the work force was out of work in the worst years of the Great Depression. As we have noted, the unemployment situation in eastern Europe was even worse than elsewhere. Because of its rearmament program, Germany solved her unemployment problem by 1938. During World War II Germany experienced an acute labor shortage. Nevertheless, even when Jews ceased to be economically redundant, they remained superfluous because of the ideal of Volksgemeinschaft.

In a period of acute economic crisis, the nineteen-thirties, the number of European Jews seeking to emigrate increased as the number of countries willing to receive them declined to the vanishing point.

Already in the nineteen-twenties the flood of eastern European immigrants to the United States, the most promising destination, produced an explicitly anti-Jewish response in the Congress. The Report of the Congressional Committee on Immigration entitled "Temporary Suspension of Immigration" and dated December 6, 1920, is concerned almost exclusively with bringing Jewish immigration to a halt. The report cites the published statement of a "commissioner of the Hebrew Sheltering and Aid Society of America": "If there were in existence a ship that could hold 3,000,000 human beings, the 3,000,000 Jews of Poland would board it to escape to America."[67] By 1924, the year the membership of the Ku Klux Klan reached an all-time high, Congress passed the Johnson Act, which established an annual quota of 5982 immigrants from Poland, 2148 from Russia, and 749 from Romania. The Johnson Act of 1924 did to Jewish immigration to the United States in the between-the-wars period what the Chinese Exclusion Act of 1882 did to Chinese immigration in the nineteenth century.[68]

There may have been an element of hyperbole in the 1919 statement that all 3,000,000 Polish Jews would immigrate to America if they could, but the vast majority desperately wanted to get out. Moreover, both the political and economic situation of the Jews of Poland, the country with by far the largest number of Jews in the between-the-wars period, grew progressively worse with every passing year. The restoration of Poland's independence in 1918 was accompanied by a violent wave of anti-Semitism. Although thousands of Jews had fought under Pilsudski for Polish independence, the Jews were regarded by the Poles as unassimilable foreigners. The situation was worsened by the fact that the Jewish population was overwhelmingly urban, giving Jews a disproportionate representation in Poland's cities, whereas the Polish population was overwhelmingly rural, and, in addition to the miserable condition of Polish peasants noted above, between seven and eight million Poles were unemployed or woefully under-employed in a country of 32,500,000.[69] The Polish government reacted to the economic predicament by enacting a series of ever more stringent measures designed to transfer whatever jobs and resources there were from Jewish to Polish hands. The downward mobility of the Jews was immediately evident in government service and state-owned enterprises. To illustrate, as long as Galicia had been a part of the Austro-Hungarian empire, thousands of Jews worked in the state-owned railroad, post office, and other bureaus. After Poland gained independence in 1918, Jews were barred from positions in all state bureaus and state-owned enterprises.[70] In both the private and the public sector, the government acted to deprive Jews of their ability to earn a livelihood on the highly questionable assumption that what was loss to Jews was gain to Poles. At no time did the Polish government attempt effectively to expand the economy so that both Jews and Poles might be gainfully employed.

The anti-Jewish measures were actively supported by Poland's Roman Catholic Church, which regarded the Jews as agents of secularization, liberalism, and bolshevism. Roman Catholic faith was regarded as an indispensable component of authentic Polish identity, and religious hatred of the Jews attained a virulence of far greater intensity in Poland than in any other European country, including Nazi Germany. In 1936 the Primate of Poland, August Cardinal Hlond, openly supported the anti-Jewish measures. Although he opposed overt violence, he counseled the faithful: "One ought to fence oneself off against the harmful moral effects of Jewry, to separate oneself against its anti-Christian culture, and especially to boycott the Jewish press and the demoralizing Jewish publications."[71] In effect, Cardinal Hlond advocated a policy of religiously sponsored apartheid.

By 1939 the explicit, officially stated policy of the Polish government was to seek by all available means to compel the Jews to emigrate from Poland. As a successor to the Czarist government, it pursued a Jewish policy that was identical in ultimate aim. The theme of Poland's "surplus" Jewish population was constantly reiterated in official statements by Poland's leaders throughout the late thirties.[72] Even the threat of German invasion made no difference. Poland's determination to be rid of the Jews was not deterred by the threat of invasion and war. In July 1939 the official government journal Gazeta Polska declared: "The fact that our relations with the Reich are worsening does not in the least deactivate our program in the Jewish question — there is not and cannot be any common ground between our internal Jewish problem and Poland's relations with the Hitlerite Reich."[73]

By 1939 the Jews of eastern Europe were caged in a deathtrap from which there was to be no escape. Poland was determined to make life as miserable for them as possible as a way of inducing them to leave, while Germany was preparing to murder them. Emigration had ceased to be a possibility for the vast majority. Even Palestine was closed by the British White Paper of May 1939, which ended all Jewish immigration save for 15,000 a year to be admitted for the next five years.

Nevertheless, while the Polish and the National Socialist governments shared a common aim in their Jewish policy, few Poles seriously entertained the possibility of establishing a system of mass extermination camps in their country. An important reason for the Polish preference for old-fashioned methods of harassment was the complex attitude of the Roman Church. As we have seen, the Roman Catholic Church in Poland also sought the ultimate elimination of the country's Jews, but the Church was limited in the methods it could actively foster by its traditional moral constraints. Although the Church defined the Jews as unwanted aliens, it also was influential in setting limits on what the Polish state could do to them. When the invading Germans exterminated the Jews, they achieved the objective of the Jewish policy of Poland's Church and state. They did so, however, by resorting to measures the Poles themselves had been unwilling to adopt. Yet in spite of numerous instances of Poles saving Jewish lives at the risk of their own, the sober weight of historical scholarship points to the dreary but inescapable conclusion that the majority of the Poles regarded the Germans as doing their dirty work. When the War was over, the Poles took up the killing where the National Socialists left off. There were pogroms in Kielce, Krakow, Chelm, Rzeszow, and elsewhere.[74]

The Poles were neither modern enough nor secular enough to plan and execute a systematic program of mass extermination. The Germans were. There is evidence that Adolf Hitler understood the difference between an old-fashioned program of Jew-hatred and a modern program of legally sanctioned, bureaucratically administered mass murder from the very beginning of his political career. His earliest political writing characteristically deals with the question of the elimination of the Jews. Early in September 1919 Hitler was asked by Staff-Captain Karl Mayr, who had put him to work as a propaganda officer for the army, to formulate a statement on anti-Semitism. In a letter dated September 16, 1919, a few days before he joined what was to become the National Socialist Party, Hitler outlined the difference between the "rational anti-Semitism" he advocated and "anti-Semitism on purely emotional grounds":

Anti-Semitism on purely emotional grounds will find its ultimate expression in the form of pogroms. The anti-Semitism of reason [rational anti-Semitism] however, must lead to a systematic and legal struggle against, and eradication of, what privileges the Jews now enjoy over other foreigners...Its final objective, however, must be the total removal *[Entfernung]* of all Jews from our midst."[75]

Thus, in his earliest political document Hitler revealed himself to be a thoroughly modern figure who had little faith in the efficacy of pogroms and looked forward to a deliberately, calculated, systematic struggle against the Jews that would begin with legal measures and end with their "total removal."

The acceptability of the "rational" solution Hitler had in mind was undoubtedly facilitated for him as well as millions of others by their experience in World War I. Hitler reported that on October 29, 1914, in its first major clash, the battle of Ypres, his unit, the Bavarian List Regiment, lost 1700 of its 3500 men. In spite of the extraordinary slaughter or perhaps because of it, Hitler, like so many others of his generation, found in the war the only home that suited him.[76] But World War I was a different kind of a war from any ever fought on the European continent. It was a war of mass death in which massed men were fed for 1500 days to massed fire power so that more than 6000 corpses could be processed each day without letup.[77] When it was over, 10,000,000 soldiers and civilians had been killed and mass death had become an acceptable part of the experience and values of European civilization. Worse still, after the war Europe was filled with men who looked back nostalgically to their war experience as the only period of real living they had ever known.[78]

In Germany, there was regret, not so much that so many lives had been lost, but that the sacrifice had been in vain. No sooner had the guns fallen silent than influential groups resolved that, whatever the cost, the enormous blood sacrifice would be made good in the victorious war of the future. At this point, the inherent indifference to moral constraints of the value-free calculating rationality of the post-enlightenment world and the revisionist passions of the defeated Germans found their synthesis. Mass extermination had become an acceptable method of restructuring European civilization. The road to Auschwitz was still obscure, but the moral constraints standing in the path of those who traveled on that road were in the process of being cleared away. Within a few years the problem of Europe's "surplus" Jewish population would find its "Final Solution."

The fate of Europe's Jews points to some of the more gruesome consequences of the modernization process and the rise of capitalism, although it would be a mistake to assume that capitalism has a monopoly on programs of mass population elimination as a means of social reconstruction. As we have observed, few groups have been as drastically affected by the modernization process as were the Jews. The political, social, religious, economic, and perhaps psychological transformations experienced by Jews were far more radical than those experienced by any other European group. A greater proportion of their number changed their domicile and a far greater proportion were murdered by the state than any other group. By the beginning of the twentieth century an urbanized Jewish mass was to be found for the first time in the national centers of England, France, Germany,

Austria, Hungary, Poland, and the United States. In Europe the cities where the Jews congregated became the breeding ground of the first anti-Semitic political parties. Modernization had brought forth mass production, mass migration, and mass politics. In due time it would bring forth mass murder.

The concentrated presence in the metropolitan centers of people whose cultural and religious traditions were alien to the national consensus became a source of social, cultural, political, economic and religious conflict. The conflict was strongest and most dangerous where cultural and religious life had previously possessed a strong degree of ethnic and religious homogeneity. Moreover, the Jewish situation did not automatically improve when Jews acquired the culture of their adopted land. Hostility was often intensified when a generation of "assimilated," university-educated Jews came to maturity. Jews were more likely to be regarded as a destabilizing element in the national culture after they had acquired the skills with which to communicate effectively in the new language than when they exhibited easily identifiable signs of foreign origin. Of paramount importance is the fact we have emphasized throughout this chapter: the Jews had ceased to be an economically complementary group and were forced to become competitors of an endangered and insecure indigenous middle class.

There was also a highly dangerous conflict of social and cultural values between the Jews and other migrants to the urban centers. Although both the Jews and the displaced peasants were victims of modernization, most of the Jewish migrants felt they had no alternative but to embrace the very process that had uprooted them as well as the nontraditional values it engendered. Modern secular society seemed to offer Jews their only hope of full membership in the larger community, since it alone seemed to be sufficiently pluralistic to allow Jews a measure of civic equality and vocational mobility. Unfortunately, what Jews took to be a pluralistic community, influential members of the dominant majority took to be no community at all, but a congery of atomized strangers. This was the reason they sought to restore older bonds of community based upon kinship and shared origins. Of necessity there could be no place for Jews in such a community. Confronted by this development many Jews attempted to create their own community based upon kinship and common origin in the face of a hostile and disintegrating world. Zionism and the State of Israel are the fruit of their efforts.

When it was undeceived, European Zionism was rooted in the perception that religious, cultural, economic, and political motives for the elimination of the Jews from Europe were rapidly and effectively converging. On the question of the Jews, as we have stressed, the churches and the parties of the right were divided only on the question of the means by which the Jews were to be eliminated. That debate was ended by National Socialism.

The elimination of the Jews was also a non-negotiable aspect of the political program of the European left. According to the Marxists, the Jews were not a distinctive religiocultural entity, but a petit-bourgeois stratum of the larger society whose religion was the ideological superstructure mirroring the group's concrete social and economic relations.[79] The Marxists saw the petite bourgeoisie, whether Jewish or non-Jewish, as a doomed and superfluous class. In both capitalism and socialism, the rationalization of the economy would bring about their elimination. Those who were fit for membership in a socialist society would eventually divest themselves of their class origins and accept their place in the working class. Those who vainly attempted to maintain their petit-bourgeois status would in any event be eliminated, as indeed happened to millions of kulaks in Russia between 1929 and 1932 and to the ethnic Chinese in Vietnam more recently. The Jews would either disappear into the working class or be eliminated altogether. When this happened, the Marxists confidently expected, and still expect, the ideological superstructure which had mirrored the precapitalist Jewish situation to disappear because of its irrelevance. This would result in the "withering away" of the Jewish religion and, with it, Jewish identity. Thus, in addition to the Christian Church, both the European right and the left expected and were prepared to implement the elimination of the Jews as a distinctive group. According to the left, the Jews would not survive the full rationalization of the economy;

according to the right, if the rationalization of the economy was inevitable, it was not to be permitted to turn society into a marketplace to which any person, irrespective of background, could gain free access. Even the Zionists saw the elimination of the Jews from Europe as inevitable. Unwilling to abandon Jewish identity or to equate it with petit-bourgeois status, they sought an alternative basis for maintaining themselves as a distinctive community by seizing a monopoly of force in the territory which, according to their mythic inheritance, was their place of ancestral origin. As of this writing, the ultimate success of their radical attempt to escape the fate modernization had apparently meted out to their people remains in doubt.

8
THE AGONY OF INDOCHINA

THIRTY YEARS OF WAR in Indochina came to a temporary end in April of 1975. Saigon fell to the Vietnamese People's Army and Phnom Penh, the capital of Cambodia, fell to the Khmer Rouge. Although American supporters of the Vietnamese War had frequently predicted a bloodbath in the event of a northern victory, the transition to rule by Hanoi was relatively tranquil initially. This was in stark contrast to the victory of the Khmer Rouge in what was to be known henceforth as Kampuchea. Phnom Penh fell on April 17. By the 24th of the month, 2,500,000 people, the entire population of the capital city, were forcibly evacuated to face a grim and uncertain future in their country's malarial jungles. Among the first to be expelled were the city's 20,000 sick and wounded hospital patients. Throughout Kampuchea, the urban population was dumped precipitously into the jungles and countryside without even rudimentary provisions. It is difficult to know exactly how many died. Whole groups within the population were executed immediately. The Vietnamese estimate that 3,000,000 out of a total Kampuchean population of 7,000,000 were eliminated. The American estimate is 2,000,000. The attitude of the Khmer Rouge toward their own urban population can best be summed up in a sentence often heard in Kampuchea at the time: "There is nothing to gain by keeping them alive, nothing to lose by doing away with them."

Apologists for the Khmer Rouge claim Phnom Penh had a food supply for only a few days when captured. In addition, they maintain, the urban population was largely "unproductive

165

and totally dependent on foreign aid." It would have been impossible to supply Phnom Penh and the other cities with domestically produced rice without disrupting the nation's delicately organized system of agricultural production. With the cities suddenly deprived of a constant infusion of foreign supplies, there was danger of a total breakdown of urban services and the outbreak of a major epidemic. The only remedy was speedily to evacuate the population of the cities to the countryside, where the evacuees might at least produce their own food. This apology fails to account for the extraordinary proportion of fatalities to the total population. Never before in history has any government with a relatively homogenous population been willing deliberately to rid itself of so great a proportion of its own people.[1]

In the face of such horror, the characteristic response has repeatedly been to stress the atypical nature of such behavior and to characterize it as a form of uncivilized madness. Reactions to the horror in Kampuchea frequently resemble reactions to the discovery of the Nazi death camps at the end of World War II. In both cases, there was the same sense of surprise and horror that the constraints of civilization have been breached so barbarously. Yet, if the current study has any lesson, it is that, though we cannot control our sense of horror, we have little reason to be surprised at the events in Indochina.

Saigon fell on April 30, 1975. In the weeks immediately before the end, there was considerable disorder and panic. Yet, a combination of small craft and the United States Sixth Fleet managed to evacuate the first 130,000 Vietnamese refugees.[2] Most of this group were skilled, well educated, and able to speak English. By December 1978, 94.8 percent had found jobs in the United States.[3]

Although the initial takeover period in South Vietnam was infinitely less bloody than in Kampuchea, the situation became progressively worse between 1976 and 1978. After the American withdrawal, the victors were confronted with monumental economic and social problems. More than 2,000,000 people in North Vietnam had been made homeless as a result of American bombing. In excess of 20 percent of Vietnam's arable land had been seriously damaged or destroyed by American defoliants. North Vietnam was dependent upon the Soviet Union and China for technological assistance and even much of its food supply.[4]

However, the situation in the south was far worse. The postwar demobilization had thrown over 1,200,000 members of the South Vietnamese armed forces and government on a labor market which was incapable of absorbing them. It was estimated that 11,000,000 people had left their homes over the years because of wartime dislocations. There were 800,000 orphans and abandoned children, many of them the offspring of foreign soldiers and Vietnamese women, as well as thousands of redundant prostitutes. Drug abuse was rampant. Health-care facilities had broken down and several hundred thousand people were afflicted with diseases such as malaria, tuberculosis, leprosy, and the plague.[5]

The south was also beset by overrapid urbanization. Before the beginning of American military intervention in the early sixties, only 15 percent of the people of South Vietnam lived in the cities. By 1975 the figure had climbed to 65 percent. This contrasted with the north where only 10 percent lived in urban areas at the end of the war. Moreover, the urbanization was almost exclusively the result of an artificial service economy sustained by American wartime spending and American aid rather than the result of the expansion of South Vietnam's own productive resources. In addition to the direct expenditures of the American armed forces, approximately $2,000,000,000 a year was given by the American government to the South Vietnamese government. When the war ended, the government collapsed, American spending was terminated, and approximately 3,000,000 people, most of whom were in or around Saigon, suddenly found themselves unemployed and, unless retrained, unemployable. Moreover, almost all who owned businesses were fated to lose them by 1978, and professionals had every reason to expect that their working conditions and status would quickly deteriorate.

Simply finding work for Vietnam's growing population was an insuperable task. In spite of the war, Vietnam had experienced something of a population explosion. In 1950 the population was around 26,000,000. By 1975 it had grown to at least 44,000,000.[6]

In December 1981 the total population was estimated to be 54,000,000.[7] The rate of population increase was exceptionally high, about 3 percent per annum. The labor force was estimated to be 22,000,000 and was growing at a rate of some 1,000,000 a year! Given Hanoi's commitment to communism, a commitment fortified by thirty years of war and victory over the world's leading capitalist power, there was little reason to doubt the bourgeois and professional classes of South Vietnam were destined to be eliminated. The only question was whether it was possible to eliminate a class without eliminating the human beings who constitute the class. In Kampuchea the ruling elite apparently decided it was not. Moreover, the Pol Pot regime seems to have decided it was necessary to eliminate potential as well as actual members of the bourgeois and professional class. As we have noted, this was accomplished by the sudden and total emptying of all of the urban communities of Kampuchea. The rejection of the professional class by the Khmer Rouge was so unrelenting that doctors and nurses from the cities were not permitted to practice after the forced evacuations. Instead, they were compelled to work as common laborers in the rice paddies, even when diseases such as malaria had reached epidemic proportions among the evacuees.[8]

By contrast, Hanoi's initial postwar policy was announced as one of "gradualism." Hanoi hoped to attract investment and technological assistance from the noncommunist world. As late as 1977 Saigon, now known as Ho Chi Minh City, still had a free market in consumer goods and many private businesses were in operation. Ho Chi Minh City was, however, living on borrowed time. The consumer goods were largely American leftovers. Almost nothing had been imported since the war.

In order to solve its economic problems, Hanoi was planning to relocate more than 10,000,000 people. They were to be put to work reclaiming and reforesting millions of acres. The relocated people were also to form the population base of new industrial communities being planned away from both Hanoi and Ho Chi Minh City.[9] In 1976 about 1,400,000 people were "relocated": 1,000,000 returned to their native villages and 400,000 settled on reclaimed acreage.[10] The reclaimed acreage was the fruit of the "new economic zone" program (NEZ) which was supposed to provide productive work for part of Vietnam's growing surplus population. However, those who settled in the NEZs found that they received little, if any, help from the government. They were expected to clear land, erect dwellings, and create new communities for themselves using only the most primitive tools. A very high proportion of those sent to the NEZs were families whose members had cooperated with the Americans and the former regime. Some politically reliable settlers from the north were mixed with settlers from the south in order to reeducate them ideologically. The NEZ program was thus both an attempt forcibly to restructure Vietnamese society along socialist lines and a means of punishing families who had had a wartime leadership role in the south.[11]

Nevertheless, in order to get a balanced picture, we must keep in mind Hanoi was faced with a major economic crisis. Theoretically, the NEZs were designed to give people who no longer had any opportunity to lead productive lives a chance to produce the essentials for their subsistence. Unfortunately, the very people for whom the NEZs were designed, the urbanized middle class, were those least suited to life in an agrarian commune, especially in its initial stages. Even slum dwellers found life in the NEZs unbearable. Many returned to the city in spite of the high unemployment.[12]

In addition to the NEZs, Hanoi established a series of Reeducation Camps. All members of the defeated armed services were required to register for "reeducation," which involved a process of critically examining one's capitalist past and acquiring new socialist values. At the lower ranks "reeducation" was usually perfunctory and was completed in a week or less at home or on the job. Intermediate ranks to the level of captain were sent to camps for periods of up to a year. Senior army officers and civil servants, as well as more "difficult" cases from the intermediate ranks, were incarcerated in camps in remote areas without running water and electricity. Many inmates from urban areas were unable to survive in the camps, which the French newspaper Le Monde called "the Vietnamese Gulag."[13] In December 1981 thousands remained in the camps, although it was difficult to arrive at an accurate figure.[14] Nevertheless, our judgment of the camps must be tempered by our knowledge of the way in which the neighboring Pol Pot regime dealt with former officers and senior civil servants in Kampuchea. With few exceptions they were summarily executed.

Although the conditions of life in postwar Vietnam encouraged many to think of leaving the country, Hanoi at first imposed a ban on emigration, which was partly lifted in 1978 and then lifted altogether in 1979. This is evident in the figures we possess for the total number of boat people arriving at a first-destination receiving country from 1975 onward. In 1975 there were 377 such people; in 1976, 5619; in 1977, 21,276. In 1978 the number jumped to 106,489, and for the period between January 1 and July 31, 1979, there were 292,315.[15]

In the south, the situation was further complicated by the fact that a very large proportion of the commercial and professional class was not Vietnamese but ethnic Chinese, called the Hoa in Vietnam. As is well known, throughout Southeast Asia the ethnic Chinese control a disproportionate share of the business and professional life. Like the Jews and Armenians, the ethnic Chinese of Southeast Asia can be regarded as an "elite minority." Because of their role as middlemen and professionals, the ethnic Chinese have been called "the Jews of South East Asia."[16] Moreover, their distinctive script gave the Chinese an advantage in international commerce because it could be read by any literate Chinese regardless of differences in their spoken dialect. Before modern times, Hebrew, Yiddish, and Ladino (a Judeo-Spanish dialect), all of which were written in the Hebrew script, gave the Jews of Europe and the Middle East a similar advantage in international commerce.

Having played a business and professional role in Southeast Asia similar to that of the Jews in the West, the ethnic Chinese attracted a degree of hostility and envy not unlike that directed towards the Jews, although hostility to the Chinese was not compounded by the distinctive religious conflict between Judaism and Christianity. Ethnic conflict was especially strong in countries such as Malaysia, the Philippines, Indonesia, and Thailand, the very nations in which the largely ethnic Chinese boat people sought temporary asylum after leaving Vietnam.

The ethnic Chinese had come to Vietnam in large numbers in the nineteenth and twentieth centuries. Before the end of the war, there were about 300,000 in the north, most of whom lived in the provinces adjacent to the Chinese border. In the north the ethnic Chinese were more likely to be wage workers than in the south, where they numbered 1,400,000, dominated much of the professional life, and controlled financial and commercial establishments of all sizes. Of especial importance was their monopoly of the rice trade, Vietnam's principal export. With their high literacy and international contacts, the ethnic Chinese became practically unbeatable competitors in intra-Asian commerce. Their success did not enhance their popularity among the majority communities in the countries where they had settled.[17] Thus, the elimination of the bourgeoisie as a class in Vietnam also involved the elimination of the country's most important ethnic minority.

Ethnic hostility between the Chinese and the Vietnamese has had a long history. A dominant theme in Vietnam's history has been that country's attempt to maintain its independence of China. As long as the French dominated Indochina, the Hoa had little reason to fear their right to remain would be seriously challenged. It was not in the interest of the French to dislodge them and thereby to create the conditions under which a purely Vietnamese business and professional class could develop. With the departure of the French, the situation of the Hoa became more precarious. There were certain parallels to the situation of the Jews in Poland after the departure of the Russians in 1917, as well as the situation of the Indian and Pakistani middle class in Kenya and Uganda after the departure of the British. Very often, the successful struggle for national liberation against a foreign overlord has been followed by intensified hostility against minority groups within the newly independent country.[18]

As long as the Vietnamese were engaged in both civil war and war with the United States, it was in the interest of both Hanoi and Saigon to mute the internal ethnic conflict. In the case of Hanoi, China's role as a communist ally also served to discourage ethnic conflict. With Hanoi's victory, the situation of the Hoa rapidly deteriorated. The Hoa were both an envied minority and a predominant element in the very class any communist government would seek to eliminate, if not as human beings at least as a class. Their situation was further aggravated by the renewal of the age-old hostility between China and Vietnam. The conflict raised the issue of whether the Hoa would be loyal to Vietnam in a Sino-Vietnamese war. The question of loyalty was made more urgent by the fact many urbanized Hoa in the north had not taken out Vietnamese citizenship even after the Chinese government had urged them to do so in 1955. Most Hoa, even those who had married Vietnamese, considered themselves Chinese in both citizenship and loyalty, in spite of the fact that the majority in the south were noncommunist.

Hanoi's attitude toward emigration began to change in December 1977 when a border conflict erupted between Kampuchea and Vietnam. According to Hanoi, about 750,000 Vietnamese were driven from their homes in the border regions as a result of bombardment by the Kampucheans using long-range artillery made in China. The Khmer Rouge was emboldened to attack because they were convinced that the Vietnamese, fearing China, would refrain from retaliation. The Vietnamese in turn were convinced China was partly responsible for the hardships caused by the Kampuchean attacks. These included a food shortfall of 1,300,000 tons of rice, a result of some of the worst weather in thirty years, and 321,400 refugees who had fled from the Pol Pot regime. More than half of the refugees from Kampuchea were ethnic Vietnamese. Moreover, the economic situation in Ho Chi Minh City was seriously deteriorating. On March 23, 1978, all private "trading and business operations" in the south were abolished. The decree had the effect of closing 30,000 business establishments in Ho Chi Minh City alone, most of which were owned by ethnic Chinese. On May 3, 1978, the government unified the currency of the north and the south. This had the effect of wiping out the savings of the South Vietnamese middle class and drastically reducing the value of the compensation received by those whose businesses had been purchased by the state. A further cause of the economic ruin of the middle class was the stepping up by the government of the socialization of agriculture. This affected both Vietnamese rice farmers and Chinese traders.[19]

It was now clear that the middle classes were facing ruin. Consequently, there was, as we have seen, a very large increase in the number of those departing. In April 1978, 5012 Vietnamese landed in first-destination receiving countries, a number eight times as great as in the previous year.[20] Having suffered the most from the economic changes, the ethnic Chinese constituted the majority of the emigrants. However, a large number of Vietnamese who had served in the political and military establishment of the defeated government or who had been identified with anticommunist political parties also left. Many were fearful of being sent to a NEZ or to a reeducation camp if they remained. The evidence seems to suggest that in the south the government's interest in eliminating an unwanted class was stronger than its interest in eliminating an unwanted ethnic group.[21] Anticommunist Vietnamese who had been prominent in the former regime were considered as undesirable by Hanoi as the ethnic Chinese.

Nevertheless, there was a strong element of ethnic hostility in the population elimination program. In March 1978 Peking accused Hanoi of a policy of "ostracism, persecution and expulsion" toward the ethnic Chinese.[22] Shortly thereafter, Hanoi announced that all Chinese who wanted to leave the country need only apply for exit visas. In four months 130,000 Chinese departed, overwhelming towns in the Chinese border provinces of Guangxi and Yunnan by their numbers. In some Chinese towns there were four times as many refugees as ordinary inhabitants. In July Peking called a halt to the refugee traffic, claiming that China had taken in 160,000.[23] The flow of refugees did not stop at this point. Barred from entering China by land, the refugees took to the sea to reach Hong Kong.[24]

The long-simmering Sino-Soviet dispute played a part in the plight of Vietnam's ethnic Chinese. Hanoi was friendly to Moscow, the more distant communist power, and hostile to Peking, the neighboring communist power. In September there was an unresolved dispute between Vietnam and China concerning whether the ethnic Chinese in Vietnam were to be considered citizens of China or Vietnam. In November Vietnam and the Soviet Union signed a twenty-five year treaty of "friendship and cooperation." Vietnam had already joined the Soviet-sponsored Communist Council for Mutual Economic Assistance (COMECON) in July. The treaty with the Soviet Union was thus the final ratification of Vietnam's military and economic alliance with China's principal adversary. Not surprisingly, the United States and China agreed to establish diplomatic relations in December 1978. Fortified by the treaty with the Soviet Union, Vietnam invaded Kampuchea, China's ally, in the same month.

In January 1979, Vietnam occupied Phnom Penh and replaced the Pol Pot regime with the government of Heng Samrin, who was entirely dependent upon the Vietnamese for his survival. This was a challenge China could not ignore. In February 1979, China initiated her "punitive" invasion of the border provinces of Vietnam. The Chinese began their phased withdrawal a month later. As the Sino-Vietnamese conflict had worsened during 1978, persecution of the ethnic Chinese in the north also intensified. Some ethnic Chinese were dismissed from their jobs both in government and factories in spite of long years of service and membership in the Vietnamese Communist Party. However, the systematic expulsion of the Chinese seems to have begun in earnest in the wake of the Chinese invasion of February and March 1979.[25] The new policy was apparently announced at a meeting for leading public officials and party members organized by the Public Security Bureau (PSB) in Hanoi in mid-March. The Hoa were accused of having aided and abetted the Chinese invasion and of having even assisted in the massacre of Vietnamese troops. Moreover, it was asserted that some of the traitors were government and party officials. As a result, the government had decided to remove Vietnamese of Chinese origin from all positions of public responsibility and to resettle them in two areas several hundred kilometers south of Hanoi where they would be put to "productive labor."[26]

The full implications of the policy became evident when: (1) ethnic Chinese in responsible positions in the party, government, and the armed forces were summarily dismissed; (2) Chinese were fired from lower-level positions in government and other employers were instructed not to hire them; (3) Chinese children were barred from school; (4) Chinese were warned that their food rations would be stopped if they did not leave by a certain date; and (5) the Chinese were subject to a curfew. There were other harassments, including nocturnal police visits to Chinese homes, whose inhabitants were asked why they hadn't left yet and were warned to depart lest they lose all civic protection.[27] It was evident the government was actively engaged in getting rid of the Hoa on the basis of their origin. In the aftermath of the Chinese invasion, Hanoi had decided that no Chinese could be trusted and that in one way or another Vietnam had to eliminate them.

The situation in the south was somewhat different. In addition to getting rid of the Chinese minority, the government also undertook to rid itself of those Vietnamese who could not be integrated into the new society by reason of their economic or political background. Moreover, the expulsion operation was systematized by the public security bureacracy in a manner calculated to yield maximum financial gain to the state while controlling the number of departing refugees as if they were water flowing from a tap.

When the flow of Vietnamese refugees was at its height, Prime Minister Lee Kuan Yew, of Singapore, himself of Chinese background, expressed the apprehension that other Southeast Asian countries might follow Vietnam's example in "solving" their Chinese problem. He observed that there were extremists in each country who liked the idea, provided it could be done less crudely than in Vietnam.[28] The Prime Minister knew whereof he spoke. His own predominantly Chinese city-state, Singapore, had been expelled from the Malaysian federation in 1965 largely because of the inability of the federation to cope with Chinese economic domination of Singapore and, through Singapore, of the rest of Malaysia.[29]

After elimination of the Hoa became official policy, responsibility for its implementation was turned over to a bureaucratic
agency, the Public Security Bureau.[30] However, just as there were
economic and political differences between the north and the
south, there were differences in the way emigration policy was
implemented in each region. In the south there was an element
of capitalist enterprise in the program. Affluent Chinese with
access to capital financed the acquisition and modification of the
refugee boats, as well as the purchase of fuel and supplies for the
voyage. Since the boats were usually small and in need of repair,
a small boom developed in the shipyards where the boats were
overhauled and prepared for the journey.[31]

Refugees in the south initiated the emigration process by paying
a middleman two taels of gold as a "registration" or "application" fee. The price for children was half that of an adult. A tael
is about an ounce and a third. Payment was almost always in gold.
In 1979, on average gold was worth about $300 an ounce. A
further payment of five to eight taels was paid at embarkation.
The proceeds were divided 50 percent for the government, 40 for
the cost of the boat and supplies, and 10 percent for the
organizer.[32] The actual amount extacted from each refugee varied
according to ability to pay, as well as the honesty of the
bureaucrats, police, middlemen, and boat owners. Because
expulsion of the ethnic Chinese had become state policy, it was
normally cheaper for Chinese to leave than for Vietnamese, the
cost of departure for the Chinese being $2400 to $3000 a head.[33]
Many refugees also had to list all their valuables on the departure
applications. Such valuables were often confiscated, save for two
taels of gold per person. Frequently the PSB would add groups
of people to a departing boat without warning. Since no provision
had been made for the extra refugees, they overloaded the boats
and seriously increased the risks of the voyage. Many of the boats
were barely seaworthy even after they had been repaired. This
made no difference. The fundamental objective of the program
was the elimination of ethnic Chinese and bourgeois Vietnamese
from Vietnamese society, not their safe passage to a new domicile.
Whether the refugees arrived safely or drowned at sea, the

policy objective would be achieved. One is reminded of the conditions under which the Irish crossed the Atlantic during the famine years. Then too, the fundamental objective was to get rid of people, not their safe passage to a new domicile.

As noted, the first large-scale wave of refugees consisted of ethnic Chinese who fled to China between March and July, 1978. There were between 140,000 (the Vietnamese figure) and 160,000 (the Chinese figure) in the group, The second wave began after the Chinese invasion of February-March 1979. Since the overland route to China had been closed, small boats from the north headed to Hong Kong, which consistently had a more open and humane policy toward receiving the refugees than any of the other receiving communities.[34]

In the north the visits by security force to the homes of the ethnic Chinese had their intended effect. The Hoa joined together in small groups, made the appropriate departure arrangements with the PSB, and sold their possessions at distress prices in order to purchase a small boat and the necessary provisions.

The cost of departing from a northern port was considerably cheaper than from the south, and the sea voyage was usually safer. In the north the total price for a single departure averaged four taels in contrast to ten taels in the south.[35] Only 10 percent of the northern boats were motorized, whereas all the boats from the south were. The northern boats hugged the China coast. The trip to Hong Kong took as long as six weeks. When the refugees needed provisions, it was possible to buy them from Chinese fishermen often by exchanging gold watches.

In contrast to the Hong Kong voyage, the motorized trip to Malaysia and Thailand took as little as three days, a week at most, but it was far more dangerous. Most refugees set out in small boats using old motors which often broke down at sea. The small boats were also a prey for Thai pirates, who by the fall of 1978 were attacking two out of every three small boats.

After mass elimination became official Vietnamese policy, converted freighters capable of carrying several thousand refugees were put into service. The *Southern Cross* was the first of the freighters to come to general notice. In September 1978 her skipper sent word by radio that the ship had rescued more than a thousand refugees. His highly suspect story was that his ship had developed "engine trouble" in the Gulf of Thailand, whereupon the refugees abandoned their small boats for the larger and safer ship. He claimed that the ship was low in both food and water. The ship was anchored outside Malaysian territorial waters near Mersing, a location close to a refugee camp maintained by the United Nations High Commission for Refugees (UNHCR). Malaysian authorities had their doubts about the skipper's veracity. Although the Malaysian government was willing to give the ship provisions, it was unwilling to permit the refugees, who numbered 1220, to disembark without a guarantee from other countries that the refugees would be given permanent homes. The *Southern Cross* finally discharged her passengers on Pengibu, an uninhabited island belonging to Indonesia. After considerable delay, the United States, Canada, and Australia finally gave assurances that most of the refugees would be granted permanent asylum.

As a result of the arrest of four men by Singapore authorities, the true story of the *Southern Cross* became known. The *Southern Cross* was one of a number of freighters purchased by syndicates operating out of Hong Kong and Singapore for the purpose of transporting refugees from Vietnam. It was obvious that no business syndicate would have invested in the conversion and provisioning of large ships to transport refugees from a country as tightly controlled as Vietnam without government approval. After the freighters had been converted, they were sent to Vietnam, where the authorities set up arrangements similar to those used with the smaller boats, save that the cost of travel by freighter was higher and the profits to the government and the entrepreneurs were enormous. In the case of one freighter, the *Hai Hong,* 1200 people paid ten taels of gold each, well over $3000, for passage. Shortly before the boat departed, Vietnamese authorities insisted on adding 1300 refugees. Even after making allowances for all possible discounts, the yield from this one sailing was estimated at over $4,000,000.[36] There were many such sailings. When the story of ships like the *Southern Cross,* the *Hai Hong,* the *Skyluck,* and the *Huey Fong* was revealed, it became clear that the massive exodus of ethnic Chinese had been systematically planned and executed by the Vietnamese government, using Chinese entrepreneurs within Vietnam and elsewhere in Southeast Asia to supply the venture capital and much of the organization for the project.

In spite of utterly squalid conditions on board the big ships were more or less immune from attack by the pirates infesting the waters off the coast of Thailand. When the refugees began to leave the south in boats, their initial destination was Thailand. By 1977 the flow of refugees by sea had shifted to Malaysia because of the predatory activities of the Thai pirates.[37] The pirate attacks were despicable in their viciousness and gratuitous in their violence. Vessels were frequently attacked several times by teams of pirate ships that kept in radio contact with each other. Refugees were robbed of their possessions on the first attack. On the second their food and provisions were taken. Very often the men were murdered and mothers gang-raped in front of their children. Boats were deliberately disabled, rammed, and sunk. The stories of the sadistic treatment of the refugees by the pirates match in horror the record of abuse of any small group by another.[38] The attacks continued as late as the winter of 1981.[39]

When attacked, the refugees seldom resisted. They calculated that more of their number were likely to escape if they submitted passively and surrendered their possessions than if they offered resistance. Their behavior was not unlike that of unarmed Jews under similar circumstances.

There were also a number of incidents in which patrol boats of both the Singapore and Malaysian naval forces deliberately rammed refugee boats, cast helpless people adrift, and refused aid to drowning refugees. One disabled refugee boat, the *MH3012,* was dragged at high speed in a zigzag course by a Malaysian patrol boat, the *Renchang,* until it capsized. The refugees were then prevented from boarding the *Renchang* for a half hour. When the refugees were finally permitted on board only 122 out of 246 survived.[40]

Most observers agree that the pirate activity was not unwelcome to the Thai government as a means of discouraging the refugees from attempting to land in Thailand.[41] In spite of the numerous, well-publicized incidents, the Thai government ceased all action against the pirates in September 1981. Moreover, at no time did the Thai government take more than token measures. As one observer commented, the priority of both the Thai and Malay navies was to discourage refugees, not pirates.[42] The pirates had a primitive grasp of some of the fundamental realities of modern politics. They intuitively understood that persons without political status, that is, without membership in a community ready and able to defend their "human" rights, have no rights whatsoever. When rights carry no practical significance, they are not rights but illusions. The Thai pirates were confident that they could with impunity inflict any act of violence, no matter how obscene or vicious, upon the refugees. Further on we shall discuss the extent to which the experiences of the boat people were like those of the Jews in Nazi-occupied Europe. For the present we note that, like the boat people, the European Jews had been expelled from their native communities and were members of no community willing or able to guarantee them even minimal human rights. Hence, there was nothing their captors could not freely and without penalty inflict upon them.[43]

Had the Thai pirates attempted to carry out comparable attacks against citizens of Thailand, Malaysia, Singapore, Vietnam, or any other power, their actions would have been swiftly brought to a halt. No government would have tolerated the kind of sustained attack on its citizens that the Thai pirates inflicted upon the Vietnamese refugees. The boat people were compelled to endure the full horror entailed in a human existence devoid of political status.

Nevertheless, the Thai government's toleration, if not covert encouragement, of the pirates cannot be divorced from the overall problems it faced as a neighbor of both Vietnam and Kampuchea. The sudden influx of ethnic Chinese refugees posed a threat to the political and social stability of all nations of Southeast Asia. Each had a sizable Chinese population that played a predominant role in its commercial and professional life. None of the countries was willing to introduce into its midst a large new contingent of talented ethnic Chinese refugees. In the case of Thailand, the one receiving country that could be reached by land after the closing of the Chinese border, the situation was further complicated by the presence of large numbers of Kampuchean and Laotian refugees and the tendency of the warring factions in Kampuchea to seek temporary asylum in Thailand. By the end of 1979 there were a total of 410,000 refugees in Thailand.

Thailand had problems with more than one ethnic group. The ethnic Chinese were actually less troublesome to the Thais than were the ethnic Vietnamese, Kampucheans, Laotians, and Hmong tribesmen. In the aftermath of the war, the Thais were apprehensive concerning the political and military intentions of the battle-hardened Vietnamese. The Thais had been pro-American during the Vietnamese war and regarded the Vietnamese as historic enemies. In 1979 about half of the 9000 boat people who arrived in Thailand were Vietnamese rather than ethnic Chinese.[44] The presence of these Vietnamese in significant numbers upset the Thais more than did the Kampucheans and Laotians in border refugee camps.

At one point, the heavy influx of Kampuchean refugees produced a violent reaction from the Thais. In June 1979, 42,000 Kampucheans in Thai refugee camps were told by Thai soldiers that they were to be taken by bus for "resettlement," a deception with deadly intent that the Nazis had used with the Jews. Instead of "resettlement," the refugees were pushed over the Cambodian border at gunpoint. They were warned to follow a narrow trail down a steep incline. Those who tried to turn back were shot at; those who left the path were blown up by mines. The gunpoint explusions continued for four days. When some refugees refused to believe the resettlement story, babies were torn from their mothers' arms and put on the buses in order to force parents into the buses. Thai soldiers killed several hundred who refused to get on the buses. The area in which the refugees were dumped was on the edge of a forest in one of the worst malaria-infected regions in the world. Most of the refugees were middle-class professionals, intellectuals, and merchants who died when their food ran out. Shortly before the "repatriation," refugee officials were told by the Thai government that they could make a selection of people to be saved, provided that they could guarantee their resettlement outside Thailand; 1300 were rescued. On the day the repatriation began, American refugee officials had buses ready to rescue another 1500. It was too late. The convoys were already rolling to the dumping point. Among those dumped off in the malarial jungle and left to die were the former head of Cambodia's supreme court, a number of bank presidents, doctors, and other skilled professionals. In spite of their skills, without a political community to guarantee their rights, these people were so much refuse to be disposed of in a human dumping ground. The UNHCR called the situation the "worst case of forcible repatriation" in the organization's thirty-year history."[45] The incident was followed by emphatic international protests. The Thais were unimpressed with the protests and, in effect, told the protesting nations to do something about the situation if they wanted any improvement. However, after the protests, the repatriations came to an end.

Singapore absolutely refused to take in any refugees, and its navy had a policy of chasing away refugee boats even when disabled. The city-state has a population that is 75 percent Chinese. In order to meet its labor shortage, it must import more than 20,000 "guest workers." Nevertheless, it initially limited the number of refugees who could be given even strictly temporary asylum to 450. This figure was later raised to 1000. The Singapore authorities were anxious not to exacerbate tensions among their non-Chinese minorities by admitting large numbers of ethnic Chinese. In explaining his approach to the refugee problem, Prime Minister Lee Kuan Yew said, "You must grow calluses on your heart otherwise you will bleed to death."[46]

The situation was somewhat similar in Malaysia, where the population was delicately balanced between Chinese and Malaysians. There are 4,000,000 Chinese in Malaysia. In spite of official discrimination, they enjoy the same kind of predominance in business and the professions that they do elsewhere in the region. In addition to the normal elements of economic and social conflict, the Malays and the Chinese are separated by an unbridgeable religiocultural gap. For example, Malays are predominantly Moslem and abhor pork products. Pork is a staple part of the Chinese diet. Thus, even the smell of food coming from the Chinese quarters is a source of group antagonism. In 1969 there were race riots, an experience the government did not want to see repeated. Understandably, the Malay government, as well as the governments of the other Association of Southeast Asian Nations (ASEAN), saw Hanoi as solving Vietnam's "Chinese problem" by creating one in its neighbors. One newspaper, the *Malay Straits Times,* likened the refugee flow to a bomber attack.[47] The Malays responded to the boat people with a "tow out/throw out" policy. On January 15, 1979, Premier Hossein announced a ban on refugees entering Malaysia. The official policy was to give all boats food and water before forcing them out to sea. However, some refugees complained that the Malaysian navy confiscated their maps and navigational aids and left them with disabled motors before casting them adrift.[48] In the first six months of 1979, the policy was applied to 47,000 refugees whose small boats were towed out to sea and left to fend as best they could.

The policy created a special group of refugees, the "beach people," consisting of those who had somehow managed to evade the Malaysian blockade and land on the beaches. These refugees were usually placed in makeshift camps on or near beaches under Malay rather than UNHCR control. Journalists and refugee officials were denied access to these camps. From February to June 1979, 5000 of the beach people were placed in boats, towed out to international waters, and cast adrift without adequate food, fuel, or water. Like the Thai "resettlement" of 42,000 Cambodian refugees, the Malay policy had the effect of doing away with thousands of refugees without Malay officials actually killing them. Nevertheless, the objective was the same: nobody wanted the refugees and the government had decided upon their riddance. Without rights, cut off from all outside contact, never knowing whether they would be taken out to sea and cast adrift, the beach people were living in an earthly purgatory.[49]

When the policy became known, there were the usual protests from other governments. The Malay government responded that the world was quick to criticize but slow to do anything to alleviate the situation. The United States had promised to take 4000 refugees a month in 1977, but by June 1979 only 13,000 had been accepted. In Thailand only one refugee in ten was resettled. The proportion was smaller in Malaysia but the problem was similar.

Thai and Malay officials also complained that the Western powers tended to skim off the best refugees, leaving them with "the garbage of the garbage."[50] There was some hypocrisy in the complaint. In reality, the skilled and educated refugees were at least as unwelcome as those who were likely to become public charges. Even when they created new wealth in their adopted lands, they were accused of diminishing the opportunities available to the general population. When they had no resources, they were accused of being a drain on the public treasury.

The most populous Malay beach camp was located on a previously uninhabited island known as Pulau Bildong. In mid–1979 more than 40,000 refugees were settled in an area of less than one square kilometer. The camp reminds us once again that people who have been rendered surplus often possess advanced education, talent, and skills. It is as easy for talented people to lose their place in the world as it is for those who cannot cope with the complexities of technological civilization. Sometimes it is easier for the former to become worldless, especially in the aftermath of a social revolution. A very high proportion of Pulau Bildong's inhabitants were both capable and resourceful. The camp was run by the refugees themselves. It was largely supported by the UNHCR. The refugees also built the camp's shelters, using scrap and material supplied by the UNHCR and the Malaysian Red Crescent, the Islamic counterpart of the Red Cross. Refugees without funds were housed in dangerously overcrowded shanties. Those with funds could purchase more desirable quarters, the best being closest to the beach and the camp center. There was a camp clinic staffed by the numerous refugee doctors, nurses, and pharmacists.

While the normal UNHCR rations were sufficient to sustain

life for adults, they were insufficient for the very young and the aged. An extremely active black market in food developed, as did a commercial area in which most services of a normal city were soon available. These even included pawnbrokers, real estate firms dealing (illegally) in desirable camp locations, and a black market in currency. There were also coffeehouses, restaurants, nightclubs featuring former Vietnamese movie stars, English classes, and several churches and pagodas. Characteristically, the commercial life of Pulau Bildong was dominated by the Chinese. In the midst of hopelessly squalid conditions, the refugees had resolved to make a life for themselves, however tenuous. Not all of the beach camps were as resourceful as Pulau Bildong, but all were under the constant threat of being overwhelmed by more people than they could handle even under emergency conditions.[51]

Many of the people towed out to sea by the Malays were given temporary shelter by the Indonesians. As with the Malays, the predominant religion of the Indonesians is Islam. Indonesia also had a history of anti-Chinese race riots and violence. The Chinese constituted only 3 percent of the population, but they dominated much of the commercial life in Indonesia, which was as reluctant to welcome the refugees as any other ASEAN country. Fortunately for the refugees, the words of Indonesian officials tended to be worse than their deeds. It is estimated that thousands of refugees survived because the Indonesians sheltered them temporarily.[52]

Even China proved to be a problematic refuge, especially for refugees from South Vietnam. Some of the Hoa regarded China as a temporary asylum. It was difficult for them to adjust to life in any communist country. However, the UNHCR and the other countries of the region saw China as their permanent destination.[53]

The time-honored tradition of rescue at sea was an important casualty of the refugee crisis. Captains who rescued refugees in disabled boats found that Singapore and the other ASEAN nations refused to permit the refugees to disembark unless resettlement elsewhere was guaranteed. Moreover, before such ships could discharge their normal cargo in Singapore, a bond of $4665 each had to be posted for the refugees as a surety that they would not jump ship. As a result, by summer 1978 many ships, especially of Asian and convenience registry, were instructed by their owners to ignore disabled refugee boats because of the trouble and financial expense rescue entailed. The United States and a few other nations were prepared to guarantee the resettlement of refugees rescued by their ships.[54] Britain avoided the issue. Japan refused to accept refugees but did offer them temporary asylum. The refusal of the big ships to rescue the refugees in distress resulted in thousands of deaths at sea.

The tradition of rescue at sea was viable in a world in which the rescued were members of an established political community. The tradition was often honored even by wartime enemies. When a skipper rescued people with normal political status, he knew he had undertaken a limited responsibility which would end when he reached port. In the case of the boat people, no skipper could be certain rescue entailed a limited responsibility. In a world in which the leaders of all nations were reluctant to grant even temporary asylum to stateless persons, a skipper who rescued refugees at sea had to reckon with the possibility of his charges remaining on board for a very long time.

Again, we note the relation between human rights and political status. Shipowners were reluctant to rescue men and women whom no country wanted. The open-ended liabilities such rescues might entail were inconsistent with the commercial nature of the modern shipping industry. For many, it seemed better to look the other way while the sea claimed those whom no landed power would shelter.[55]

There has been considerable debate concerning the proportion of boat people who perished at sea. In June 1979 Richard Holbrooke, then Assistant Secretary of State for East Asian and Pacific Affairs, estimated that about half of the boat people were lost at sea. Holbrooke spoke at a time when the crisis was at its height. Subsequent estimates have been lower. About 290,000 people who left Vietnam between May 1975 and August 1979 are known to have reached land elsewhere. At least 28,000, or about 10 percent, are believed to have died at sea. This is, however, a minimum estimate. Other estimates are as high as 30 percent. The exact number will never be known.[56]

In December 1978 a United Nations conference on the refugee problem was held in Geneva which resulted in a guarantee of 3500 more places for the refugees. In view of the fact that hundreds of thousands were fleeing Vietnam at the time, the conference can be considered a failure. Within a month Malaysia announced its "tow-away-throw-away" policy and there was a general hardening of attitudes among the leaders of all of the ASEAN nations who saw their nations as burdened by a problem for which others were responsible. In the months following, the flow of refugees continued to increase and little was done to relieve the hard-pressed ASEAN nations.

The crisis came to a head when Mahathir Mohamad, Deputy Prime Minister of Malaysia, was quoted as saying his country had reached the end of the line. Henceforth, there would be no more beach camps like Pulau Bildong. The 70,000 in the camps would be sent back to sea. If they attempted to return, they would be shot on sight.[57] Mohamad's words came a week after Thailand had pushed 42,000 Kampuchean refugees back across the border at gunpoint. If the ASEAN nations were not acting in concert, they were certainly acting simultaneously.

Mohamad's words caused an international sensation. The Malaysian government followed the statement with the comment that, although there would be no shooting, no further asylum would be provided to any refugees. At the same time, Indonesia announced it would accept no further boat people. A second international refugee conference was then convened in Geneva, with considerably better results.

On previous occasions Hanoi's leaders had given assurances to the leaders of the ASEAN nations that the flow of refugees was about to diminish. Nevertheless, the number of refugees continued to increase. After the second Geneva conference in July 1979, Hanoi finally kept its word. A sure sign of a change of policy in a communist country is the arrest of those responsible for implementing the old policy. After the Geneva conference many of the ethnic Chinese middlemen who had facilitated the mass exodus were arrested, tried, and convicted.[58] In June 1979, 56,941 people left Vietnam; in December 1979 only 2745 departed.[59] For the time being, the crisis was at an end.

In the opinion of many diplomatic observers Hanoi had the upperhand at Geneva. By entering into an understanding with Hanoi concerning the flow of refugees, the receiving nations had, perhaps unintentionally, collaborated with Hanoi's harsh policies toward the ethnic Chinese and Vietnamese dissidents. These people had been told by their own government that they could hope for no viable place in Vietnamese society. As a result of the informal agreement between Hanoi and the receiving nations, escape had become impossible for the majority. Moreover, the nations of the world had in effect abandoned all concern for the fate of those who remained in Vietnam. Were the receiving nations to protest Hanoi's treatment of its minorities or its dissidents, Hanoi had the power to engulf the world in a flood of refugees who were neither wanted nor easily absorbed anywhere. Thus, one result of the international understanding to control the number of people leaving Vietnam was to condemn the ethnic Chinese and the noncommunist Vietnamese to total domination by the Vietnamese government. The world was faced with a choice between the agony of an uncontrolled mass exodus and abandoning any effective concern for those seeking to escape. It chose the latter alternative. The fate of these people was now entirely in the hands of a government which had publicly proclaimed they could have no meaningful place in their country's life.

The final chapter of the story of the Indo-Chinese refugees has yet to be written, but one can begin to reflect on the lessons of this tragedy. For example, it would appear that Prime Minister Lee Kuan Yew of Singapore was essentially correct when he observed, "You must grow calluses on your heart otherwise you will bleed to death." Had the ASEAN countries not taken such extreme measures as the gunpoint "resettlement" of 42,000 Kampucheans and the absolute refusal to take any more refugees, it is doubtful that the leaders of countries like the United States would have felt under any compulsion to take the political and social risks involved in accepting so large a number of talented strangers. Between 1975 and 1981 1,014,596 refugees were resettled. The United States received 480,912; China 265,588;

Canada 72,484; France 71,011; and Australia 47,637. In February 1981 there were 193,626 in camps and processing centers and about 150,000 Kampuchean refugees in Thailand.[60]

Unfortunately, it is impossible to say that the crisis is over. The Vietnamese government can reconstitute the crisis at any time by once again forcing thousands into mass flight or by consigning its minorities and dissidents to Vietnamese-style gulags. Hanoi's leaders are in a position to tell the rest of the world, "If you do not like the way we treat our minorities, take them yourselves." Nor is Vietnam the only country that has adopted a policy of solving minority and dissident problems by encouraging the departure of the unwanted people. On January 25, 1981, Prime Minister Wojciech Jaruzelski of Poland announced that dissidents wanting to leave would henceforth be free to go. The practical effects of the new policy have yet to be felt, but it is not difficult to imagine the difficulties that will face the noncommunist world should every communist country follow the example of Cuba and Vietnam and permit the free emigration of its dissidents and unwanted minorities.

When one studies the recent history of Vietnam, it seems difficult at first to avoid the conclusion that there was an extraordinary measure of villainy in the actions of the Vietnamese communist leaders. Yet, the more one reflects on the agony of Vietnam, the more is one likely to see all of the actors as trapped by a political, social, and economic tragedy of oceanic proportions. Unfortunately, many of the elements of the tragedy threaten to engulf other nations as well. Vietnam is by no means the only developing country with resources currently insufficient to support its rapidly growing population. Moreover, even if those countries beset by an imbalance between population and resources were to succeed in slowing down their rate of population increase, they would not necessarily solve the problem of surplus population. On the contrary, if every nation achieved zero population growth, modernization would still pose the threat of unemployment to large numbers of unskilled laborers and skilled professional workers as well as to owners of undercapitalized small enterprises.

Nor is Vietnam the only modern state confronted with difficult and perhaps insoluble class and ethnic conflicts. It cannot be said, for example, that Vietnamese fears concerning the loyalty of the ethnic Chinese were entirely without foundation. This observation is not offered in any spirit of reproach against the Chinese. On the contrary, it is offered in recognition of the fact that abstract, legally defined ties, such as that of citizenship in a modern state, do not elicit the same degree of loyalty from most people as do ties of kinship and common origin. Racist ideologies have been responsible for the death of millions of human beings, but liberal political philosophies have failed to offer any basis for a shared sense of community as emotionally compelling as ties of kinship and common origin. Although communism promises an end to racism and stresses the international unity of the working class, Vietnam is by no means the only communist country that has attempted to build a common life on the basis of common origins, as the recent history of Polish communism demonstrates.

In the case of Vietnam's ethnic Chinese, Peking has on many occasions insisted that the majority of the overseas bourgeois Chinese are "patriotic" and that every effort should be exerted to create a "united front" with them.[61] It would only be natural for Vietnam's ethnic Chinese to feel a measure of loyalty to their ancestral homeland, especially as they entered Vietnam when it was a French colony rather than an independent nation with its identity tested in war. As we have seen, even when the ethnic Chinese became Vietnamese citizens, their Chinese identity remained intact. The loyalty of those Hoa committed to socialism was further strained by Vietnam's commitment to Soviet rather than Chinese communism.

After the Sino-Vietnamese war of February 1979, the Vietnamese government found itself irrevocably confronted with the inherent conflict between the modern state as a legal and territorial institution and the nation as an ethnic institution. In the north it was as little possible for the Vietnamese to gamble on the loyalty of the ethnic Chinese as it would be for the Israelis to admit Palestinian Arabs to its armed forces or its intelligence services. Nor ought we to forget the mass expulsion of the

Germans at the end of World War II from those parts of the Third Reich already ceded to Poland, or the expulsion of the ethnic Germans, the *Volksdeutsche,* from the countries of eastern Europe in which their families had been settled for centuries. Almost 13,000,000 Germans were expelled. Although the vast majority of the ethnic Germans supported Nazi expansionist aims, no distinction was made by the postwar communist governments of eastern Europe between pro- and anti-Nazi Germans or between socialist and antisocialist Germans. All alike had to go.[62]

After the communist takeover in 1975, the Hoa of the south were subject to double jeopardy: they were both alien and bourgeois. Moreover, as we have seen, the country's bourgeoisie had been artificially enlarged by the war economy. Most members of the middle class were faced with almost certain downward social mobility regardless of what economic system carried the day in South Vietnam. Under communism the middle class is being ruined by the economic policies of a socialist state. Under capitalism a market economy would have produced a roughly comparable result. Without a quantum leap in productivity, it was impossible for so large a number of people to enjoy the same middle-class status and amenities after the war as during the war. Moreover, there is little reason to believe that had Vietnam been unified by a capitalist government after thirty years of war the ethnic Chinese would have fared much better than they have under Hanoi. The reasons for expelling the ethnic Chinese were largely nationalistic rather than ideological. History and geography had condemned the Vietnamese to perennial distrust of, if not outright hostility toward, the Chinese. In all likelihood, the same modernizing pull toward national homogeneity would have made itself felt in a capitalist as in a communist Vietnam.

Incidentally, the fate of South Vietnam's middle class dramatizes some of the limitations of a service economy. As such, the story may carry a warning for the middle class of other countries, including the United States. Without genuine productivity no service economy can survive. Sooner or later it must wither and die. This is a truism that even so rich a country as the United States can ignore at its peril. There is a limit to the size of the middle class that can be sustained by any economy. As we have seen, victorious Hanoi had to cope with millions of people who had been made redundant by the collapse of South Vietnam's service economy. Hanoi had no viable solution. With rampant unemployment and a labor force growing at the rate of about one million a year, the country was ripe for either a natural or a man-made demographic catastrophe. Kampuchea was condemned to experience both; Vietnam's catastrophe was largely man-made. Amid the extraordinary prosperity of Vietnam's ASEAN neighbors, the fundamental economic and social problems that led to the mass expulsions in Vietnam have yet to be solved.

At the height of the refugee crisis, the elimination of the ethnic Chinese by Hanoi was frequently likened to the Nazi extermination of the Jews. There were some obvious as well as some not-so-obvious resemblances between the two events. One of the most graphic, but by no means least accurate, observations was offered by Thailand's Supreme Command Chief of Staff, General Saiyud Kerdphol, who accused the Vietnamese of practicing "racist expulsion policies that resemble those of the Nazis during World War II." The General added that Hanoi had improved on the Nazis in cost-effectiveness: "Indeed, if Adolf Hitler had been as indifferent to world opinion as the present Vietnamese Workers' Party, his 'final solution' for the Jews might have been more cheaply and effectively achieved by casting them off on leaky boats, rather than by consigning them to the gas chambers of Auschwitz."[63]

Surely the similarities are there. In both cases there was a decision by the state to restructure society by eliminating an unwanted "elite minority"; in both cases the unwanted minority was an ethnic group that functioned largely as an urbanized business and professional middle class within the larger community; in both cases the decision-making elite perceived that willing replacements were available within the majority for slots held by the minority; in both cases no consideration of abstract "human rights" impeded the program of systematic population riddance; in both cases the target population was deprived of most of its resources by the state before being eliminated; in both cases the state security forces organized elements in the target population to facilitate the process of elimination; in both cases the process created a "refugee problem" whose solution exceeded the will if not the absorptive capacities of other states.

There were other similarities. The Nazi assault against the Jews produced its own "boat people." The plight of the Jewish boat people was dramatized in the motion picture *Voyage of the Damned,* which depicted the desperate voyage of more than 900 Jewish refugees in 1939 on the German passenger liner *St. Louis* from Hamburg to Havana. The refugees embarked on the mistaken assumption that they would be granted asylum in Cuba. When the *St. Louis* arrived in Havana, permission to land was denied. Refused asylum by the United States as well, the refugees were forced to return to Europe. At the last minute, they were given asylum by England, France, Holland, and Belgium.[64] As we have noted, there were many boatloads of Jews who were not so fortunate. Setting out from Nazi-dominated Europe in any available vessel, the Jews were forced by the British navy to return to certain death in Europe. The British navy was under orders to prevent the Jewish boat people from entering Palestine under any circumstance.[65] Finally, in both cases the fate of a goodly portion of the target population, far more in the case of the Jews than the Chinese, was the terminal expression of redundancy, namely, removal from the face of the earth.

There were, however, significant differences, the most important being that the method of population elimination favored in Europe was outright extermination. Mass murder was not Hanoi's preferred method. Admittedly, Hanoi was indifferent to the fate of the refugees and often compelled them to leave in vessels of questionable seaworthiness. There were also a number of incidents in which refugees on disabled vessels were shot and killed when they took shelter in territory belonging to Vietnam.[66] Yet, the leadership of Vietnam exhibited none of Hitler's single-minded commitment to mass extermination. Unfortunately, even this crucial difference might not hold in a future crisis. The absorptive capacities of the world's receiving nations is strictly limited. One of the nightmares facing the receiving nations is that the flow of refugees could continue until their absorptive capacities were overwhelmed. In view of the number of actual and potential refugees in an overpopulated and underemployed world, that possibility will haunt humanity for the foreseeable future.

In the refugee crisis Hanoi was confronted with overwhelmingly difficult political, economic and social problems at a time when its course of action was limited by a political ideology that had been rendered non-negotiable by the blood sacrifices of thirty years of war. Nevertheless, in attempting to get a balanced picture of the refugee crisis, it is important to remember that Hanoi rejected the most extreme measures. In the aftermath of the fall of Saigon Hanoi could have "solved" its minority problem after the manner of Pol Pot and Adolf Hitler. Undoubtedly, fear of the reaction of the Peoples' Republic of China to a radical anti-Hoa program was an important element in determining Hanoi's policies. Whatever may have been the motives of Hanoi's leaders, the wartime bloodshed was not followed by a peacetime bloodbath. As terrible as was the expulsion of the Hoa from Indochina, the majority did escape with their lives and, albeit with much difficulty, they were eventually permitted to settle elsewhere. The same cannot be said of Europe's Jews.

These reflections are not offered in defense of Hanoi's policies but as a caveat against oversimplifying a monumental human tragedy. As we have seen, the problems of Vietnam were and are hardly unique. Overpopulation in relation to resources and available skills, the dislocations caused by modernization, overly rapid urbanization followed by the collapse of an artificially bloated, nonproductive, urban service economy, and the need to integrate people of diverse background and conflicting values into a common community are hardly problems Hanoi alone has had to face. If we are indignant with the means she employed to cope with the problems, our most constructive response might well be to come up with a more humane solution insofar as these problems beset our own country.

9
REFLECTIONS ON
THE AGE OF TRIAGE

THE MEANING OF TRIAGE

ACCORDING TO the *Oxford English Dictionary,* the word triage is of French origin and comes from "trier," to pick or to cull. It denotes "the action of assorting according to quality." In the eighteenth century it was used to denote the sorting of fleece pelts. It was also used in connection with the sorting and sifting of coffee beans. In the twentieth century triage has been given both a political and a medical meaning. The word has been used to refer to the sorting of whole classes of human beings "according to quality."[1] *Stedman's Medical Dictionary* offers this definition of triage:

> French: sorting. The medical screening of patients to determine their priority for treatment. The sorting of casualties in military and civil disasters into three groups: those who will be expected to survive regardless of treatment, those who will be expected to die regardless of what is done for them, and those who will die unless given immediate aid.[2]

A very graphic example of the application of medical triage can be seen in the way penicillin was allocated in the treatment of wounded American soldiers in North African military hospitals during World War II. The new drug was in short supply. Some of the stricken men had received their wounds in battle; others in brothels. Although the battlefield casualties had a stronger claim on the government's resources, it was decided that only soldiers with venereal disease would be given penicillin, even if it meant that some of the wounded would die without it. Dr. Henry Beecher has explained the reason for the decision:

> Before indignation takes over, let us examine the situation. First, there were desperate shortages of manpower at the front. Second, those with broken bodies and broken bones would not be swiftly restored to the battle line even with penicillin, whereas those with venereal disease, on being treated with penicillin, would in a matter of days free the beds they were occupying and return to the front.[3]

In the wartime emergency, priority had to be given to the army's manpower requirements. Individual claims, no matter how just, had to be sacrificed to needs of the group.

Today, triage has acquired a sociopolitical meaning. Social triage is a term currently used in academic discussions concerning the distribution of food in a demographic crisis. The objects to be sorted "according to quality" are no longer coffee beans or even battlefield casualties but whole nations stricken by famine. The purpose of the sorting process is to determine which nations are to be given food and medical supplies and which are to be left to their own devices, no matter what the human cost. Famine-stricken nations are divided into three basic categories: those capable of returning to work if given first-aid supplies; those that would become food-viable and rehabilitate their economies with foreign assistance; and those incapable of rehabilitation even with massive foreign aid. The last group are to be written off entirely.[4]

Obviously, the most controversial aspect of social triage is the proposal deliberately to withhold food and medical supplies from famine-stricken nations. The reasoning is clearly Malthusian. Just as Malthus argued that it is best to withhold public assistance from those who cannot provide for their own maintenance lest they multiply and endanger the entire community, Neo-Malthusian advocates of social triage argue that food should be withheld from starving nations lest their population increase and further tax the world's resources.[5]

Opponents of social triage argue that triage is simply another name for genocide. The late Lord Ritchie-Calder expressed his opposition to triage succinctly: "No one dare say that starvation is a merciful way to die."[6] Another British opponent of triage,

Dr. Stuart W. Hinds, has argued that, whereas medical triage is strictly an emergency measure in which a limited number of people might be sacrificed, social triage involves the adoption of a harsh, unfeeling, permanent posture toward the problems of population growth and resource scarcity.[7] If adopted, a policy of social triage could result in the death by starvation of hundreds of millions of human beings.

ECONOMIC TRIAGE AND FEDERAL POLICY

There is yet another important area in which the sorting of classes of human beings "according to quality" is currently being practiced, although the issue is seldom discussed with the frankness it deserves. I refer to the direction the Reagan administration has taken at this writing in its policies for dealing with the unemployed and the indigent. In spite of the administration's assurances that it intends to maintain a "safety net" for the "truly needy," its policy seems to be to decrease the level of assistance allocated to the needy and to deprive large numbers of poor people of help altogether.[8]

A great deal can and should be said on this subject, but for our purpose it is important to note that welfare benefits are being drastically cut at a time when unemployment has reached its highest levels since World War II.[9] Moreover, there is considerable evidence that the actual level of unemployment is much higher than official statistics suggest.[10]

While unemployment has been increasing and welfare benefits cut, as is well known, government tax benefits to wealthy individuals and corporations have greatly increased. According to the Congressional Budget Office, in 1983 a household with an annual income of less than $10,000 will pay $120 less in taxes, but will lose an average of $360 in federal benefits, while a family with an income of $80,000 will pay an average of $15,000 a year less in taxes and will lose about $120 in federal benefits.[11] The rationale for weighing tax cuts in favor of the rich is not unlike that used in England to justify the enclosures. It was argued that by consolidating their holdings, English landowners would increase both their income and capital. This in turn would increase the wealth of the nation. Sooner or later, it was argued, the landowner's increased wealth would benefit the entire community.[12] England's aggregate wealth did increase but it took decades before the "trickle-down" process had a beneficial effect on the lower classes. Far more Americans are today without hope of improvement than was the case in England during the enclosure period. It is doubtful that the United States can afford to wait for the delayed benefits of a trickle-down process to take effect. In spite of the rhetoric about concern for the "deserving poor," the welfare policies of the Reagan administration can best be described as a modified form of triage in which the poor are being left increasingly to their own devices.

The Reagan administration has also proposed that government subsidies to higher education be governed by a form of economic triage. In addition to the poor, those most seriously affected by the new policies will be the class most dependent upon advanced education to qualify for the technical and professional slots available in a complex high technology society, namely, the middle class. Perhaps the biggest loser will be the nation as a whole. In 1981–1982 an estimated 11,000,000 students were enrolled in American institutions of higher learning. In addition to serving as training institutions, colleges and universities provide an appropriate environment in which unemployable young people can await their turn to enter the job market and, at the same time, acquire necessary vocational skills. Increasingly, the higher-education system fulfills the same function for older people. In recent years, there has been a great increase in the number of "returnees" and "retreads" in America's colleges and universities.[13] In 1978, 1,500,000 Americans had returned to colleges and universities for a second try at higher education.[14] Currently, more than one third of all post–secondary school students are 25 years old or older.[15] Without its distinctive system of higher education, with its mass student population, America's unemployment rate would be materially higher than it is now. So too would be the level of middle-class resentment.

During the decade of the seventies, the cost of higher education rose sharply. Had it not been for the availability of undergraduate scholarships for low-income students and a liberal, federally subsidized, low-cost student loan program, hundreds of thousands of low-income and even middle-class students would have been forced to enter an overly saturated job market with few skills. As unemployment rose in the nineteen-eighties, the Reagan administration proposed that grants to low-income students and support for federally guaranteed student loans be drastically reduced and that subsidies for graduate student loans be terminated altogether.[16]

Given the extraordinary size of the federal deficit and the rapidly escalating cost of the student-loan program, the administration's interest in economizing is understandable. There are areas in which student aid programs can be cut. For example, there is no reason why federally guaranteed loans should be available to students of all income levels. Nor is there any reason why an eligibility test based upon scholastic aptitude cannot be used in allocating scholarship funds to low-income students.[17]

Nevertheless, the proposed cuts in the scholarship and student-loan program can only exacerbate the problem of surplus people confronting American society while seriously wounding one of the few institutions capable of moderating the problem. Apart from the fact that the cuts are likely to damage America's ability to educate the personnel with which to compete against high-technology societies such as Japan and Germany, the proposals appear to have been formulated without considering whether it is ultimately less costly to assist students to acquire advanced training than to add their numbers to the ranks of the unemployed.

If past experience with the problem of population redundancy offers us any instruction, instead of reducing scholarship and student-loan programs, the federal government ought to expand the programs that do not subsidize the academically incompetent or those whose families can pay the full cost of higher education. If this is not feasible, the programs ought to be kept at present levels. The number of unemployed middle-class Americans is not likely to diminish in the foreseeable future; and, to repeat, a resentful middle class is a social phenomenon no modern society dare take lightly. Nor will American society be healthier or better able to compete in the world economy if talented students from low-income families are barred from the opportunities higher education can offer them.

COMPUTERIZED AUTOMATION AND
POPULATION REDUNDANCY

The seriousness of cutting the scholarship and student-loan programs, as well as other proposals to reduce federal support for higher education, becomes even more apparent when one considers the potential impact of computer-aided design and computer-aided manufacturing (CAD/CAM) on the American economy in the decades ahead. As we have seen, in the past almost all advances in the rationalization of production have resulted in large-scale human redundancies. Admittedly, the labor market has eventually absorbed a very respectable segment of the available work force, but not before monumental social dislocations intervened. With the advent of microcomputer robotics, we are on the threshold of a series of quantum leaps in office and factory automation, and there is a high probability that we will experience social dislocations of unprecedented magnitude in the decades ahead.[18]

In the past, computer-assisted manufacturing was limited because of the need to connect machines to a small mainframe computer, such as the IBM System/7. The cost of wiring an entire factory to a single computer proved prohibitive in most applications. The arrangement also lacked flexibility. By contrast, the microprocessors used in contemporary robotics are highly sophisticated computers occupying a space on a chip no more than a quarter-inch square. They are small enough and inexpensive enough to be used directly on individual machines. In addition, the capacities of the microcomputers have been enhanced by extraordinarily sophisticated computer programs which are simple to use and easy to change. One firm, Cross and Trecker, has started an FMS line (a computer-controlled flexible manufacturing system) which will enable it to produce computer-controlled machine tools on an unmanned third shift. German workers already call such a shift *die Geisterschicht* or Ghost shift. The Lockheed Corporation plans to install a painting and processing line to be operated by robots controlled by a hierarchy of computers rather than human beings.[19]

The use of microcomputers as word processors is but one example of the way automation promises to change the American office as much as robots promise radically to alter the American factory. There is little doubt office and factory productivity will increase significantly in the years ahead. There is debate concerning the effect of computerized automation on employment. According to a Carnegie-Mellon University study on the impact of robots on the labor force, current robots, plus those being developed possessing "crude sensory abilities," could perform the work now being done by 7,000,000 people.[20] According to *Business Week* magazine, experts expect 45 percent of all of the jobs in the labor force, almost 45,000,000, could be affected by automation during the next twenty years. The United Automobile Workers anticipates that, even were automobile production to increase at an average annual rate of 1.8 percent, automation will cause its membership to decrease from 1,000,000 in 1978 to 800,000 in 1990.[21]

While past productivity increases have ultimately had a beneficial effect on overall employment, benefits have not been uniform. When productivity rises more rapidly than demand, unemployment tends to increase. Moreover, even if the long-range effects of computerized automation on employment prove to be beneficial, an assumption by no means self-evident, the social dislocations promise to be monumental. A large proportion of the work force may find the jobs for which they were trained no longer exist when they are in mid-career. Many workers will have to return to school for further job training or even for training leading to a meaningful alternative to a job. This is another reason why federal support to higher education ought not to be cut. Since there is little reason to believe automation will be less disruptive of work patterns in the decades ahead, the long-term costs of controlling angry and frustrated people whose jobs cease to exist could prove far more expensive to society than subsidies permitting them to return to school.

CHANGING PATTERNS OF EMPLOYMENT

In addition to automation, changing patterns of government spending and private investment have dramatically altered the vocational opportunities available to the average American. As a result of increased defense spending by government, demand for scientists, engineers, and other skilled professionals is rising. Unfortunately, high-technology defense production requires far fewer workers than do those sectors of the economy which have felt the brunt of the restrictive side of the government's fiscal policies. These sectors had been responsible for the absorption of most of the new entrants into the labor market in the past decade. During the nineteen-seventies, the United States experienced an unprecedented growth in employment. From 1973 to 1979 almost 13,000,000 new nonagricultural jobs were created, 11,000,000 in the private sector. Seventy percent of the new jobs were in the retail trades and in services. The rest were in state and local government.[22] Most of the jobs were low-paying and offered scant opportunity for advancement. Nevertheless, millions of Americans preferred even dead-end jobs to dependence on public assistance.

Many of the new jobs have already disappeared in the current economic downturn. There have been widespread firings and layoffs of public employees. In addition, in hard times service industries tend to decline more rapidly than the economy as a whole. Fewer people eat out and retail employment has declined. The job situation is further aggravated by the facts that: American industry is being more effectively challenged by Asian and European competitors than at any time in the postwar period; multinational corporations have transferred many of their manufacturing operations from the United States to parts of the world where labor costs are a fraction of what they are in the United States;[23] and porous borders have enabled millions of "illegal" Hispanic immigrants to enter the United States in search of work.

Thus, in the midst of oceanic transformations which magnify the problem of population redundancy, the Reagan administration has initiated policies that have the effect of destroying the work opportunities of millions of men and women while seriously reducing the support given to the unemployed. Nor can it be said that these policies are the result of high-level blundering or miscalculation. On the contrary, they are, as we have argued, a form of economic triage. As in other forms of triage, resources are withheld from those who are incapable of helping themselves.

There is reason to believe that America is in the midst of a counter-revolution led by highly sophisticated opponents of the fifty-year-old welfare state who are honestly convinced the current rise in unemployment and the reduction of welfare benefits are in the nation's long-range interest.[24] The tradeoff between unemployment and inflation has long been understood by macro-economic planners. In the past, whenever inflation threatened to destabilize the economy, macroeconomic planners had a relatively simple way to lower prices, namely, to throw the economy into recession and thereby increase unemployment. With labor in over-supply, the employed and the unemployed alike were under pressure to demand less for their services. If labor costs, a substantial component in the cost of production, could not be reduced, at least wage increases could be kept to more moderate levels than when labor was in short supply, thereby reducing the rate of inflation. Whatever the campaign rhetoric of politicians of both parties, the principal anti-inflation target of macroeconomic planners has been the labor force.

Toward the end of the nineteen-sixties, the strategy of trading off unemployment and inflation ceased to work as expected. Neither wages nor prices declined during recessions. It is now thought the new development was a consequence of the social-welfare programs enacted during the nineteen-sixties and seventies which shielded the poor from the worst effects of unemployment.[25] When the value of all health, subsistence, job training, and income maintenance programs was added up, few Americans found themselves forced to work simply to avoid hunger. The relative independence of the poor and the unemployed also strengthened the bargaining position of those within the work force.

As the nineteen-seventies came to an end, macroeconomic planners recognized that recessions could only play their historic role in reducing inflation if the bargaining position of the poor were weakened. This could only be achieved by reducing the support given to the poor and the unemployed by federal, state, and local government. Even the extraordinarily high deficit in the Reagan administration's budget helped to achieve this end. At first glance, it seemed strange that an administration claiming to be both conservative and fiscally responsible had proposed budgets with annual deficits exceeding $100,000,000,000. If, however, one perceives there is little that is genuinely conservative about this counter-revolutionary administration save, on occasion, its rhetoric, one will begin to comprehend why it has insisted on drastically reducing the national tax base while increasing both military spending and the budget itself. The purpose of the deficit is to mortgage the American future and limit the resources available to the federal government so as to cripple its social-welfare programs, thereby stripping the poor of the economic protection they previously enjoyed.[26] The "less eligibility" principle of Jeremy Bentham and Edwin Chadwick is once again becoming the basis for the administration of poor relief.

The rationale behind the Reagan strategy is not unlike that expressed by Patrick Colquhoun in 1806 in his book, *A Treatise on Indigence.* As noted, Colquhoun saw poverty as indispensable to the progress of civilization, comfort, and refinement. He argued that "without a large proportion of poverty, surplus labour could never be rendered productive in procuring either the convenience or luxuries of life."[27] According to Colquhoun, poverty alone is the goad capable of forcing the poor to labor for a miserable pittance, thereby facilitating the accumulation of wealth within England.[28] Not surprisingly, Colquhoun is also credited with being "the inventor of the modern police system."[29] It cannot be said that this strategy has been unsuccessful either in Colquhoun's time or in ours. In the face of an economic downturn of unprecedented severity, one large American labor union after another has agreed to effective cuts in real wages and benefits.

THE AMERICAN UNDERCLASS

As structural unemployment has worsened in the United States, a massive underclass has arisen.[30] People with nothing to hope for save dependence on public relief are likely to become victims of a pernicious culture of poverty and hopelessness. When no amount of effort or training leads to a job, there is little incentive to discipline oneself to acquire work skills. Delayed gratification, the fundamental presupposition of all education, is a plant that must be nurtured by hope. One accepts the learner's subordination in the expectation that learning will lead to improvement. Learning involves disciplined control of instinct at every age. Such control does not come easily. Learning makes no sense for those with nothing to hope for.

When men and women are uprooted from a sustainable social matrix and transformed into an anonymous urban mass for whose energies there exists no legitimate need, it is impossible to integrate them into the religious, cultural, or moral universe of the normal working population. One does not have to resort to elaborate social theories to understand that such people are likely to become an anomic underclass. As noted, Hegel saw this as early as 1803.[31] Unless all who seek work can find it, we are likely to witness the rise of a permanent American underclass.

I shall never forget a conversation I had recently with an intelligent seventeen-year-old young woman of Irish background at Boston's Commonwealth School. She told me why she had decided to attend a private school: "I considered myself a liberal. I had planned to go to a public high school, but what do you do when, at fifteen, most of your classmates are already third-generation welfare mothers? They have no interest in learning and it is impossible to learn anything in a class with them."

Private-school tuition is a tax hundreds of thousands of middle-class parents are currently paying because America has no viable way of coping with its underclass. Incidentally, the Commonwealth School does not discriminate against blacks or other minorities. Class rather than race was the crucial factor in the young woman's choice of school.

Apparently, the fifteen-year-old welfare mothers feel that state-supported single parenthood is the best option available to them. Given the grim alternatives available to the hopelessly poor, an adolescent's choice of a child of her own is by no means the least rational for the individual if not for society. Nor is the choice of crime or vice necessarily less rational for those without hope of gainful employment. This is in no sense a defense of crime or a plea to lessen vigilance in law enforcement. Crime and vice are obviously antisocial and must be dealt with as such. Nevertheless, they are often expressions of a socioeconomic predicament which is itself profoundly antisocial. Most societies since the days of Tudor England, if not earlier, have cast off their workless poor as little more than human refuse. Is it surprising such individuals have a less than wholehearted respect for social norms?

Our civilization prizes successful self-aggrandizement. Even today, few Americans would find fault with Adam Smith's observations concerning the primacy of self-interest: "It is not from the benevolence of the butcher, the brewer, or the baker that we expect our dinner, but from their regard to their own interest. We address ourselves, not to their humanity but to their self-love, and never talk to them of our own necessities but of their advantages."[32]

Ironically, we expect from those whom society casts aside a greater degree of selflessness than we do from those whom society rewards. Barred from the legitimate pursuit of "their advantages," the underclass is nevertheless expected to conform to society's norms even when there is little to be gained in so doing.

It is difficult to go to the movies or watch television today without being bombarded with the message that the underclass is dangerous and must be controlled. This perception is in some measure accurate. It is also an oversimplification. The underclass is as much a "product" of contemporary civilization as the automobile, the computer, and the nuclear bomb. Between 1940 and 1970 more than 4,000,000 American farm workers lost their jobs because of agricultural mechanization and were compelled to migrate to an unfamiliar urban world in search of work.[33] The story is a familiar one. We have seen it unfold from the Tudor enclosures to mass urbanization in contemporary Latin America.

As is well known, a large proportion of the displaced farm workers were blacks whose ancestors had been forcibly imported into an expanding American economy when labor was in short supply. Their urbanization began when they were no longer needed in rural areas. Incidentally, it would be a mistake to assume that the American underclass is entirely black and Hispanic. Poor whites are well represented. The final chapter of the story of American rural emigration has yet to be written. Most of the migrants, both black and white, came to the cities when America was either at war or enjoying a period of prolonged economic growth and could absorb a large proportion of their number into the urban labor force. That period seems to have ended. The rural emigrants who failed to find work in the cities have become the unhappy vanguard of millions of others.[34] Even without computerized automation, the threat of permanent economic superfluity confronts millions of American workers.

THE INDIGENT AND THE UNEMPLOYED IN A TIME OF CRISIS

In spite of the spreading social pathology in America's cities, macroeconomic planners do not regard the current level of unemployment as unacceptable. However, if unemployment continues to increase, crisis-ridden government leaders may eventually feel compelled to reconsider the ways in which the problem is to be managed. Should this happen, the probable scenarios are not very pleasant. When we consider them, we enter upon an effort to think about the unthinkable. Yet, lest we dismiss as implausible the grim scenarios we are about to consider, let us remember that the moral barriers which once prevented governments from eliminating large numbers of their own citizens have often been breached in the twentieth century. Although there is no need to indulge in unwarranted sensationalism or apocalypticism, much that is apocalyptic has already taken place in our century. Unfortunately, even more sorrowful misfortunes may await us if we permit ourselves the foolish luxury of pretending our problems are self-correcting.

If one assumes that the Reagan administration is fully cognizant of the social consequences of its fiscal policies, it is difficult to avoid viewing its response to the problems associated with mass destitution and population superfluity as triage-like. Those who cannot help themselves are to be left to their own devices. Moreover, some policy makers may even find a certain utilitity in the growth of the underclass. This view is consistent with the sociological theories of Emile Durkheim and Kai Erikson, who see society as encouraging deviance in order to define the boundaries of acceptable behavior and life style.[35] As with all other forms of deviance, the underclass's economic deviance can be seen as a paradoxically important element binding the "normal" community together. It goes without saying that the underclass also serves as a reserve labor force. Nevertheless, in a period of acute economic hardship a future administration might conclude that mass unemployment and destitution no longer serve the national interest. If such a time ever comes, the problem of surplus people will admit of only two possible solutions: *redistribution of resources and work opportunities or elimination of surplus people.* In the past, most governments have chosen the latter alternative, as the extraordinary emigration of Europeans to the New World demonstrates. Without the emigration opportunities available to nineteenth-century European governments, an American population-elimination program will of necessity be draconian.

Unless present trends are altered, there is little likelihood that redistribution would be the method preferred by government. Although a serious national effort to reduce destitution and unemployment through redistribution might ultimately result in a more uniformly prosperous America, it would initially involve painful sacrifices, especially for middle-income Americans. Given the class, racial, religious, ethnic, and ideological divisions pervading American life, such an effort would be extremely difficult, though not impossible, to sustain.

Since most Americans understandably find both redistribution and population elimination unacceptable, we are likely to drift along in the hope that the problem can somehow be managed without disturbing the way of life of the working majority. In reality, the drift has already proved costly. Our inability to deal effectively with unemployment and destitution has resulted in constantly rising costs to both individuals and society. We have already noted that a large number of middle-class parents can no longer trust the education of their children to the public school system. Other social costs include the escalating incidence of vicious, often gratuitous, criminality in America's cities, the cost of the protective measures law-abiding citizens are compelled to take to defend themselves, the spreading use of hard drugs, the rise of an underground drug-based economy, and the massive deterioration of large urban neighborhoods.[36] The list is by no means inclusive. In truth, the phenomena of population redundancy and mass poverty have already had a dramatic impact on the way of life of the average American.

As long as the perception holds that the situation is manageable, decision-makers are likely to prefer a policy of drift to one involving major sacrifice. However, if the economy deteriorates over an extended period, political leaders may feel compelled to take decisive action.

There are a number of strategies future leaders might employ to "solve" the problem of surplus people. Some have been explored in a fictional work that has its bitterly serious side, *Triage* by Leonard Levin.[37] The book depicts a future administration in which "the President's Special Commission on National Priorities" secretly initiates an extensive program to eliminate the "chronically unproductive and generally unemployable."[38] In the novel, the argument is advanced that "the progression of our economy" has made "a high proportion" of the population "totally disposable." It is further argued that although most surplus people "were formerly sources of latent productivity, they are now, functionally, slag piles."[39] In order to eliminate the problem, a series of artificially induced "natural" disasters are planned and executed. Although the members of the commission recognize that the effects of the program cannot be limited to the target population, they are willing to accept the death of 35 productive members of society in every 100 who are to be eliminated.

The mass misfortunes depicted in the novel include:

1. A dramatic increase in the mortality rate of older people. Most of the increase takes place in institutions caring for terminal patients.

2. The outbreak of a large number of localized epidemics as a result of deliberately contaminated food and water supplies. The epidemics tend to be restricted to public hospitals and prisons. Some also take place in rural and urban slum areas.

3. A spectacular increase in drug-related deaths due to the sudden availability, unknown to users, of heroin of lethal purity. The problem of drug abuse is speedily reduced to manageable proportions by the elimination of the worst addicts.

4. An outbreak of catastrophic fires of unknown origin in urban slums. The fires kill 22,000 persons and render 200,000 homeless.

5. The "accidental" distribution of lethally contaminated surplus food to people on welfare.

The novel's list of horrors includes many more apparently accidental but, in reality, deliberately contrived attempts by government leaders and influential private citizens to put into practice their own Neo-Malthusian program for reducing "the numbers of people who contribute disproportionately to the intensification of both our particular and our more general breakdowns."[40] It is the author's thesis that properly planned disasters would not be unwelcome to a government despairing of its ability to manage the nation's economic and social problems. Perhaps the most frightening aspect of the novel is that the mass killings are coolly justified on the basis of the same kind of amoral, rationalized cost-benefit analyses currently employed in both business and government.

Levin's novel is not the only serious literary attempt to deal with the problem. In 1933, in the midst of the Great Depression, Allen Tate, a distinguished American poet, suggested, albeit with tongue in cheek, that the gassing of the unemployed and their families might "solve" the problem of unemployment, which, then as now, was plaguing American society:

...unless we deal with the permanently unemployed, we shall have trouble. The masses of the unemployed are not consuming. They are beginning to engage in anti-social pursuits...and in twenty years...this class may increase to fifty million men. If the number increases or is even allowed to remain constant, it will... constitute a dire menace to public order...Society would suffer the least rupture...if it quietly, and in the ordinary routine of industrial technology, *killed off about eight million workers and their families.*

It should be done, all things considered, gradually, but completed in a year lest there should be an abnormal increase of that class of persons, with the attendant perils...

I need not suggest that the method be painless. We are too humane for the axe, guillotine, rope or firing squad. *I should personally prefer some kind of lethal gas,* but not being a chemist, I leave that proposal to the specialists...

I have said that this method of disposing of the residue X would relieve us of the whole problem of unemployment. That is not strictly true. It assumes as accomplished a long moratorium on the invention of labour-elimination devices; it requires for its success a stabilization of our technology. Yet should our technical equipment still further improve, the method is still workable. There would merely be a certain number of newly unemployed to kill off every year. [italics mine][41]

Tate was a member of that group of Southern writers known as the Agrarians. They did not admire industrial society and were deeply concerned with its social costs. Tate was keenly aware of some of the destructive tendencies imminent in our rationalized technological civilization. His article was entitled "The Problem of the Unemployed: A Modest Proposal." Undoubtedly when he made his "modest proposal" Tate had in mind an earlier article by Jonathan Swift entitled "Modest Proposal for Preventing the Children of Poor People from Being a Burden to Their Parents or the Country."[42] Swift's solution to the problem of redundant poor children in his time was simple: fatten them and eat them. The proposals of both Swift and Tate are examples of black humor, but, like Levin's novel, they have their hideously serious side.

Another example of black humor was one which made the rounds in the nineteen-seventies during New York City's financial crisis. In other parts of the United States it was suggested that if the Russians "nuked" New York, the budget crisis would be solved, a lot of public money saved, and some unpopular minorities would be eliminated. One of the functions of black humor is to permit the expression of morally repugnant ideas in a form that disguises their fundamental seriousness.

What is black humor in a period of relative stability could become a real temptation in a period of chronic instability. As every child of this century knows, the problem of surplus people can be "solved" by outright extermination. On a small scale, there are already institutions in the United States in which a death-dealing form of triage is regularly practiced and the question of life or death hangs on a cost-benefit analysis. There are hospitals in which the plug has regularly been pulled on mentally alert paraplegics who are wholly dependent on the "iron lung" for survival.[43] Old-age homes sometimes have an inexplicable way of going up in flames with few or no survivors. Automobile manufacturers have knowingly produced lethally defective cars after deciding that a given level of fatal accidents is preferable to a minor increment in production costs. Air lines make similar calculations concerning the tradeoff between human lives and the additional cost of equipment that could materially improve their passengers' chances of surviving a crash.[44] Nor ought we to forget Parson Malthus' earlier proposal that the poor be settled in the most disease-ridden, unhealthy neighborhoods in order to reduce their numbers.[45]

The list could be lengthened indefinitely. The point is simple. Within the logic of triage, there is nothing sacred about human life. It is simply another component to be calculated in amoral cost-benefit analyses. Unfortunately, such thinking contains no credible restraint on its own excesses.

Lest these scenarios seem implausible, let us remember that in earlier times there were American leaders who had no qualms about exterminating Indians and placing Japanese-Americans in concentration camps. As noted, a number of leading population experts have recently advocated withholding food and medical supplies from foreigners in a crisis. At first glance, it is hard to believe respectable political leaders would favor applying the same policy to their fellow citizens. Nevertheless, if past experience is any guide, it is unlikely that economizing decision-makers would refrain from harsh measures against the indigent in a period of acute social stress. At the very least, one must ask whether the bonds of community between Americans would be sufficiently strong to protect the poor in a crisis?

In this regard, it is interesting to note that even conviction at Nuremberg for the enslavement and mass murder of 200,000 inmates at Auschwitz did not bar one of the major German war criminals of World War II, Dr. Otto Ambros, from employment as a high-level technical advisor to a major American corporation, W. R. Grace and Company, and as a consultant to the Department of Energy. When queried about Dr. Ambros in March 1982, a spokesman for the W. R. Grace Company is reported as having declared: "We do not feel there was anything wrong in employing this man in a technical position years after whatever he did." The spokesman added that J. Peter Grace, chairman of the board, "is extremely proud" of his relationship to Ambros and did not find the appointment "embarrassing in any sense." James W. Nance, a special assistant to President Reagan for national security, confirmed with apparent approval that Ambros had "recently" served as a consultant to the Department of Energy. A White House spokesman declared that Ambros, who served three years for his crimes, "had paid his debt to society."[46] If nothing else, Ambros' welcome in the highest levels of American business and government after conviction for mass murder demonstrates the degree to which technical and administrative competence have been divorced from moral values in contemporary society.

There is, of course, nothing unique about the attenuated bonds of community within American society. One of the more depressing lessons of the enclosure movement is that even the ancient bonds between lord and peasant were not strong enough to prevent the mass depopulation of the English countryside.

Moreover, when unemployment became a serious problem in seventeenth-century England, poverty was seen as a mark of moral inferiority. Both the unemployed and the working poor were regarded as incapable of a fully rational life and hence unworthy of the right to participate in political society.[47] This view was held by no less a figure than John Locke, who regarded the unemployed as depraved by choice![48] According to Tawney, the harsh attitude of English economic writers toward the working poor in the second half of the seventeenth century had "no parallel except in the behavior of the less reputable of the white colonists towards coloured labor."[49]

According to English historian Christopher Hill, the harshness with which the poor were viewed reflected the Calvinist division of humanity into the elect and the non-elect.[50] In Calvinism and Puritanism, poverty was a condition far worse than mere economic misfortune. It was seen as evidence of divine condemnation, from which it followed that one need not concern oneself with the fate of those whom God himself has rejected. The Calvinist-Puritan view of poverty served to legitimate the harshness with which the poor were treated in both England and the United States. Regrettably, there is little reason to believe that those who today advocate triage in dealing with foreigners would refrain from applying it to the American poor in a crisis.

The likelihood that a future elite might resort to radical measures in a crisis was graphically expressed to one of my academic colleagues by a group of retired army officers several years ago. He had been invited to lecture to the group on the subject of the population explosion and resource scarcity. My colleague advocated an equitable distribution of resources as the preferred way to cope with the problem. Responding on behalf of the group, one retired officer said: "We know there isn't going to be room in the boat for everybody, but we know there'll be room for us, no matter whom we have to throw out."[51]

One of the most harrowing lessons of both National Socialism and bolshevism is that for a dominant elite the most "rational" and "economical" method of dealing with surplus people is to dispose of them. In previous decades of this century, mass warfare provided an effective means of killing off the population surplus. This "solution" is no longer realistically available because of the unpredictable hazards of nuclear war. In a crisis, government leaders are likely to prefer controlled methods of eliminating surplus people to the imponderables of nuclear conflict.

ELITE SECRECY

It is unlikely that the question of doing away with permanently superfluous people would ever surface in a popular referendum. Such a decision is more likely to be taken *in secret* by the ruling elite and conveyed only to the appropriate police and civil service personnel. In addition, a "tough solution" can be self-legitimating. Few situations can reinforce an elite's sense of class pride as one in which its members have the power secretly to play god and decide the fate of millions of ordinary men and women, while regarding themselves as exempt from the consequences of the awesome judgments they mete out.

Moreover, there are convergent structural and religiomythic elements in American civilization which could affect the way a permanently superfluous population might be dealt with. One of the most important consequences of the bureaucratic organization of political and economic institutions in the modern era has been the dichotomous division of the world into a secret-bearing elite and a largely inarticulate mass of outsiders. After Watergate, there was strongly felt popular revulsion at the abuse of secrecy in the federal government. The Freedom of Information Act was enacted in response to the public reaction. But at present, the pendulum is swinging in the other direction and the Reagan administration has taken a number of steps to tighten the conditions under which material can be made available.[52] This return to greater secrecy was predictable. Max Weber's 1916 observations concerning secrecy and bureaucracy are, as usual, extremely prescient: "Every bureaucracy seeks to increase the superiority of the professionally informed by keeping their knowledge and intentions secret. . . . The conception of the 'official secret' is the specific invention of bureaucracy and nothing is so fantastically defended by bureaucrats as this attitude. . . ."[53]

CALVINISM AND SOCIAL DARWINISM

Although this dichotomous division is a structural consequence of modern social organization, it bears a strong resemblance to the biblical division of humanity into the elect and the reprobate, expressed most rigorously in the Calvinist theory of double predestination: namely, that from the beginning of creation God has predestined the elect to eternal salvation and the reprobate to eternal damnation. Furthermore, the resemblance between structure and doctrine may not be entirely fortuitous. Calvinism and Puritanism have played a decisive role in the formation of American civilization. Of special importance is the Calvinist tendency to view worldly success as certification of divine election and worldly failure as attesting a double rejection: the poor are regarded as both social outcasts and objects of divine condemnation.[54] Their plight is thus seen as well deserved, an attitude we have often encountered in this study.

In the past, the ideology of elite election and mass condemnation, especially of the indigent, has had the effect of intensifying the harshness with which the disinherited were dealt, especially in the administration of poor relief.[55] However, during a time of economic extremity in the United States, any "harsh," "objective," triage-like solution to the problem of the permanently poor could be reinforced by the Calvinist elements in our culture. In a crisis, a secularized equivalent of the division of mankind into the elect and the reprobate could easily become a controlling image. It would be difficult for a decision-making elite motivated by Calvinist values to expend scarce resources on those who can neither help themselves nor respond effectively to the help of others.

Lest I be mistaken, when I refer to Calvinist values I do not restrict that designation to members of Presbyterian or Reformed churches. On the contrary, the Calvinism to which I refer long ago left the confines of the sanctuary and entered the worldliest domains of secular society. Almost all Americans who have achieved elite status are likely to conduct the business of life and train their offspring in accordance with a secular version of the

Puritan work ethic and the Calvinist division of humanity into the elect and the preterite.[56]

The temptation to employ triage in dealing with the dependent poor in a crisis would be reinforced by the strong affinity between Calvinism and Social Darwinism. On the surface, Darwin's theory appears to be anti-Christian and is so regarded by religious conservatives. Darwin contradicted the literal account of human origins in Scripture. Yet, as both David Bakan and Richard Hofstadter have observed, Social Darwinism can be seen as a secularized form of Calvinism in which the "survival of the fittest" is the Darwinian equivalent of the Calvinist "salvation of the elect."[57] The full title of Darwin's great work is *On the Origin of the Species by Means of Natural Selection, or The Preservation of Favored Races in the Struggle for Life* (1859). In the title it is the "favored races" that survive. Darwin could hardly have come closer to the Judaeo-Christian term, "the elect," without abandoning his posture of scientific neutrality altogether.

According to Hans-Günter Zmarzlik, European Social Darwinism became increasingly popular with the rise of the new imperialism and the Second Industrial Revolution in the last quarter of the nineteenth century. There was at the time, in Zmarzlik's words, a tendency toward "the naturalization of political thinking" and "the brutalization of political methods." The idea of a universal "struggle for existence" became dominant among the bourgeoisie at a time when imperialist expansion became the order of the day.[58]

Nowhere was Social Darwinism more influential in the closing decades of the nineteenth century than in the United States. The expanding American economy gave successful Americans the conviction that they were winning the harsh struggle and were the most favored members of the world's most favored race. In his well-known study, *Social Darwinism in American Thought, 1860–1915,* Richard Hofstadter has observed that, although England gave Darwin to the world, Darwinism received its most sympathetic hearing in the United States. The English sociologist and Social Darwinist, Herbert Spencer (1820–1903), was far more popular in the United States than in England.[59] Darwinist ideas were especially appealing to success-oriented men who had taken their chances in a highly competitive industrial society in which all honor went to the winners and the losers were relegated to economic and social obscurity.

The winners in the bitter struggle regarded their victory as "merely the working-out of a law of nature and a law of God." This judgment was offered by John D. Rockefeller in a Sunday school address.[60] Another magnate, James J. Hill, argued that the absorption of small railroads by the larger ones was determined by "the law of the survival of the fittest."[61] The kind of men whom Max Weber regarded as incarnating the Protestant ethic in their success as capitalist entrepreneurs looked upon Darwinism, especially as expounded by Spencer, as fully congruent with their own experience.

In Zmarzlik's opinion the core of Darwin's theory is the postulation of "a process of selection in which value judgments play no part."[62] Zmarzlik may have overstated the case. Belief in an all-powerful God, such as is found in Calvinism, facilitates the merging of fact and value. Value judgments need play no visible part for those who believe that facts are the work of such a God.[63] Since God has predestined the entire course of history from the beginning, everything that has ever happened is as it should be. Belief in predestination has the paradoxical effect of merging fact and value and fostering the strictly objective, value-neutral study of both nature and history. If all that has come to be expresses unconditionally the will of the all-powerful Lord of History, it is pointless to speculate on whether things have turned out well or badly. If one wishes to discern God's will as it manifests itself in the world, one must study things as they are. Whatever has happened is as it should be, if not in the understanding of fallible, corruptible men, then certainly in the light of God's overall plan.

Without the merging of fact and value made possible by the biblical view of God, it is unlikely that Darwin could have formulated a theory of natural selection in which "value judgments play no part." For Darwin, as for Malthus, the course of events is as it should be, especially with regard to the demise of those unfit for survival. While the "fittest" survive, there is, according to Darwin, little reason to regret the passing of those who fall by the wayside: "When we reflect on this struggle, we may console ourselves with the full belief, that the war of nature is not incessant, that no fear is felt, that the vigorous, the healthy and the happy survive and multiply."[64]

Darwin's vision has obvious biblical overtones: the plight of those who suffer must be viewed from the larger perspective of the Great Plan. In the Bible, God is the Author of the Plan; in Darwin it is Nature. Moreover, in both Darwin and the Bible, history derives its ultimate meaning from the fate of the fortunate few. Thus, both Calvinism and Darwinism provide a cosmic justification for the felicity of the few and the misery of the many. It is precisely this common feature that could prove dangerous in the years ahead.

There are other links between Darwin and the Protestant doctrine of God's lordship over nature and history that are important to our theme. As an undergraduate at Christ's College, Cambridge, from 1828 to 1831, Darwin was a student of divinity. In 1838, he read and was deeply influenced by Malthus' *Essay on the Principle of Population.* Darwin explicitly credited Malthus as the source of the idea of natural selection: "...I saw on reading Malthus on Population that natural selection was the inevitable result of the rapid increase of all organic beings; for I was prepared to appreciate the struggle for existence having long studied the habits of animals."[65]

Although Darwin's ideas on natural selection came from Malthus, Malthus himself, as we have seen, regarded the process by which unchecked population increases exponentially and food supply increases arithmetically as an expression of the wise and providential design of the Creator.[66] Thus, a crucially important source for Darwin's scientific theory of natural selection was Malthus' theodicy!

Like Darwin, Malthus studied divinity at Cambridge. Unlike Darwin, he took Holy Orders and served as an Anglican parson for part of his career. Malthus did not feel under any constraint to avoid theological argument in his writings. On the contrary, he insisted that the ultimate author of his grim scenario was none other than the wise and providential Creator.

In addition to being a crucial figure in the formulation of the harsh Poor Law Reform of 1834, Malthus also anticipates Social Darwinism and reveals the powerful convergence of religious and scientific themes in this overwhelmingly important philosophy of life. Not only are his ideas on population the indispensable starting point of the contemporary debate, but his views opposing the use of public funds for poor relief are among the earliest serious expressions of the opinion that favors cutting adrift those who do not have the resources to feed themselves.[67]

Opposition to poor relief has remained a consistent theme among Social Darwinists and Neo-Malthusians to this day. Herbert Spencer was especially harsh in his opposition to public maintenance of the poor. He argued that "the whole effort of nature is to get rid of such [the poor], to clear the world of them, and make room for better."[68] For Spencer, as for all Social Darwinists, nature is the final arbiter of who shall live and who shall die. According to Spencer, those who do not pass nature's test of survival die "and it is best that they should die."[69] Although Spencer did not study divinity as did Malthus and Darwin, during his adolescence he was strongly influenced by his uncle, the Reverend Thomas Spencer, a dissenting clergyman who undertook to give the young man his formal education.

The career of the celebrated Yale sociologist William Graham Sumner (1840–1910) offers another important link between Protestantism and Social Darwinism. Sumner believed that untrammeled competition for property and status had the beneficial effect of eliminating the unfit and of preserving a community's racial soundness and cultural vigor. According to Richard Hofstadter, Sumner was brought up "to respect Protestant economic virtues."[70] In his later life, Sumner wrote that the holder of a savings bank account was "a hero of civilization." Like Darwin and Malthus, Sumner studied theology. Upon graduation from Yale, wealthy friends supplied the funds permitting him to secure a substitute to take his place in the Union Army, an interesting variation on the theme of the "survival of the fittest." We do not know the fate of the soldier who took his place, but while the Civil War raged and millions died, Sumner took himself to

Europe, where he studied theology at Geneva, Göttingen, and Oxford. When the war was over, he returned to America and was ordained a priest of the Episcopal Church. He served as rector of the Episcopal Church in Morristown, New Jersey, for a number of years before joining the Yale faculty. Most of his professional career was spent at Yale.

Like Darwin and Spencer, Sumner was strongly influenced by Malthus. He was also an unwavering supporter of free-enterprise capitalism, as were Spencer and the other American Social Darwinists of the period. He regarded the system of unbridled economic competition that was regnant in post–Civil War America as a social expression of the process of natural selection and, as such, nature's providential means of advancing the progress of civilization. Sumner had no doubt that millionaires are nature's elect: "The millionaires are a product of natural selection, acting on a whole body of men to pick out those who can meet the requirements of certain work to be done."[71]

As in other variants of Calvinism and Social Darwinism, Sumner invoked the dichotomous division of mankind. Like Spencer, he was utterly devoid of sympathy for those who had faltered in the competitive struggle. Their misery was further evidence of the wisdom and beneficence of nature's ways. The damned receive their just desserts:

> Many are frightened at liberty, especially under the form of competition...They do not perceive that here "the strong" and "the weak" are terms which admit no definition unless they are made equivalent to the industrious and the idle, the frugal and the extravagant. They do not perceive, furthermore, that if we do not like the survival of the fittest, we have only one possible alternative, and that is the survival of the unfittest. The former is the law of civilization; the latter is the law of anti-civilization.[72]

The only kind of "civilization" Sumner could envisage was one in which the happy few prosper and the "idle," whom this son of the Gilded Age equated with the "extravagant," perish as omnipotent nature separates the wheat from the chaff.

Writing during World War II, Hofstadter concluded his book on Social Darwinism in America with the observation that the

Darwinian apotheosis of tooth-and-claw competition no longer reflected the mood of members of the middle class, the class that had been its most enthusiastic advocates. Nevertheless, Hofstadter warned that the resurgence of Social Darwinism was always possible as long as the predatory element remains strong in society. Had Hofstadter lived to the present time, he would undoubtedly have concluded that Social Darwinism has once again become a very potent ideology among those responsible for formulating the economic and social policies of the current administration.

Thirty-five years after Hofstadter set down his concluding reflections, the related value-systems of Social Darwinism, Neo-Malthusianism, and secular Calvinism have yet to be discredited. On the contrary, they gain in apparent plausibility every day as the world economic situation worsens. H. Richard Niebuhr observed that Calvinism "repelled" the poor and gave "religious sanction to the enterprise of the business man and the industrialist by regarding it as a divine calling."[73] What Calvinists proclaim in the name of God, Social Darwinists assert in the name of a strangely providential Nature.

Social Darwinism or secular Calvinism fulfills one of the most important functions of a viable religion. It provides an overarching structure of meaning in terms of which a group's experiences and values can be comprehended. It enables its adherents to believe that their social location, way of life, and fundamental values are cosmically grounded rather than the accidental product of precarious human invention.[74] In a time of acute socio-economic crisis, Social Darwinism could provide decision-makers with the legitimating ideology for political decisions that would spell disaster to millions of their fellow citizens. Regrettably, one of the lessons of this study is that the dependent poor have almost always been treated as reprobate strangers. Moreover, Social Darwinism is not merely one ideology among many. It is a conceptualization of the pre-theoretical foundations of the way the American middle and upper classes have tended to perceive social reality. The plausibility of Social Darwinism is enormously enhanced by its roots in both the predominant religious and scientific traditions of American civilization. Nor ought we to forget that even the worst scenarios we can foresee as future possibilities have already taken place in our era. Unless we find a humane way to solve the long-range problem of unemployment and population redundancy, we cannot rule out the possibility that in an acute crisis we shall turn to inhumane methods.

10
IS THERE A WAY OUT?

Is THERE THEN no escape from a situation in which millions of Americans become redundant and could eventually be eliminated altogether? It is my conviction that we are by no means helpless in meeting the challenge confronting us. While it is not my intention to offer a detailed prescription for the kinds of economic, political, and social transformations required to meet the challenge, an indispensable requirement for averting social tragedy must be the restructuring of the American economy to provide a decent job for every American willing to work. Until private industry meets this need, we will have no alternative but to insist that provision of full employment become a permanent function of the federal government. Unfortunately, during the postwar period America's economy has had a far worse unemployment record than any other major industrial society.

I find myself largely in agreement with economist Lester Thurow concerning the outlines of such a federal job program.[1] Thurow has suggested: (1) the program must offer all able-bodied Americans the kind of work opportunities and the range of earnings currently available to fully employed white males; (2) it must be designed to provide such work regardless of age, race, sex, and education; and (3) the program must be seen as a permanent part of American life rather than as a temporary expedient to help people weather a recession. This does not mean that all jobs in the program would be permanent. Some people would enter the program for short periods and some only on a part-time basis. Indeed, automation may compel us to revise downward our understanding of what constitutes full-time work.[2]

As Thurow points out, there are a number of important advantages to such a program. The moral advantages are obvious. In a civilization which holds honest work to be the morally acceptable way to provide for one's livelihood, the program would make it possible for all Americans to have the kind of self-respect that can never be the possession of those permanently dependent on welfare assistance. Since large numbers of Americans are without work through no fault of their own, such a program would go a long way to restoring the morale and, indeed, the mental health of millions.

As we have seen, macroeconomic planners are willing to trade reductions in the rate of inflation for large increases in unemployment. Given the alternatives of increased unemployment or reduced inflation, macroeconomic planners currently have few qualms about electing policies that can throw millions of people out of work. If macroeconomic planners knew their anti-inflationary policies would automatically result in increased levels of government employment instead of increased unemployment, they would be less likely to resort to fiscal policies that hobble private enterprise. Policies depending upon increased unemployment run the risk of an implosion effect resulting in a prolonged depression. For example, as automobile workers lose their jobs, they must cut back on all but the most necessary expenditures. If the downturn persists, many workers will be unable to meet their mortgage payments. As the economy contracts, layoffs in the automobile industry are followed by layoffs among the industry's subcontractors. Similarly, a dying housing market affects the lumber industry, the home appliance industry, and the capital assets of almost all American homeowners. Since World War II we have been fortunate in having more or less recovered from all downturns. Nevertheless, there is always the danger that a serious business recession will feed on itself and precipitate a deep depression.

A state-guaranteed jobs program minimizes such dangers. Such a program need not further strain the federal budget. In 1978 welfare and other transfer payments of the federal government stood at $224,000,000,000; at the same time the government spent only $10,000,000,000 for subsidized jobs.[3] A full employment program would reduce the amount paid for welfare. Moreover, people with steady jobs are better customers of private enterprise than the unemployed. The tax revenues of the federal government are more likely to increase if the gross national product increases than through tax reductions for the well-to-do. Instead of unprecedented levels of business failures due to an imploding economy and high interest rates, the climate for business activity would materially improve.

Nor need a full employment program be an exercise in creating work where none is needed. There is enough to be done in America to keep its entire population at work indefinitely even with automation. In the past, the private sector has tended to oppose state-guaranteed jobs programs because of the fear that the government would compete with private enterprise and because the state is not subject to the same fiscal constraints as the private sector. However, such a program need not have a negative effect. Those businesses, such as defense industries, for whom government is the most important customer, are by no means worse off than those without government patronage. As government employment programs grow, the role of the government as the most important customer of private enterprise will also grow. In addition, with a national commitment to full employment, there would be less reason to fear the increased productivity and reduced workload made possible by computerized automation. Automation would enrich rather than impoverish America.

Our fundamental choice is between work and idleness. To date we have chosen idleness whenever the private sector has been unable to make a profit. But this is an insane choice. Mass idleness and diminished productivity are infinitely more dangerous to the social fabric than enhanced productivity and full employment, whether brought about by the private or the public sector.

Obviously a government commitment to full employment will involve a massive restructuring of the economy. It will certainly involve changes in tax policy that would redirect the way money is invested. Such a program will inevitably be attacked as socialistic and even godless, as if an honest attempt to reduce the number of wasted American lives could ever be unholy. It is, however, not a proposal to dismantle private enterprise but to supplement it in those areas where the private sector has failed to function effectively. It is a serious effort to save and even to encourage the growth of those aspects of capitalism and private enterprise that are viable. We have already considered the possible ways American society might respond should the problem of unemployment continue to worsen. None of the scenarios are pleasant. They are morally corrosive, destructive, and humanly wasteful. If sin has any social meaning, there can be few social phenomena more sinful that a society willing to tolerate the waste of millions of its citizens. Mass unemployment may lower inflation, but it increases the real cost of living, not in terms of the price of goods and services but in terms of the violence society must both endure and employ in order to cope with its redundant population. Furthermore, even if it were possible to eliminate all of the "surplus" people, the problem would soon reappear with the progress of automation or with a change in the business cycle. In reality neither violence nor segregation of the unemployed can solve the problem.

A change in the way human beings sustain themselves, such as would be entailed in a government-guaranteed full-employment program, would affect almost every aspect of public and private life. As work patterns are altered, so too would be patterns of leisure. As job descriptions change, so too would job training. As work hierarchies are altered, so too would be social hierarchies. Art, literature, and music would soon reflect the transformations; so too would religion.

It is my conviction that the proposed economic and social transformations constitute a conservative rather than a radical program. There is nothing radical in attempting to halt mass despair before it destroys civilization as we know it. There is nothing unholy about seeking to maximize productivity with the help of government when the private sector fails. Large corporations do it all the time. When the middle class came to understand that higher education would remain a monopoly of the rich and the religious without state support, they turned to government to create the public university system. Is there any reason why the state's resources can be used to educate the middle class but not to rescue the unemployed from permanent worklessness?

There is nothing radical about insisting that *no human being ought to be considered surplus.* On the contrary, the real radicals are those who do not know the difference between a genuine human community and a jungle. Survival of the fittest may indeed be the law of the jungle, but a human community is not a jungle. Human beings have banded together to create an artificial space in which they can protect themselves from the ravages of the jungle and in which decency and civility can govern the relations between them. When advocates of free-enterprise capitalism and Social Darwinism naturalize the human condition and claim that, as with all animals, the fundamental law of human existence is the survival of the fittest, they are in reality insisting that even in civil society the condition of mankind is one of the war of all against all. They are the real radicals.

There is nothing conservative about a social philosophy that subordinates human relations to the impersonal and unpredictable tyranny of the marketplace. What could be more radical or destructive of human values than a society so organized that millions of men and women are permanently denied any opportunity to lead productive lives? If we are seriously interested in preserving private property in a complex, vulnerable, high-technology civilization, we had better be prepared to abolish welfare not by cutting the welfare budget but by providing job opportunities for all who are willing to work. A full-employment program is neither radical nor utopian. On the contrary, it is the only viable response to an explosive and morally corrosive social crisis.

Sooner or later, America will have a full-employment program. The only question is whether we are wise enough to initiate it before or after a monumental social tragedy. It is a sad fact of human nature that we are more likely to take corrective action after a tragic event than before. Yet, as we have noted throughout this essay, the tragic events we fear have already happened elsewhere. It remains to be seen whether they must happen to us *before* we take effective action.

THE NEED
FOR A RELIGIOUS TRANSFORMATION

One of the principal obstacles to a workable full-employment program is the kind of possessive individualism fundamental to the value-system and the self-understanding of most upper middle-class Americans. Possessive individualism has helped to make ours a society of universal otherhood rather than brotherhood.[4] Such individualism mistakenly dichotomizes the individual and society. It also misconstrues self-realization as largely a private affair. It is congruent with free-enterprise capitalism and Social Darwinism. Unfortunately, it is incongruent with any theory of obligation that would make the fate of one's neighbor more than a prudential concern. Dichotomizing, possessive individualism is rooted in American religion and historical experience. According to H. Richard Niebuhr, in bourgeois religion the problem of personal salvation is far more urgent than that of social redemption.[5] In an earlier age, Protestant individualism was functional for uprooted, masterless men who had been thrust out of the organic life of the agrarian village into the city or the frontier. It was also functional for businessmen and artisans whose claims to an honorable place in their communities were based upon personal achievement rather than ancestral inheritance.

However, the values inherent in dichotomizing individualism have lost much of their relevance in today's interdependent, high-technology civilization. Unfortunately, they have yet to be replaced by a synthesis of individual and communal values more congruent with contemporary experience. On the contrary, American religion continues to reinforce older individualistic values long after they have lost their social and cultural relevance. While this situation persists, we are not likely to deal effectively with the social problems confronting us. Ironically, continued affirmation of individualistic values is even crippling us in the very arena in which they were supposed to be supreme, the world of commerce. According to informed observers, the ability of Japan and other East Asian nations effectively to compete with us is in large measure due to the fact that their religious and cultural values offer a more harmonious integration of the private and public spheres than do ours.[6]

In so far as our individualism is rooted in religion, we may require a new American religious consensus before we can shape the kind of community capable of halting our satanic proliferation of wasted lives. (I hasten to add such a religious consensus cannot be achieved by amending constitutional guarantees of religious freedom.) Much of the strength of the American fundamentalist revival stems from the growing realization that a purely secular society cannot provide the values with which to respond to our multiple crises. Unfortunately, by its insistence on the priority of the individual's quest for personal salvation, its sectarian division of humanity into the chosen few and the reprobate majority, its uncritical identification with free-enterprise capitalism, and its failure to comprehend the structural nature of the problems besetting the economy and society of the United States, American fundamentalism fails to offer a viable basis for an American religious consensus. On the contrary, as with all sectarian movements, its initial premise is that religious consensus is neither desirable nor possible.

We began this study by observing that modern civilization is largely the unintended consequence of a religious revolution. In all likelihood, the modern secular world could not have come into being without a religiously legitimated transformation in consciousness. Reverence and awe of sacred institutions, traditions, and powers can be instilled in human beings long before the faculty of critical reflection begins effectively to function. If, for example, a person is taught from earliest childhood to regard trees as the abode of powerful spirits, it would be very difficult for a university course in biology or philosophy to change his feelings about tree spirits. He could, however, liberate himself from fear of tree spirits through a religious conversion in which he became convinced that one and only one God is the sovereign Creator of all things in heaven and earth. He would thereafter regard trees as part of creation rather than powers to be reckoned with.

Only a religious faith radically polemic to magic and to belief in earth's indwelling spirits could have brought about the cultural revolution in which an entire civilization came to reject what men and women had revered as sacred from time immemorial. Moreover, only one religious tradition proclaimed the existence of an absolutely sovereign Creator unremittingly hostile to the powers of magic and polytheism. In his claim to total and exclusive worship, the transcendent God of biblical monotheism demanded that his followers regard all other gods and spirits as of no account whatsoever. Belief in the God of the Bible involved a radical rejection of any sort of faith in intermediary spirits dwelling in men or nature. This attitude is characteristically expressed by the Psalmist:

Great is the Lord and worthy of all praise.
He is more to be feared than all gods.

For the gods of the nations are idols every one;
But the Lord made the heavens. [Ps. 96:4-5]

A similar attitude is to be found in Deutero-Isaiah:

Thus saith the Lord, King of Israel,
the Lord of hosts, his Redeemer:
"I am the first and I am the last,
And there is no God but me." [Isa. 44:6]

If one wishes to find the beginnings of the modern secular world one can find it here. Only those who believed in God's unique sovereignty could abandon belief in magic, spirits, and powers and begin rationally to construct a world almost as subject to humanity's sovereign mastery as men were to God's mastery. *The paradoxical precondition of the rationalizing and secularized attitude that has effectively eliminated religious and ethical values from the economy and the productive processes of the modern world was a religious revolution.*

This insight is, of course, entirely consistent with Max Weber's thesis on the role of Calvinism in the emergence of rational bourgeois capitalism. Crucial to Calvinism's role in helping to create the modern world has been the fact that it affirmed with far greater consistency than ever before the radical transcendence, exclusiveness, and sovereignty of the biblical God.[7] Unlike Judaism, which was the religion of a small group of outsiders, Calvinism was the predominant religious force precisely in those communities in which capitalism experienced its initial impetus.

There are many reasons why Weber remains worthy of study; not the least is his insight that modernization is Christian in origin and, even today when it has lost its original religious motivation, it nevertheless represents a sociocultural expression of the triumph of what he called "ascetic Protestantism." Put differently, the Weber hypothesis suggests that modernization represents a highly successful form of Christianization even when it is adopted by non-Christians who continue to be faithful to their ancestral traditions. Lest I be misunderstood, I do not offer these observations because of any desire to foster Christianity among non-Christians, but because I see no other way to interpret the sociocultural meaning of the phenomenon of modernization.

If, however, we are correct in holding that a religious revolution brought about the transformations of consciousness leading to modernization, then another transformation of consciousness originating in religion may be necessary to overcome our present predicament, if for no other reason than the fact that *a purely secular, rationalistic approach to our social problems is unlikely to produce the collective altruism our situation demands.* Without religious values, the preferred solution to a social problem is likely to be the one involving fewest costs. If it were strictly a matter of fiscal reckoning, the least costly way to "solve" the problem of surplus people would be to get rid of them. Regrettably, we have seen examples aplenty of this "solution" throughout the modern period.

But, it will be argued, is not a unifying religious consensus contrary to the American tradition of religious pluralism and religious freedom? Not necessarily, if as some scholars believe, there exists in America a "well-institutionalized civil religion" alongside the official beliefs and traditions of the churches and synagogue.[8] Whether they are correct or not, it is helpful to recognize the direct connection existing between the establishment of a free market in commodities and free religious institutions. In those communities in which men and women had a fixed and secure place, the Church was a territorial institution and there was little room for religious diversity. In general, modern religious pluralism began as an urban phenomenon among the uprooted and reflected the developing class, ethnic, and structural differentiations, as well as the anonymity, of the urban centers. Nor is it accidental that religious pluralism and tolerance first took hold in the United States, the country which, from its inception, has been the most hospitable to free-enterprise capitalism.[9]

It is also interesting to note that John Locke, the most influential advocate of religious toleration among the English philosophers, saw "the preservation of their property" as the principal motive for men banding together in civil society.[10] Nevertheless, even Locke did not want to extend toleration to atheists. His reasons are important: "Promises, covenants, and oaths, which are the bonds of human society, can have no hold upon an atheist. The taking away of God, though even but in thought, dissolves all."[11]

According to Locke, no society can function unless men can be trusted to keep their word even when keeping a promise is contrary to their material interests and cannot be enforced by the magistrate. Obviously, a person who pledges his word before both God and man may break it. Nevertheless, such a breach is a far graver matter than a breach of trust by a person who is convinced that he need reckon no interest beyond his own. There is a point beyond which Locke was not prepared to go in religious toleration because he knew that the bonds uniting men and women in a community required religious legitimation. The alternative is a world in which nothing is sacred and the fate of millions can hang upon bureaucratic cost-benefit analyses. Without a binding religious consensus, we are left with a Hobbesian congery of self-aggrandizing individuals and the power of the state as the only force making for civic tranquility.

Unfortunately, genuine religious transformations cannot be brought into being simply because their need is deeply felt. Moreover, such transformations must originate with men and women of credible inspiration. It is difficult to say how such inspiration might arise but it is doubtful that it will originate with contemporary, Western-trained clergymen, theologians, or religious scholars. The theological training received by most religious leaders in the West, whether Protestant or Jewish, and to a certain extent Roman Catholic, is an expression of the same spirit of rationality which gave birth to the modern world. It is, for example, impossible to receive a theological degree from any mainstream Western institution without studying the basic texts of the biblical religions as if they were literary documents to be investigated in the same spirit of rational, critical inquiry as any other historical document.[12] One might say the modern secularization of consciousness even expresses itself in training of contemporary religious professionals. This is understood by those Orthodox Jews and Fundamentalist Christians who continue to regard the Bible as literally the word of God. Nevertheless, it is impossible for Western religious communities to overcome this secularization of consciousness which, when carried to an extreme, can lead to mass murder. The way they train their professionals is itself an expression of the same secularization process.

When I express doubt that modern religious professionals are likely to be the source of the religious transformation our situation requires, it is not because of any distinctive flaw in their character but because of the unavoidably secular nature of the training that is an indispensable prerequisite of their certification. In spite of themselves, contemporary religious professionals are fully a part of the rational spirit of our age. This is part of what I meant when I said in an earlier work, "We live in the time of the death of God."[13]

Lest the idea of a religious consensus appear either utopian or reactionary, it is important to note there are a number of memorable historical instances in which people who shared neither common origin nor religious inheritance united to form a new community by accepting a common faith. In its formative period, Islam was able to create such a community for those who previously had no common bond.[14] One can also discern the seeds of a new community transcending older political and tribal affiliations in Paul of Tarsus' proclamation that: "There is neither Jew nor Greek, there is neither slave nor free, there is neither male nor female; for you are all one in Christ Jesus." (Gal. 3:28)

Perhaps the most influential example of a congery of strangers forming a community by adopting a common faith is that of the "Hebrews" at Sinai. As the story of the Exodus and the theophany at Sinai is recounted in Scripture, the "Hebrews" who were enslaved in Egypt appear to share common tribal and religious roots. In reality, Scripture offers ample hints that the group who escaped from Egypt with Moses did not possess a common inheritance. Referring to Moses' band in the wilderness, Scripture tells us: "Now there was a mixed company of strangers who had joined the Israelites." (Num. 11:4)

For several centuries before the Exodus, people from Palestine and Syria had entered Egypt, some as hostages and prisoners of war, some as merchants, and some who had been forced to take up residence in Egypt after engaging in activities hostile to their Egyptian overlords. It is the opinion of the majority of modern biblical scholars that the name "Hebrews" designated a number of alien peoples who shared a common condition and social location in Egypt but were of diverse origins.[15] Each group of resident aliens retained something of its own identity, especially insofar as its indigenous religious traditions involved elements of ancestor worship.[16] Not all were slaves, but their situation tended to deteriorate over time. In some respects, the situation of the "Hebrews" was similar to that of members of a modern multi-ethnic metropolis, in which diverse groups share common problems in the present but remain distinct because of differences in origin, religion, and culture.

When the time came to flee from Egypt, the "Hebrews" shared a common yearning for liberation and a common hatred of their overlords, but little else. This was enough to unify them for the escape. However, as soon as they were beyond the reach of the Egyptians, a compelling basis for unity beyond shared antipathy and a desire to flee had to be found if the band of fugitives and outcasts was to survive the natural and human hazards of the wilderness. Fortunately, the escape provided a further shared experience, the Exodus itself.

In the ancient Near East, where the distinction between group membership and religious identity was unknown, there could be only one basis for communal unity. The diverse peoples could only become a single people if they were united by a common God who was the author of their shared experience. This new basis for unifying the ethnically diverse band was proclaimed in the prologue to the Decalogue: "I am Yahweh your God who brought you out of Egypt out of the land of slavery." (Exod. 20:2)

Moreover, the God of the new religion had to be one whose power exceeded that of Pharaoh, the Egyptian god-king. Nor could any of the diverse peoples among the escapees claim that its particular ancestral god (or gods) was the true God of the entire band without arousing the mistrust and the hostility of the others. Ancestral gods were an impediment to unity. The "Hebrews" shared a common historical experience rather than kinship. Only a God who was regarded as the author of their shared experience could unify them. This too was proclaimed at Sinai: "You shall have no other gods to set against me... for I am Yahweh, your God, a jealous God." (Exod. 20:3–5)

Yahweh's insistence on exclusive worship had both political and religious implications. It united those who accepted his worship into a community and barred them from returning to the disuniting worship of their ancestral gods. *After* they had been unified under the new God, it was natural for the assorted peoples to claim they had been kin all along and to read back elements of continuity between their common God and their ancestral gods. The process is visible in Scripture.[17]

We know that under Moses the new faith and the new unity were found. Within a relatively short time the united escapees also experienced an extraordinary increase in numbers and energy and were able to gain control of much of Palestine and Jordan. The details of the conquest need not detain us. What is important is that the new community was formed by a common religious bond, not common origin and kinship. All of the world religions have performed a similar unifying task in the past. If we are to avoid the destructive consequences of our unfolding predicament, either they or some new encounter with the Sacred will have to fulfill this function in the period before us.

When one argues for a religiously grounded basis for community and collective altruism, the social and political thought of Karl Marx immediately comes to mind. It has often been noted that, in spite of his self-proclaimed atheism, his thought contained a secularized version of some of the most powerful religious themes which have moved men and women throughout the generations. One commentator has identified the principal religious themes in Marx as: "...the severity of human alienation, the apocalyptic sense of the imminence of the coming revolution, and the messianic aspiration that infuses much of Marx's thinking."[18]

One does not have to be a Marxist to understand the profound religious hunger that has made Marxism one of the most potent, if not the most potent, ideology of our secular age. If Marxism demonstrates nothing else, it demonstrates an enormously widespread yearning to overcome the moral, psychological, and cultural bankruptcy of self-aggrandizing bourgeois individualism. Neither of the two figures who have moved men and women most deeply in the Western world, Christ and Socrates, were self-regarding individualists. On the contrary, both demonstrated with their own lives there are values beyond egoism worth dying for. By contrast, there is little to inspire us in the self-preoccupied, bourgeois individualist. Whether he seeks his own material advantage or his personal salvation, he must nevertheless hope some providential Invisible Hand will provide him with the community even he in his egoism finds indispensable.

Nevertheless, though we have much to learn from Marx, his path is not the way. How often do we have to be told, despite the fact that the experiment with socialism has so often yielded bureaucratized terror rather than the humanitarian society Marx envisaged, that it is within our power to achieve a "truly" socialist society? How many mass horrors will take place before intellectuals realize a secular socialism is as incapable as a secular capitalism of providing the basis for the community our times require? Even if we grant that all societies, including those founded on religion, have been grievously flawed, the mass horrors to which this essay offers testimony ought to engender within us a measure of caution before we place our faith in any purely secular society as capable of achieving the kind of civic altruism humanity requires.

Although we require a religious transformation, it does not necessarily follow that we require a theistic transformation. Unless we are prepared to deny that Buddhism, Confucianism, and perhaps Shinto are religions, we ought to recognize that some of the world's most important religions are nontheistic. In an age in which Asia has regained a central role in human history, such a rejection of that continent's major religions would indeed be provincial, shortsighted, and unwise. Our historical experience has taught us that neither secular capitalist individualism nor collectivist communism exclude the kind of human desolation described in this essay. If we continue in a secular path, there is little reason to doubt that the tragedies of the past are but a foretaste of those to come. There simply has to be a better way for human beings to dwell together on this planet.

Here we reach the limits of analysis. The historian, the social theorist, the philosopher, the theologian — none of them can go beyond this point. This was understood by Hegel. Both hope and despair are expressed in the oft-quoted reflections in the Preface to the *Philosophy of Right:*

> One word more about giving instructions as to what the world ought to be. Philosophy in any case always comes on the scene too late to give it. As the thought of the world, it appears only when actuality is already there cut and dried after its process of formation has been completed... When philosophy paints its grey in grey, then has a shape of life grown old. By philosophy's grey it cannot be rejuvenated but only understood. The owl of Minerva spreads its wings only with the falling of the dusk.[19]

For Hegel, philosophy is "the wisdom of ripeness."[20] It can understand what has been. It can announce the dissolution of what is; but more is needed if a new and better world is to come into being.

Before we conclude, let us recall another observation by Hegel: "[History is] the slaughter bench at which the happiness of peoples, the wisdom of states, and the virtue of individuals have been sacrificed..."[21]

For Hegel, as for the Calvinists and the Social Darwinists, value and fact are one, and all we are left with is the slaughter bench of history. If there is to be more it will not come from the thinker, the theorist, or the theologian. It can only come from men and women of authentic religious inspiration.

If there be such persons among the religious thinkers of this generation, they have yet to make known their vocation. To date, the most important effort of this generation of theologians, the generation after Paul Tillich, has been to demonstrate that no purely intellectual enterprise in the domain of religious thought can overcome the "death of God." This badly misused and misunderstood term is simply a verbal instrument, utilizing the vocabulary of religion, to point to the radical secularization of our times. In reality, there was nothing new in the theologians' insight that reason had reached its destination in godlessness. It was understood as clearly by Kierkegaard and Karl Barth, who were believers, as by Nietzsche and Max Weber, who were not. They all understood that the revolution of rationality, the glorious and terrible revolution which brought forth the modern world, had reached its limits. Those who fear nuclear annihilation have come to the same insight in their own way. But to understand the limits of reason and reflection is not to be reduced to impotent despair. It is rather to acknowledge the need for a path beyond those familiar to the critics and the thinkers.

The story we have told is one of the extraordinary achievements and the terrible costs of human rationality in modern times. The worst cost has obviously been the incredible waste of human potential and indeed of life itself from the English enclosures of Tudor times, the Great Famine in Ireland, the Armenian massacres, and the destruction of the European Jews to genocide in Kampuchea and the millions upon millions of men and women who are today condemned, through no fault of their own, to the damnation of permanent worklessness.

Unlike other nations, both in the past and in our own century, the United States cannot solve the problem of mass unemployment and other forms of population redundancy by sending its unwanted people elsewhere. Neither unending growth nor unending movement offers a solution. In this new political and social environment, our worst pollution may very well be what we do to ourselves. That is why a religious transformation is crucial. But, if it is to come, it must be an inclusive vision appropriate to a global civilization in which Moses and Mohammed, Christ, Buddha, and Confucius all play a role. We can no longer rest content with a humanity divided into the working and the workless, the saved and the damned, the Occident and the Orient. Our fates are too deeply intertwined. The call for religious transformation is in reality a call to conversion, a call to change ourselves. Our preachers have rightly told us that we must be converted, that we must be born again. Unfortunately, what has been understood as conversion has all too often been devoid of the inclusive social component our times demand. In truth, we must be born again as men and women blessed with the capacity to care for each other here and now.

NOTES

Chapter 1
Overview: The Revolution of Rationality

1. Carlo M. Cippola, *The Economic History of World Population*, 6th Edition, pp. 115–18. See also André Armengaud, "Population in Europe, 1700–1914," in Carlo M. Cipolla, ed., *The Fontana Economic History of Europe*, Vol. 3, *The Industrial Revolution*, pp. 22–77; Franklin D. Scott, ed., *World Migration in Modern Times*, pp. 9–58; Oscar Handlin, *The Uprooted*.

2. David S. Landes, *The Unbound Prometheus: Technological Change and Industrial Development in Western Europe from 1750 to the Present*, p. 21.

3. Max Weber, "The Social Psychology of the World Religions," in H. H. Gerth and C. Wright Mills, eds., *From Max Weber: Essays in Sociology*, p. 293.

4. Landes, loc. cit.

5. Ibid.

6. Max Weber, "Science as a Vocation," in Gerth and Mills, op. cit., p. 139.

7. See Max Weber, *Ancient Judaism*, trans. H. H. Gerth and Don Martindale, pp. 222ff; Peter Berger, *The Sacred Canopy: Elements of a Sociological Theory of Religion*, pp. 113ff.

8. Landes, op. cit., p. 24.

9. G. W. F. Hegel, Preface to *Phenomenology of Spirit*, trans. A. V. Miller, p. 14. On the intellectual and spiritual relationship between Goethe and Hegel, see Karl Löwith, *From Hegel to Nietzsche: The Revolution in Nineteenth-Century Thought*, trans. David E. Green, pp. 14–30.

10. G. W. F. Hegel, *Jenaer Realphilosophie I, Die Vorlesungen von 1803/4*, ed. J. Hoffmeister, p. 239, originally published as *Jenenser Realphilosophie*. I am indebted to Shlomo Avineri, *Hegel's Theory of the Modern State*, for the reading of Hegel's economic thought presented in this section. See also Georg Lukacs, *The Young Hegel: Studies in the Relations Between Dialectics and Economics*, trans. Rodney Livingstone, pp. 319–397.

11. G. W. F. Hegel, *Philosophy of Right*, trans. T. M. Knox, par. 246. Reference in the *Philosophy of Right* is to the enumerated paragraphs rather than pages. See Avineri, op. cit., pp. 153f.

12. Hegel, *Philosophy of Right*, par. 244.

13. Hegel, op. cit., par. 245.

14. Hegel, op. cit., addition to par. 244.

15. Hegel, op. cit., par. 246.

16. Hegel, op. cit., par. 248.

17. Hegel, *Jenaer Realphilosophie II: Die Vorlesungen von 1805/6,* ed. J. Hoffmeister, pp. 256–57, originally published as *Jenenser Realphilosophie;* cited by Avineri, op. cit., p. 107.

18. Thomas Hobbes, *Leviathan,* ed. C. B. Macpherson, Part I, Ch. 10, pp. 151–2.

19. Hobbes, op. cit., Part II, Ch. 24, p. 295.

20. Max Weber, *Economy and Society,* ed. Guenther Roth and Claus Witich, Vol. 2, p. 636.

21. Weber, op. cit., p. 637.

22. Benjamin Nelson, *The Idea of Usury: From Tribal Brotherhood to Universal Otherhood.*

23. See Talcott Parsons, *The Structure of Social Action,* Vol. 2, pp. 686–694; Bryan Wilson, *Religion in Sociological Perspective,* pp. 163–68. Wilson aptly titles this section "The Moral Community and the Rational Society."

24. Karl Polanyi, *The Great Transformation: The Political and Economic Origins of Our Time,* p. 40.

25. See Richard L. Rubenstein, *The Cunning of History: Mass Death and the American Future,* pp. 9ff.

26. Polanyi, op. cit., p. 35.

27. See Michael J. Arlen, *Passage to Ararat,* p. 119. For a bibliography on the Armenian genocide, see Richard G. Hovannisian, *The Armenian Holocaust: A Bibliography Relating to the Deportations, Massacres of the Armenian People, 1915–1923.* For an account of the events as told by the American Ambassador to Turkey, see Henry Morgenthau, *Ambassador Morgenthau's Story;* see also Dickran H. Boyajian, *Armenia: The Case for a Forgotten Genocide;* Vigen Guroian, "A Comparison of the Armenian and Jewish Genocides: Some Common Features."

28. Viscount James Bryce, *The Treatment of the Armenians in the Ottoman Empire, 1915–16: Documents Presented to the Secretary of State for Foreign Affairs by Viscount Bryce,* p. 624. According to Richard G. Hovannisian, Abdul Hamid's massacres were a response to what he perceived to be European meddling in Turkey's internal affairs. His objectives were thus limited. See Hovannisian, *Armenia on the Road to Independence,* p. 28.

29. Bryce, loc. cit.

30. Arlen, op. cit., p. 129; Hovannisian estimates that between one and two hundred thousand were killed; *Armenia,* loc. cit.

31. This telegram is quoted in Manuel Sarkisyanz, *A Modern History of Transcaucasian Armenia,* p. 196.

32. All commentators are agreed upon the modernity of the operation. See, for example, Arlen, op. cit., pp. 343–44.

33. See the excerpt from the minutes of a secret meeting (undated) of leaders of the "Ittihad ve Terraki," the dominant "Committee for Union and Progress Party," at which the pros and cons of genocide were coldbloodedly discussed: James Nazer, *The Armenian Massacres,* pp. 7-9.

34. This information was presented by Professor R. Hrair Dekmejian in a lecture at the Seminar in Commemoration of the 65th Anniversary of the Armenian Genocide, St. Vartan's Cathedral, New York, N.Y., April 25, 1980.

35. Bryce, op. cit., p. 648.

36. Arlen, op. cit., p. 179.

37. Weber, *Economy and Society,* Vol. 3, p. 983.

38. Bryce, op. cit., p. 634.

39. Morgenthau, op. cit., p. 336.

40. Richard Grenier, "The Horror, The Horror" in *The New Republic,* May 26, 1982, pp. 28-29. See Robert Conquest, *The Great Terror: Stalin's Purge of the Thirties,* pp. 699-713 (Penguin edition); Alexander Solzhenitsyn, *The Gulag Archipelago: 1918-1956,* trans. Thomas. P. Whitney, p. 432ff, (a translation of Parts I and II of the Russian version.); Gil Eliot, *The Twentieth Century Book of the Dead,* pp. 218ff.

41. Grenier, loc. cit.

42. Grenier, op. cit., p. 29.

43. Solzhenitsyn, op. cit., pp. 81-83, 237-51.

44. Adam B. Ulam, *Stalin: The Man and His Era,* p. 325.

45. On the destruction of Russia's peasant class, see Ulam, op. cit., pp. 289ff; Conquest, op. cit., pp. 41-47; Alexander Solzhenitsyn, op. cit., pp. 54ff; Solzhenitzyn, *The Gulag Archipelago Three,* pp. 350-68.; Alan W. Gouldner, "Stalinism: A Study of Internal Colonialism" in *Telos,* 34 (Winter 1977-78), pp. 5-48.

46. Winston S. Churchill, *The Second World War,* Vol. 4, pp. 447-48. For this citation I am indebted to Conquest, op. cit., p. 46.

47. Grenier, op. cit., p. 28. Solzhenitzyn estimates that 15,000,000 died. See *Gulag Archipelago Three,* p. 350.

48. See Frances Fox Piven and Richard A. Cloward, *Regulating the Poor: The Functions of Public Welfare,* pp. 200-21; Roger Beardwood, "The Southern Roots of the Urban Crisis" in *Fortune,* August 1968.

49. See Ken Auletta, *The Underclass;* "The Blackout: Night of Terror" in *Time,* July 25, 1977; "The American Underclass" in *Time,* August 29, 1977.

50. "Thousands of Aliens Held in Virtual Slavery in U.S." in *The New York Times,* October 19, 1980.

51. See H. Richard Niebuhr, *The Social Sources of Denominationalism.* Although much work has been done in recent years on the relationship between denominationalism and sectarianism on the one hand and class structure on the other, Niebuhr's book remains a classic.

52. See Liston Pope, *Millhands and Preachers.*

53. See Max Weber "Capitalism and Rural Society in Germany" in Girth and Mills, eds., op. cit., pp. 363–85. Weber's study of the employment of seasonal Polish workers in Prussian agriculture was originally undertaken for the *Verein für Sozialpolitik* in 1891. See Wolfgang J. Mommsen, *The Age of Bureaucracy: Perspectives on the Political Sociology of Max Weber,* pp. 26ff.

54. Rubenstein, op. cit.

55. See Ezra F. Vogel, *Japan as No. 1: Lessons for America,* pp. 11ff.

56. For an overview of the political, economic and social impact of the microprocessor, see Christopher Evans, *The Micro Millennium.*

57. "Robots Enter the Limelight" in *The New York Times,* March 4, 1982.

58. See Clifford D. May, "Mexico City: Omens of the Apocalypse" in *Geo,* Vol. 3, May 1981, pp. 10–36.

59. Armengaud, op. cit., pp. 66ff.

60. Gil Eliot estimates that 100,000,000 have been killed. See Eliot, op. cit., pp. 211–33. I used his estimate in *The Cunning of History.* I now believe that the figure is much higher. Eliot estimates that 50,000,000 Russians have been killed whereas there is a developing consensus that at least 80,000,000 citizens of the Soviet Union have been killed by their own regime since the Russian Revolution. Moreover, much has happened since the publication of Eliot's book. It is very likely that even the figure of 150,000,000 is too low!

61. See Roderick MacFarquar, "The Challenge of Post-Confucian Asia" in *The Economist,* February 9, 1980. For an informed study of reasons why the nations of East Asia may soon follow the example of Japan as the world's leading technological, industrial and economic powers, see Roy Hofheinz, Jr., and Kent E. Calder, *The East Asia Edge.*

62. Hofheinz and Calder, op. cit., p. 7.

63. See "Taiwan's Car Industry" in *The Economist,* 6–12 March 1982, p. 78.

64. On the euthanasia program, see Pierre Joffroy, *A Spy for God: The Ordeal of Kurt Gerstein,* pp. 84–89, 119–23, and 130–69.

65. For a contrasting view of the destruction process as pathological, see Lucy S. Dawidowicz, *The War Against the Jews,* pp. 3–28.

66. See below, Chapter 9.

67. See Jonathan Schell, "The Fate of the Earth: I–A Republic of Insects and Grass" in *The New Yorker,* February 1, 1982.

Chapter 2
The Enclosure Movement in England and Its Social Consequences: The Tudor Period

1. The literature on the enclosures is voluminous. For a balanced recent study, see William E. Tate, *The Enclosure Movement*. R. H. Tawney's *The Agrarian Problem in the Sixteenth Century* remains an important study of the movement in the Tudor period. The most influential, literate and controversial study is that of John L. and Barbara Hammond, *The Village Labourer, 1760-1832: A Study in the Government of England before the Reform Bill*. The Hammonds are frequently accused of being biased against the landowners. Nevertheless, their work remains very readable and indispensable for anyone interested in the subject. For a view more or less defending the enclosures, see the second edition of Edward C. K. Gonner, *Common Land and Enclosure* with a new introduction by G. E. Mingay. For a collection of legal documents dealing with the sixteenth century enclosures and a long introduction that is critical of Tawney and generally defends the enclosures, see Eric Kerridge, *Agrarian Problems in the Sixteenth Century and After*. For a discussion of the enclosures by a scholar of impressive authority, see John Thirsk, "Enclosing and Engrossing" in H. P. R. Finberg, gen. ed., Joan Thirsk, ed., *The Agrarian History of England and Wales, 1500-1640* (Vol. 4). See also Hermann Levy, *Large and Small Holdings: A Study of English Agricultural Economics,* trans. Ruth Kenyon. For an authoritative review of the literature, see Jerome Blum, "English Parliamentary Enclosure," *Journal of Modern History,* Vol. 53, pp. 477-504, September 1981.

2. See Thirsk, op. cit., p. 200; Tate, op. cit., pp. 91-120; Gonner, op. cit., pp. 70-95; Wilhelm Hasbach, *A History of the English Agricultural Labourer,* trans. Ruth Kenyon, pp. 107-113.

3. Tate, op. cit., p. 44.

4. Tawney, op. cit., pp. 258 and 301-10.

5. For a contemporary Marxist defense of the enclosures, see Barrington Moore, Jr., *Social Origins of Dictatorship and Democracy: Lord and Peasant in the Making of the Modern World*. Moore sees the enclosures as a necessary form of "revolutionary violence" that made modern English democracy possible through "the final solution of the peasant question." (p. 426). Moore argues that the violent destruction of the peasantry was a social necessity. It eliminated a class that could otherwise have served "the reactionary ends of the landed upper classes as in Germany and Japan" (p. 426); see also p. 29.

6. Tate, op. cit., p. 22.

7. Tate, op. cit., p. 40.

8. Ibid.

9. Tate, op. cit., p. 32.

10. Tate, op. cit., p. 34.

11. See Tawney, op. cit., pp. 91ff.

12. See Tawney, op. cit., pp. 40–54; Tate, op. cit., pp. 174–75.

13. Tate, op. cit., p. 45.

14. See Tawney, op. cit. pp. 6ff; Thirsk, op. cit., pp. 209ff.

15. Tawney, op. cit., pp. 308–10.

16. On the abuses of emparcation, see especially the Hammonds, op. cit., pp. 163ff. The Hammonds describe conditions at the beginning of the nineteenth century, but the eviction of people in order to turn the land into parks for the enjoyment of landowners occurred as early as the sixteenth century. See Tawney, op. cit., pp. 148, 201.

17. By the Parliamentary Act of 1828, third offenders were subject to transportation to Australia for as long as fourteen years. See the Hammonds, op. cit., p. 166.

18. Thirsk, op. cit., pp. 209–10; Hasbach, op. cit., pp. 160–2.

19. Tawney, op. cit., pp. 112–13.

20. See Tawney, op. cit., pp. 78–86 and 381–82; Hasbach, op. cit., pp. 65–66, 108.

21. Tawney, op. cit., pp. 192–213; Hasbach, op. cit., p. 160.

22. Tawney, op. cit., pp. 242ff.

23. Tawney, op. cit., pp. 281–312.

24. Tate, op. cit., p. 63.

25. Johanni Rossi, *Historia Regum Anglie,* 2nd ed., (Oxford: 1745), pp. 122–3; cited by Tate, loc. cit.

26. Sir Thomas More, "Utopia," in Burton A. Milligan, ed., *Three Renaissance Classics,* pp. 124–27.

27. Tate, op. cit., p. 122.

28. Tawney, op. cit., p. 188.

29. Tawney, op. cit., pp. 377–400; Tate, op. cit., pp. 124–27. In spite of the attempts of Charles I to limit the enclosures, Tawney (p. 391) writes concerning the agrarian policy of his Council that "the whole of it is smeared with the trail of finance." According to Thirsk, under the Stuarts the government lost much of its anti-enclosure zeal and punishment of the enclosures became in large measure a "revenue-raising device." Thirsk, op. cit., p. 213.

30. Tawney, op. cit., p. 189.

31. Tawney, op. cit., p. 360.

Chapter 3
The Enclosure Movement in England and Its Social Consequences: The Age of Enlightenment

1. A number of sources rely on Gilbert Slater, *The English Peasantry and the Enclosure of the Small Fields,* pp. 140-7. See John L. and Barbara Hammond, *The Village Labourer, 1760-1832,* p. 17; William E. Tate, *The Enclosure Movement,* p. 88.

2. See Hammonds, op. cit., pp. 12ff; Tate, op. cit., pp. 80ff.

3. Tate, loc. cit.

4. Tate, op. cit., pp. 152f. See E. J. Evans, "Some Reasons for the Growth of English Rural Anti-Clericalism 1750-1830," *Past and Present,* Vol. 66 (1975), pp. 95-96; Hammonds, op. cit., pp. 143-44.

5. See Tate, op. cit., p. 143.

6. John Billingsley, *Report on Somerset,* (London: 1794); p. 52; cited by Hammonds, op. cit., p. 13.

7. J. Bishton. *Report on Shropshire,* (London: 1794); cited without pagination by Hammonds, op. cit., p. 14.

8. "The rage for order and symmetry and neat cultivation was universal." Hammonds, op. cit., p. 16.

9. Tate, op. cit., p. 130.

10. Arthur Young, "An Inquiry into the Propriety of Applying Wastes to the Better Maintenance and Support of the Poor" in *Annals of Agriculture,* (London: H. Goldney, 1801), Vol. 36, pp. 497-658. See also John G. Gazley, *The Life of Arthur Young,* pp. 435-84.

11. See J. R. Poynter, *Society and Pauperism: English Ideas on Poor Relief, 1795-1834,* pp. 109-11. For a contemporary study of Malthus' life and thought, see William Petersen, *Malthus;* see also the earlier work by James Bonar, *Malthus and His Work.*

12. Thomas R. Malthus, *An Essay on the Principle of Population,* p. 205 (Penguin ed.).

13. Malthus, op. cit., p. 202.

14. Malthus, op. cit., p. 215.

15. Ibid.

16. This is the view of Petersen, op. cit.

17. This passage is to be found in Chapter 8 of the revised edition of 1803. It is reprinted in Thomas Robert Malthus, *Essay*, ed. Philip Appleman, p. 135.

18. Cited by Allan Chase, *The Legacy of Malthus: The Social Costs of the New Racism*, p. 6.

19. As the Irish famine intensified, Lord John Russell, the Prime Minister, Sir Charles Wood, the Chancellor of the Exchequer, and Sir Charles M. Trevelyan, the permanent head of the Treasury, came to favor a policy of letting nature take its course. See Cecil Woodham-Smith, *The Great Hunger: Ireland, 1845–1849*, p. 375 and infra., Ch. 6.

20. See Hannah Arendt's discussion of the difference between the public and the private realm, in *The Human Condition*, pp. 22–78.

21. Malthus, pp. 187–88, (Penguin ed.).

22. On Turkish use of Social Darwinism as a legitimating ideology, see "The Secret Meeting of the Ittihad" in James Nazer, *The Armenian Massacre*, pp. 7ff. On the German use, see Hans-Günter Zmarzlik, "Social Darwinism in Germany Seen as a Historical Problem," in Hajo Halborn, ed., *Republic into Reich: The Making of the Nazi Revolution*, pp. 435–74.

23. Max Horkheimer and Theodore Adorno, *Dialectic of Enlightenment*, p. 5.

24. Francis Bacon, "Valerius Terminus: Of the Interpretation of Nature" (Miscellaneous Tracts Upon Human Knowledge) in *The Works of Francis Bacon, Lord Chancellor of England*, ed. Basil Montagu (London: W. Pickering, 1825), Vol. I, pp. 254ff. Cited in Horkheimer and Adorno, loc. cit.

25. Weber, *Economy and Society*, Vol. I, p. 93.

Chapter 4
The Fate of the Defeated Peasants

1. See Wilhelm Hasbach, *A History of the English Agricultural Labourer*, pp. 131–38.

2. See Hasbach, op. cit., pp. 116–70; John L. and Barbara Hammond, *The Village Labourer, 1760–1832: A Study in the Government of England Before the Reform Bill*, pp. 73–98.

3. See Edward C. K. Gonner, *Common Land and Enclosure*, pp. 388ff; William E. Tate, *The Enclosure Movement*, pp. 63ff.

4. R. H. Tawney, *The Agrarian Problem in the Sixteenth Century*, p. 67.

5. Tawney, op. cit., p. 267.

6. Sidney and Beatrice Webb, *English Poor Law History: Part I, The Old Poor Law*, p. 356. This is Vol. 7 of the Webbs' work, *English Local Government*.

7. See J. Thomas Kelly, *Thorn on the Tudor Rose: Monks, Rogues, Vagabonds, and Sturdy Beggars*, pp. 83ff.

8. Robert Cushman, "Reasons and Considerations Touching the Lawfulness of Removing Out of England and into America," in E. Arber, *The Story of the Pilgrim Fathers* (Boston: Houghton, Mifflin, 1897), pp. 495–505.

9. Ibid.

10. "London Orders of 1517 for Restraining Vagabonds and Beggars," Journal 11, pp. 337ff, in Frank Aydelotte, *Elizabethan Rogues and Vagabonds*, pp. 140–42.

11. Kelly, op. cit., p. 83.

12. Aydelotte, op. cit., pp. 17–20; Kelly, loc. cit.

13. Kelly, op. cit., p. 85.

14. For abbreviated texts of the Acts of 1601 and 1662, see Maurice Bruce, ed., *The Rise of the Welfare State: English Social Policy, 1601–1971*, pp. 39–42.

15. Hammonds, op. cit., pp. 88ff; on the abuses of the Law of Settlement and Removal, see Sidney and Beatrice Webb, op. cit., pp. 314–49. For Adam Smith's opposition to the Law of Settlement, see *The Wealth of Nations*, p. 245 (Penguin ed.).

16. For an abbreviated text of the Poor Removal Act of 1795, see Bruce, op. cit., p. 42. See also the Hammonds, op. cit., pp. 89f; Geoffrey W. Oxley, *Poor Law Relief in England and Wales, 1601–1834*, pp. 19–21; Sidney and Beatrice Webb, op. cit., pp. 338ff.

17. Hammonds, op. cit., pp. 89–92.

18. Hammonds, loc. cit.

19. See Sidney and Beatrice Webb, op. cit., pp. 211–21 and 246–54.

20. See Norman McCord, "Aspects of the Relief of Poverty in Early 19th-Century England," in R. M. Hartwell, et al., *The Long Debate on Poverty: Eight Essays on Industrialisation and "The Condition of England,"* pp. 89–108.

21. Beatrice and Sidney Webb, op. cit., p. 407.

22. Raymond G. Cowherd, *Political Economists and the English Poor Laws*, p. 268.

23. John L. and Barbara Hammond, *The Town Labourer, 1760–1832: The New Civilisation*, p. 144.

24. Hammonds, op. cit., pp. 32–34; E. P. Thompson, *The Making of the English Working Class*, pp. 243–44. For a study of the abuses of industrialization that takes issue with the Hammonds, see "Industrialisation and Poverty: In Fact and Fiction," Hartwell, et al., op. cit., pp. 189–238.

25. Hammonds, *The Town Labourer,* pp. 146–49.

26. Hammonds, op. cit., pp. 172–76.

27. Hammonds, op. cit., pp. 176–93.

28. Hammonds, op. cit., p. 145; Sidney and Beatrice Webb, op. cit., pp. 298–99.

29. Sidney and Beatrice Webb, *English Poor Law History: Part II, The Last One Hundred Years,* Vol. 1 of Part II, pp. 156–57. On Chadwick, see S. E. Finer, *The Life and Times of Sir Edwin Chadwick;* Cowherd, op. cit., pp. 216–282; Sir Edwin Chadwick, *The Papers of Sir Edwin Chadwick.*

30. J. R. Poynter, *Society and Pauperism: English Ideas on Poor Relief, 1795–1834,* p. 126; Finer, op. cit., p. 75.

31. Edinburgh Review, Vol. 63 (1836), p. 490; cited by Cowherd, op. cit., p. 246.

32. Cited in Sidney and Beatrice Webb, op. cit., Part II, *The Last One Hundred Years,* Vol. 1 of Part II, p. 66.

33. Sidney and Beatrice Webb, op. cit., Part I, *The Old Poor Law,* pp. 254–260.

34. Sidney and Beatrice Webb, op. cit., Part I, pp. 256–57.

35. Sidney and Beatrice Webb, op. cit., Part I, pp. 190–7; Oxley, op. cit., pp. 110–11, 116–7; Hammonds, *Village Labourer,* pp. 140–41.

36. Sidney and Beatrice Webb, op. cit., Part I, p. 190.

37. Sidney and Beatrice Webb, op. cit., pp. 191ff. See Karl Polanyi, *The Great Transformation: The Political And Economic Origins of Our Time,* pp. 77–85.

38. Sidney and Beatrice Webb, op. cit., Part I, pp. 222, 232–33.

39. Sidney and Beatrice Webb, op. cit., Part I. pp. 170–71, 272–75.

40. Jeremy Bentham, *Pauper Management Improved: Particularly by Means of an Application of the Panopticon Principle of Construction,* pp. 21–2; cited by Poynter, op. cit., p. 133. For a succinct overview of Bentham's views, see Poynter, op. cit., pp. 106–144. See also Leslie Stephen, *The English Utilitarians,* Vol. 1, p. 203; E. Halevi, *The Growth of Philosophical Radicalism;* Gertrude Himmelfarb, "Bentham's Utopia: The National Charity Company," *The Journal of British Studies,* Vol. 10, No. 1 (November 1970); Cowherd, op. cit., pp. 82–101. Sidney and Beatrice Webb, op. cit., Part II: Vol. 1 of Part II, pp. 26–32.

41. Bentham, op. cit., pp. 57–74.

42. Poynter, op. cit., pp. 130–44.

43. Sidney and Beatrice Webb, op. cit., Part II, Vol. 1 of Part II, pp. 26–29.

44. Sidney and Beatrice Webb, op. cit., Part II, Vol. 1 of Part II, p. 29.

45. See Richard L. Rubenstein, *The Cunning of History,* pp. 48–67; Joseph Borkin, *The Crime and Punishment of I. G. Farben;* Benjamin B. Ferenc, *Less Than Slaves: Jewish Forced Labor and the Quest for Compensation.*

46. According to Sidney and Beatrice Webb, "It is to Jeremy Bentham, the prophet of the Philosophic Radicals, that we owe the insidiously potent conception

of a series of specialised government departments supervising and controlling from Whitehall, through salaried officials, the whole public administration of the community, whether police or prisons, school or hospital, highways or the relief of destitution." Sidney and Beatrice Webb, op. cit., Part II, Vol. 1 of Part II, pp. 26–27.

47. Patrick Colquhoun, *A Treatise on Indigence,* pp. 7–9. Malthus shared Colquhoun's belief in poverty as a necessary goad to industry. Concerning poverty, Malthus wrote: "Such a stimulus seems to be absolutely necessary to promote the happiness of the great mass of mankind, and every attempt to weaken this stimulus, however benevolent its apparent intention, will always defeat its own purpose." Malthus, *An Essay on the Principle of Population,* p. 98 (Penguin ed.).

48. See Polanyi, loc. cit.; Hammonds, *The Village Labourer,* pp. 137–41.

49. See Eric J. Hobsbawm and George Rude, *Captain Swing,* pp. 72ff; Hammonds, *The Town Labourer,* pp. 105ff.

50. See Hobsbawm and Rude, op. cit., pp. 97–194.

51. Sidney and Beatrice Webb, op. cit., Part II, Vol. 2 of Part II, p. 46.

52. Sidney and Beatrice Webb, op. cit., Part II, Vol. 2 of Part II, pp. 56ff.

53. *Report of Poor Law Inquiry Commissioners, 1834,* Appendix A, Part III, p. 29; cited by Sidney and Beatrice Webb, op. cit., Part II, Vol. 2 of Part II, p. 67.

54. Sidney and Beatrice Webb, op. cit., Part II, Vol. 2 of Part II, pp. 137–42.

55. Sidney and Beatrice Webb, op. cit., Part II, Vol. 2 of Part II, p. 148.

56. Sidney and Beatrice Webb, op. cit., Part II, Vol. 2 of Part II, pp. 161–62.

57. Sidney and Beatrice Webb, op. cit., Part II, Vol. 2 of Part II, pp. 163–64.

58. Sidney and Beatrice Webb, op. cit., Part II, Vol. 2 of Part II, pp. 179–82.

59. "Report from the Select Committee on the Andover Union" cited in Bruce, *The Rise of the Welfare State,* p. 67.

60. Sidney and Beatrice Webb, op. cit., Part II, Vol. 2 of Part II, pp. 167–72 and 183–88.

61. George Lansbury, *My Life,* pp. 135f.

Chapter 5
The Safety Valve of Emigration

1. Stanley C. Johnson, *A History of Emigration: From the United Kingdom to North America, 1763–1812,* pp. 2–3. In addition to eliminating the economically redundant, emigration was seen as a means of eliminating members of dissident religious sects. For example, of the 50,000 Quakers in England at the time William Penn's petition for a grant of land in the New World was approved by King Charles II, 20,000 had spent some time in jail (1681). Penn wrote to a friend that "the crown would be glad to be rid of us..." See E. Digby Baltzell, *Puritan Boston and Quaker Philadelphia: Two Protestant Ethics and the Spirit of Class Authority and Leadership,* p. 114.

2. Johnson, loc. cit.

3. H. J. M. Johnston, *British Emigration Policy, 1815–1830: "Shoveling Out The Paupers,"* p. 7.

4. See Eric J. Hobsbawm and George Rude, *Captain Swing,* pp. 72–80; Johnston, op. cit., p. 5; Johnson, op. cit., pp. 38–47.

5. Johnston, op. cit., pp. 11–12.

6. Thomas R. Malthus, *An Essay on the Principle of Population* (London: 1817), pp. 304–5; cited by Johnston, op. cit., pp. 12–13. For Malthus' views on emigration, see G. Talbot Griffith, *Population Problems in the Age of Malthus,* pp. 89–100.

7. W. G. Hayter, *Proposals for the Redemption of the Poor's Rates by Means of Emigration,* cited by Johnston, op. cit., p. 13.

8. Robert Torrens, "A Paper on the Means of Reducing the Poor's Rates" in *The Pamphleteer,* Vol. 10, No. 20, 1817.

9. Johnson, op. cit., pp. 18–20; Johnston, op. cit., pp. 16–17.

10. Johnston, op. cit., pp. 19–20.

11. Johnston, op. cit., pp. 37–40.

12. Johnston, op. cit., pp. 36–37.

13. See Johnston, op. cit., pp. 56–68.

14. Ibid.

15. Johnston, op. cit., p. 61.

16. Johnston, op. cit., pp. 63–64.

17. Ibid.

18. Johnston, op. cit., p. 64.

19. Johnston, op. cit., p. 66.

20. Johnson, op. cit., p. 299.

21. "Emigration and Industrial Training," *Edinburgh Review,* Vol. 92, No. 188 (October 1850), p. 493.

22. See R. N. Ghosh, "Malthus on Emigration and Colonization: Letters to Wilmot-Horton," *Economica,* February 1963; Donald Winch, *Classical Political Economy and Colonies,* pp. 56–60; Johnston, op. cit., pp. 135–37; Cowherd, *Political Economists and the English Poor Laws,* pp. 161–63.

23. *Cobbett's Weekly Political Register,* March 13, 1830, p. 350, March 20, 1830, p. 368, April 9, 1831, p. 80; cited by Johnston, op. cit., p. 130. On Cobbett, see John W. Osborne, *William Cobbett: His Thought and His Times.*

24. See Johnston, op. cit., pp. 145–62.

25. Johnson, op. cit., p. 38. The figures given by Johnson are: 9,798,934 to the United States; 2,918,328 to "British North America." However, many who emigrated to Canada proceeded to the United States.

26. Carlo M. Cippola, *The Economic History of World Population,* p. 33.

27. Ibid.

28. Arnold Toynbee, *Lectures on the Industrial Revolution of the Eighteenth Century in England,* p. 84. It should be noted that this Toynbee (1852–1883) was the uncle of the famous historian.

29. R. M. Hartwell, "The Consequences of the Industrial Revolution in England for the Poor" in Hartwell et al., *The Long Debate on Poverty,* pp. 1–22.

30. R. M. Hartwell, *The Industrial Revolution and Economic Growth,* p. 129; see also, Hartwell, "Economic Change in England and Europe 1780–1830," in *The New Cambridge Modern History,* Vol. 9, pp. 31ff.

31. G. E. Mingay, "The Transformation of Agriculture" in Hartwell et al., op. cit., p. 25.

32. "Upsurge of Prejudice Against Immigrants in West Germany," *New York Times,* February 22, 1982, Section 1, Page 3.

33. The Know-Nothing agitation of 1852–1856 was one of the earliest expressions of hostility against the immigrants. At the time Irish immigrants were the principal targets. Practically every immigrant group has been the object of such hostility thereafter. See Marcus Lee Hansen, *The Atlantic Migration, 1607–1860,* pp. 303–5; Mack Walker, *Germany and the Emigration, 1816–1885,* pp. 171–73; Oscar Handlin, *The Uprooted,* pp. 255–68. For a comprehensive study of the influence of Neo-Malthusianism, racism and eugenics on American immigration policy, see Allan Chase, *The Legacy of Malthus.*

34. William E. Tate, *The Enclosure Movement,* p. 31.

Chapter 6
The Irish Famine

1. See Cecil Woodham-Smith, *The Great Hunger: Ireland, 1845–1849,* pp. 411–12 (1980 ed.). At the beginning of this chapter, I wish to acknowledge my profound indebtedness to Woodham-Smith for my understanding and interpretation of the Irish famine.

2. See William L. Langer, "Europe's Initial Population Explosion," *American Historical Review,* Vol. 69, No. 1 (Oct. 1963), pp. 1–17; Langer, "American Foods and Europe's Population Growth 1750–1850," *Journal of Social History,* No. 1, Winter, (1975), pp. 57–66; Redcliffe N. Salaman, "The Influence of the Potato on the Course of Irish History," (Tenth Finlay Memorial Lecture Delivered at University College, Dublin); Salaman, *The History and Social Influence of the Potato.*

3. G. Talbot Griffith, *Population Problems in the Age of Malthus;* Woodham-Smith, op. cit., pp. 35–6.

4. Griffith, op. cit., p. 50.

5. Ibid.

6. See R. B. McDowell, "Ireland on the Eve of the Famine," in R. Dudley Edwards and T. Desmond Williams, *The Great Famine: Studies in Irish History 1845–52,* pp. 66ff. Oliver Macdonagh, *Ireland: The Union and Its Aftermath,* p. 22.

7. Woodham-Smith, op. cit., p. 22.

8. Nassau Senior, *On the Third Report of the Commissioners for Inquiry into the Conditions of the Poor in Ireland,* H. C. (House of Commons), 1837 (90), Vol. LI, p. 245; cited by Woodham-Smith, op. cit., p. 32.

9. See E. R. R. Green, "Agriculture," in Edwards and Williams, op. cit., pp. 92–93; Woodham-Smith, op. cit., p. 34.

10. Griffith, op. cit., pp. 34–5.

11. Woodham-Smith, op. cit., p. 38.

12. Salaman, *The History and Social Influence of the Potato,* p. 292. Woodham-Smith, op. cit., pp. 54–55.

13. Thomas P. O'Neill, "The Organisation and Administration of Relief, 1845–52," in Edwards and Williams, op. cit., p. 213; Woodham-Smith, op. cit., p. 74.

14. See letter of Sir R(andall) Routh to Mr. Pennefather, April 6, 1846, Great Britain, Treasury, *Correspondence Explanatory of the Measures Adopted by*

Her Majesty's Government for the Relief of Distress Arising from the Failure of the Potato Crop in Ireland: Presented to both Houses of Parliament by Command of Her Majesty, (London: W. Clowes and Sons: 1846), p. 90. Hereafter referred to as *Correspondence.* See also Woodham-Smith, op. cit., pp. 71–2.

15. Woodham-Smith, op. cit., pp. 319–20.

16. Lord Londonderry, House of Lords, March 30, 1846, Hansard, Vol. 85, p. 273, cited by Woodham-Smith, op. cit., p. 72.

17. Lord Brougham, House of Lords, March 23, 1846, Hansard, Vol. 84, pp. 1396–97, cited by Woodham-Smith, op. cit., loc. cit.

18. Woodham-Smith, op. cit., p. 55.

19. Eric J. Hobsbawm, *The Age of Revolution, 1789–1848,* p. 61. See also Kevin B. Nowlan, "The Political Background," in Edwards and Williams, op. cit., pp. 138–41.

20. Woodham-Smith, op. cit., p. 62.

21. Woodham-Smith, op. cit., p. 63.

22. See Woodham-Smith, op. cit., pp. 415–6.

23. Woodham-Smith, op. cit., pp. 85–87.

24. Woodham-Smith, op. cit., p. 111.

25. Woodham-Smith, op. cit., pp. 112–13.

26. Woodham-Smith, op. cit., pp. 144, 155–6.

27. Woodham-Smith, op. cit., p. 120.

28. Letter of Sir R. Routh to Mr. Trevelyan, June 24, 1846, *Correspondence,* p. 176.

29. Woodham-Smith, op. cit., p. 121. Russell was also concerned lest government action in Ireland cause food prices to rise in England. See G. P. Gooch, ed. *The Later Correspondence of Lord John Russell,* Vol. 1, p. 156.

30. O'Neill, op. cit., in Edwards and Williams, op. cit., p. 228. Woodham-Smith, op. cit., p. 185.

31. Woodham-Smith, op. cit., p. 288. O'Neill, op. cit., in Edwards and Williams, op. cit., p. 234.

32. Sir William L. MacArthur, "Medical History of the Famine" in Edwards and Williams, op. cit., p. 272; Woodham-Smith, op. cit., pp. 198–205.

33. Woodham-Smith, op. cit., p. 368.

34. Anthony Trollope, *The Three Clerks,* pp. 59–69. For Trevelyan's own account of the famine, see Sir Charles Edward Trevelyan, *The Irish Crisis,* (reprinted from the *Edinburgh Review,* No. 175, January 1848).

35. See Charles E. Trevelyan and Stafford H. Northcote, *Papers Relating to the Reorganisation of the Civil Service Presented to Both Houses of Parliament;* Woodham-Smith, op. cit., p. 415; O'Neill, op. cit., in Edwards and Williams, op. cit., p. 214.

36. See George Otto Trevelyan, *Life and Letters of Lord Macaulay,* pp. 278f; cited by Woodham-Smith, op. cit., p. 59.

37. Woodham-Smith, op. cit., p. 156.

38. Woodham-Smith, op. cit., p. 133.

39. Woodham-Smith, op. cit., pp. 123–24.

40. Woodham-Smith, op. cit., p. 125.

41. Woodham-Smith, op. cit., p. 162. On Skibbereen see also, O'Neill, op. cit., in Edwards and Williams, op. cit., pp. 232–33.

42. Nicholas Cummins, Letter to *The Times,* December 24, 1846; cited by Woodham-Smith, loc. cit.; Woodham-Smith, op. cit., pp. 161–4.

43. For Trevelyan's expression of satisfaction at the mass emigration, see Woodham-Smith, op. cit., pp. 375–76. Trevelyan's letter to Lord Monteagle is quoted by O'Neill, op. cit., in Edwards and Williams, op. cit., p. 257.

44. Letter of Trevelyan to Edward B. Twistleton, September 14, 1848, quoted by Woodham-Smith, op. cit., p. 371.

45. Woodham-Smith, op. cit., p. 374.

46. Charles Cavendish Fulke Greville, *The Greville Memoirs,* ed. Lytton Strachey and Roger Fulford (London: Macmillan, 1938), Vol. 6, p. 156.

47. Woodham-Smith, op. cit., p. 379.

48. Woodham-Smith, op. cit., p. 380.

49. Letter of Lord Clarendon (George William Frederick Villiers, Fourth Earl of Clarendon) to Lord John Russell, April 26, 1848, quoted by Woodham-Smith, op. cit., p. 381. At the time Clarendon was Lord Lieutenant of Ireland.

50. Between January 1, 1847, and December 31, 1854, "no less than 1,656,044 people left Ireland for North America." Of this number, 1,300,000 emigrated to the United States. See Stanley C. Johnson, *A History of Emigration: From the United Kingdom to North America, 1763–1812,* p. 50; for a historical survey of Irish emigration, see Oliver MacDonaugh, "Irish Emigration to the United States of America and the British Colonies During the Famine," in Edwards and Williams, op. cit., pp. 319–388; see also Woodham-Smith, op. cit., p. 206.

51. Woodham-Smith, op. cit., p. 276.

52. Woodham-Smith, op. cit., p. 271.

53. For a general picture of the hostility of the English, especially the English working class, toward the Irish emigrants see E. P. Thompson, *The Making*

of the English Working Class, pp. 429–44. On the reception of the emigrants in England, see Woodham-Smith, op. cit., pp. 276–84.

54. Woodham-Smith, op. cit., pp. 278–79.

55. Woodham-Smith, op. cit., p. 208.

56. See MacDonaugh, op. cit. in Edwards and Williams, op. cit., pp. 359–368; see also Woodham-Smith, op. cit., p. 212.

57. See H. J. M. Johnston, *British Emigration Policy, 1815–1830: "Shoveling Out the Paupers,"* pp. 101–30 and 131–157.

58. On the reception of the Irish in the United States, see MacDonaugh, op. cit., in Edwards and Williams, op. cit., pp. 376–87. On American immigration restrictions, see Johnston, op. cit., pp. 131–57.

59. Woodham-Smith, op. cit., p. 215.

60. Woodham-Smith, op. cit., pp. 214–38; see also MacDonaugh, op. cit., in Edwards and Williams, op. cit., pp. 370–74.

61. Marcus Lee Hansen, *The Atlantic Migration: 1607–1860,* pp. 256–261.

62. "Effects of Emigration on Production and Consumption," *The Economist,* February 12, 1853, Vol. 11, No. 494, pp. 168–69. *The Economist* reflected the views of a very important segment of the British establishment and tended to see the Irish as responsible for their own misfortune. *The Economist,* regarded mass emigration as a necessary corrective to the problems of Ireland. See, for example, "The Poor of Ireland," op. cit., June 28, 1851 and "The New Drug for Irish Maladies," *The Economist,* October 4, 1851. There was also an element of smug anti-Catholicism in *The Economist*'s treatment of Ireland's problems. The Irish were regarded as primitive and incompetent, priest-ridden members of an inferior race. See, for example, "The Irish Priesthood and the Irish Laity," *The Economist,* June 19, 1852.

63. See Peter Berger, *Pyramids of Sacrifice: Political Ethics and Social Change.*

64. Woodham-Smith, op. cit., pp. 407–10.

65. For a study of the British military in the Crimean War, see Cecil Woodham-Smith, *The Reason Why.*

66. See Martin Middlebrook, *The First Day on the Somme.*

67. G. Talbot Griffith, *Population Problems,* p. 50. For an influential English statement of the desirability of diluting the Roman Catholic component of Ireland's population, see "The Irish Priesthood and the Irish Laity," *The Economist,* June 19, 1852.

68. On British policy towards the Jews of Europe immediately before and during World War II, see Bernard Wasserstein, *Britain and the Jews,* pp. 54ff; Martin Gilbert, *Exile and Return: The Struggle for a Jewish Homeland,* pp. 236ff; Leni Yahil, "Select British Documents on the Illegal Immigration to Palestine (1939–1940)" in *Yad Vashem Studies,* No. 10, pp. 241–76.

69. Raul Hilberg, *The Destruction of the European Jews,* p. 771.

Chapter 7
The Unmastered Trauma:
The Elimination of the European Jews

1. See Raul Hilberg, *The Destruction of the European Jews,* pp. 1-16; Richard L. Rubenstein, *After Auschwitz,* pp. 1-21.

2. See Hilberg, op. cit., pp. 11ff.

3. The literature on this subject is voluminous. See Franklin H. Littell, *The Crucifixion of the Jews,* pp. 24-43. See also Rosemary Reuther, *Faith and Fratricide: The Theological Roots of Anti-Semitism;* Malcolm Hay, *Europe and the Jews: The Pressure of Cristendom on the People of Israel for 1900 Years;* Rudolph M. Loewenstein, *Christians and Jews: A Psychoanalytic Study.*

4. Hilberg, op. cit., p. 16.

5. See Richard L. Rubenstein, "Response to the Issue on Judaism and Psycho-History of the Journal of Psycho-history," *Journal of Psycho-History,* Spring 1979.

6. See Richard L. Rubenstein, op. cit., pp. 61-82.

7. A characteristic example of this approach is to be found in Lucy Dawidowicz, *The War Against the Jews, 1933-1945.* See p. 221 where she characterizes post-World War I German anti-Semitism as a "delusional disorder" involving "pathological fantasies about the Jews." She also describes anti-Semitism as a "mass psychosis" which "deranged a whole people." Earlier examples include Nathan Ackerman and Marie Jahoda, *Anti-Semitism and Emotional Disorder;* T. W. Adorno, Else Frenkel-Brunswick, Daniel J. Levinson and R. Nevitt Sanford, *The Authoritarian Personality;* Otto Fenichel, "The Psycho-analysis of Anti-Semitism," *American Imago,* Vol. 1 (1940), pp. 24-39. See also Florence R. Miale and Michael Selzer, *The Nuremberg Mind: The Psychology of the Nazi Leders* (New York: Quadrangle, 1975). (For a critical rejoinder to *The Nuremberg Mind,* see Richard L. Rubenstein, "The Psychology of the Nazi Leaders," *Psychology Today,* July 1976. Max Horkheimer and Theodore Adorno, "Elements of Anti-Semitism," in *Dialectic of Enlightenment,* trans. John Cumming, pp. 168-208.

8. Among the works in which the theory of cognitive dissonance is discussed are: Leon Festinger, Henry W. Riecken, and Stanley Schachter, *When Prophecy Fails;* Festinger, *A Theory of Cognitive Dissonance;* Festinger, *Conflict, Decision and Dissonance;* Robert Abelson, ed., *Theories of Cognitive Dissonance;* Eliot Aronson, *The Social Animal;* Aronson, "The Rationalizing Animal," *Psychology Today,* May 1973; Anthony Greenwald and David L. Ronis, "Twenty Years of Cognitive Dissonance: A Case Study of the Evolution of a Theory," *Psychology Review,* Vol. 85, January 1978.

9. Festinger, "Cognitive Dissonance," *Scientific American,* Vol. 207 (October 1962).

10. Ibid.

11. The dissonance-reduction role of the theologian is especially manifest in the career of Nathan of Gaza, the theologian of the Sabbatian movement, a Jewish messianic movement of the seventeenth century. Nathan argued that the startling conversion of the Jewish "Messiah" Sabbatai Zvi to Islam was indispensable to the fulfillment of his messianic role. See Gershom Scholem, *Sabbatai Sevi: The Mystical Messiah, 1626-1676,* pp. 197-326. It is the conviction of this writer that Paul of Tarsus was also engaging in dissonance-reduction in passages such as the following: "but we proclaim Christ-yes, Christ nailed to the cross: and though this is a stumbling-block to Jews and folly to the Greeks, yet to those who have heard his call, Jews and Greeks alike, he is the power of God, and the wisdom of God..." (I Cor. 1:23, 24).

12. See Harold D. Lasswell, Daniel Lerner, and C. E. Rothwell, *The Comparative Study of Elites: An Introduction and Bibliography,* Hoover Institute Studies.

13. See Max Weber, *Economy and Society,* ed. Guenther Roth and Claus Wittich, Vol. 2, p. 613.

14. For a neglected but singularly important interpretation of Jewish economic history, see Abram Leon, *The Jewish Question: A Marxist Interpretation.* For critical reviews of the Leon thesis, see Oscar Handlin, "Does Economics Explain Racism," *Commentary,* Vol. 6, No. 1 (July 1948), pp. 79-85; Werner J. Cahnman, "Socio-Economic Causes of Antisemitism," *Social Problems,* Vol. 5, No. 1, July 1957. On the economic history of the Jews, see also article "Economic History," *Encyclopaedia Judaica,* Vol. 13, pp. 1295-1325.

15. Article "Population," in *Encyclopaedia Judaica,* Vol. 13, pp. 889-92.

16. See Stephan Kieniewicz, *The Emancipation of the Polish Peasantry,* pp. 140-90.

17. See Edward Crankshaw, *The Shadow of the Winter Palace: The Drift to Revolution, 1825-1917,* pp. 197ff; David Vital, *The Origins of Zionism,* p. 49.

18. Articles "Poland," *Encyclopaedia Judaica,* Vol. 13, pp. 735-36.

19. Leon, op. cit., p. 228.

20. Ibid.

21. Article "Poland," op. cit., Vol. 13, pp. 735-40.

22. Ibid.

23. Leon, op. cit., p. 206.

24. Leon, op. cit., p. 207.

25. See Vital, op. cit., p. 52; S. Ettinger, "Anti-Semitism as Official Government Policy in Eastern Europe," H. H. Ben-Sasson, ed., *A History of the Jewish People,* pp. 881-90. Howard M. Sachar, *The Course of Modern Jewish History,* pp. 240-46. For an older, but still useful, account of the events of 1881 and their aftermath, see Louis Greenberg, *The Jews in Russia,* Vol. 2, pp. 1-75.

26. Vital, op. cit., p. 54.

27. Crankshaw, op. cit., pp. 333–34.

28. See Stephen M. Berk, "The Russian Revolutionary Movement and the Pogroms of 1881–1882," *Soviet Jewish Affairs*, Vol. 7, No. 2 (1977), pp. 22–39; Article "Pogroms," *Encyclopaedia Judaica*, Vol. 13, pp. 695–98; Vital, op. cit., p. 56.

29. Statistics on Jewish immigration are to be found in Mark Wischnitzer, *To Dwell in Safety: The Story of Jewish Migration Since 1800*, p. 289; Leon, op. cit., p. 200; Sachar, op. cit., p. 306. For an overall view of the great European migration to the United States, see Handlin, *The Uprooted*, second edition.

30. Vital, op. cit., p. 59.

31. Alexander III, "The May Laws (May 3, 1882)," Paul R. Mendes-Flohr and Jehuda Reinharz, eds., *The Jew In the Modern World: A Documentary History*, p. 309; Sachar, op. cit., pp. 244–45.

32. Article "May Laws," *Encyclopaedia Judaica*, Vol. 11, pp. 1147–48.

33. Sachar, op. cit., p. 245.

34. Crankshaw, op. cit., p. 331. For a biography of Pobedonostsev, see R. F. Byrnes, *Pobedonostsev*. See also Greenberg, op. cit., pp. 1–3.

35. See Manuel Sarkisyanz, *A Modern History of Transcaucasian Armenia*, p. 142.

36. James H. Billington, *The Icon and The Axe: An Interpretive History of Russian Culture*, p. 441.

37. Sachar, op. cit., p. 246; Article "Pobedonostsev," *Encyclopaedia Judaica*, Vol. 13, p. 663.

38. See Carl Schorske, *Fin-de-Siècle Vienna: Politics and Culture*, p. 128. On the impact of industrial capitalism on the lower middle class, see Theodore S. Hamerow, *Restoration, Revolution, Reaction: Economics and Politics in Germany, 1815–1871*, pp. 3–94; Hamerow, *The Social Foundations of German Unification 1858–1871* (Princeton: Princeton University Press, 1972), pp. 49–97.

39. Hans Rosenberg, "Political and Social Consequences of the Great Depression of 1873–1896 in Central Europe," in James J. Sheehan, ed., *Imperial Germany*, p. 45. See also Martin Kitchen, *The Political Economy of Germany 1815–1914* (London: Croom Helm, 1978), pp. 161–179; Ismar Schorsch, *Jewish Reactions to German Anti-Semitism, 1870–1914*, pp. 36ff.

40. Adolf Stoecker's first anti-Semitic speech, delivered at the Christian Social Workers' Party on September 19, 1879, is reprinted in Paul Massing, *Rehearsal for Destruction: A Study of Political Anti-Semitism in Imperial Germany*, pp. 278–287; see also pp. 21–36; Ernst Nolte, "Germany," in Hans Rogger and Eugen Weber, eds., *The European Right: A Historical Profile*, pp. 287ff.

41. Sachar, op. cit., p. 224; Heinrich von Treitschke, "A Word About Our Jewry," in Mendes-Flohr and Reinharz, op. cit., pp. 280–84.

344448

42. Andrew Whiteside, "Austria" in Rogger and Weber, op. cit., p. 318. For a brief but illuminating study of Schoenerer, see Schorske, op. cit., pp. 120-33.
43. See Celia S. Heller, *On the Edge Of Destruction: Jews of Poland Between Two World Wars,* pp. 118-24; Geoffrey Pridham, *Hitler's Rise to Power: The Nazi Movement in Bavaria, 1923-1933,* pp. 209-15.
44. Article "Vienna," *Encyclopaedia Judaica,* Vol. 16, p. 1247. See Leon, op. cit., p. 215.
45. Article "Berlin," *Encyclopaedia Judaica,* Vol. 4, p. 644.
46. Schorske, op. cit., p. 129.
47. Rogger and Weber, op. cit., pp. 312-14.
48. For a comprehensive study of German emigration during the nineteenth century, see Mack Walker, *Germany and the Emigration, 1816-1885.* On the character of the emigration during the Bismarck period, see Walker, op. cit., pp. 175-194.
49. Ibid.
50. See George L. Mosse, *Toward the Final Solution: A History of European Racism,* p. 177ff.
51. Hegel, *Philosophy of Right,* addition to par. 182.
52. Hegel, op. cit., par. 187.
53. A. J. Ryder, *Twentieth-Century Germany: From Bismarck to Brandt,* p. 40.
54. Handlin, op. cit., p. 32.
55. A. M. Carr-Sanders, *World Population,* pp. 49ff.
56. Robert L. Waite, *The Psychopathic God: Adolf Hitler,* p. 73.
57. Adolf Hitler, *Mein Kampf,* trans. Ralph Mannheim, pp. 641ff.
58. Waite, op. cit., p. 11.
59. On the National Socialist elite, Karl Dietrich Bracher, *The German Dictatorship,* pp. 272-86.
60. See Allan Mitchell, *Revolution in Bavaria.* See also Richard Grunberger, *Red Rising in Bavaria.*
61. See Robert Pois, Introduction to Alfred Rosenberg, *Race and Race History,* pp. 15f.
62. On the wartime attitude of Pope Pius XII to National Socialist Germany, see Saul Friedlander, *Pius XII and the Third Reich: A Documentation,* trans. Charles Fullman, pp. 174-96.
63. Hitler, op. cit., pp. 622-24.
64. Heinrich von Treitschke, "A Word about Our Jewry," in Mendes-Flohr and Reinharz, op. cit., p. 281. On the impact of Jewish immigration, see also Arthur J. May, *The Hapsburg Monarchy, 1867-1914,* pp. 178-80.
65. Hannah Arendt, *The Origins of Totalitarianism,* pp. 275ff. See also Richard L. Rubenstein, *The Cunning of History,* pp. 14ff.

66. Ryder, op. cit., p. 345.

67. Congressional Committee on Immigration, *Temporary Suspension of Immigration,* Sixty-sixth Congress, Third Session, House of Representatives, Report no. 1109, December 6, 1920.

68. Sachar, op. cit., pp. 313–4.

69. See Heller, op. cit., pp. 101–7.

70. Article "Poland," *Encyclopaedia Judaica,* Vol. 13, pp. 739–49.

71. Quoted in Heller, op. cit., p. 113.

72. Heller, op. cit., pp. 136–39.

73. Cited by Edward D. Wynot, Jr., "A Necessary Cruelty: The Emergence of Official Anti-Semitism in Poland, 1936–39," *The American Historical Review,* Vol. 76, No. 4 (October 1971), p. 1057.

74. Heller, op. cit., p. 295.

75. Adolf Hitler, Letter to Staff-Captain Karl Mayr, September 16, 1919, in Werner Maser, ed., *Hitler's Letters and Notes* (New York: Harper and Row, 1974), p. 211.

76. Waite, op. cit., p. 373.

77. Eliot, op. cit., p. 23.

78. Waite, loc. cit.

79. For a scholarly survey of Marxist views on Jews and Judaism, see Julius Carlebach, *Karl Marx and the Radical Critique of Judaism.*

Chapter 8
The Agony of Indochina

1. François Ponchaud, *Cambodia Year Zero,* trans. Nancy Amphoux, p. 66. On the Kampuchean genocide, see also John Barron and Anthony Paul, *Murder of a Gentle Land: The Untold Story of Communist Genocide in Cambodia;* William Shawcross, *Sideshow: Kissinger, Nixon and the Destruction of Cambodia,* pp. 365–392; Pierre Rousset, "Cambodia: Background to the Revolution," *Journal of Contemporary Asia,* Vol. 7, No. 4 (1977), pp. 513–28; Leo Kuper, *Genocide: Its Political Use in The Twentieth Century,* pp. 154–60, 170–73. For a terse description of the conduct of the Pol Pot regime following the fall of Phnom Penh on April 17, 1975, see United Nations, Commission on Human Rights, Subcommission on Prevention of Discrimination and Protection of Minorities (ECN./4/1335, dated January

30, 1979). This description is quoted in Kuper, op. cit., pp. 155–6. See also Peter J. Donaldson, "In Cambodia, A Holocaust Clearly," *New York Times,* April 22, 1980; United States Senate, Hearings before the Committee on Judiciary, Hearing on Cambodian Crisis, October 31, 1979. For a defense of the behavior of the Pol Pot regime, see George C. Hildebrand and Gareth Porter, *Cambodia: Starvation and Revolution* and David Kline, *The New Face of Kampuchea.* For an informed rebuttal of the Kline volume, see Nayan Chandas, "A Fairy Tale of Kampuchea," *Far Eastern Economic Review,* July 20, 1979, p. 43.

2. Bruce Grant, et. al., *The Boat People: An "Age" Investigation with Bruce Grant,* pp. 12–14.

3. Grant, op. cit., p. 160.

4. Grant, op. cit., p. 20.

5. Grant, op. cit., p. 22.

6. Colin McEvedy and Richard Jones, *Atlas of World Population History,* p. 196.

7. Grant, op. cit., p. 23.

8. Ponchaud, op. cit., p. 64.

9. Grant, op. cit., p. 23.

10. Barry Wain, *The Refused: The Agony of the Indochinese Refugees,* p. 49. (Pagination of the Wain book refers to publisher's page proofs. I was unable to secure a copy of the published volume before going to press.)

11. Grant, op. cit., pp. 26–28.

12. Grant, op. cit., p. 25.

13. Wain, op. cit., p. 47.

14. Bernard Weinraub, "In Vietnam, Tears as the Past Is Remembered," *New York Times,* December 27, 1981.

15. Grant, op. cit., pp. 215–17.

16. See D. Stanley Eitzen, "Two Minorities: The Jews of Poland and the Chinese of the Philippines," *Jewish Journal of Sociology,* December 10, 1968, pp. 221–38.

17. Grant, op. cit., pp. 82ff. On ethnic conflict in Southeast Asia, see Cynthia H. Enloe, "Ethnic Diversity: The Potential For Conflict," in Guy J. Pauker, Frank H. Golay and Cynthia Enloe, *Diversity and Development in Southeast Asia: The Coming Decade,* pp. 137–82. (This book is part of the 1980s Project of the Council on Foreign Relations.) See also Stephen Fitzgerald, *China and the Overseas Chinese.* On Thailand's response to Southeast Asian ethnic conflict, see Richard Nations, "Battle for the Hearts and Stomachs," *Far Eastern Economic Review,* December 7, 1979. Incidentally, the *Far Eastern Economic Review,* published in Hong Kong, is one of the most reliable sources of information on the economic, political, and social problems of East Asia.

18. There are interesting parallels between the situation of the ethnic Chinese in Vietnam after Hanoi's victory and that of the Jews in Poland after that country gained its independence in 1918. On the Jews in Poland, see, Celia S. Heller, *On the Edge of Destruction: Jews of Poland Between Two World Wars.*

19. Grant, op. cit., pp. 97–98; Wain, op. cit., p. 74.

20. Wain, op. cit., p. 76.

21. Wain, op. cit., p. 93.

22. Wain, op. cit., p. 75.

23. Wain, op. cit., p. 78.

24. Grant, op. cit., p. 156; Wain, op. cit., p. 87.

25. Grant, op. cit., pp. 90–91.

26. Grant, op. cit., p. 93.

27. Wain, op. cit., p. 92.

28. Wain, op. cit., p. 159.

29. Emily MacFarquar, "The Survivors Who Seek Their Place in Paradise," *The Economist,* July 21, 1979, p. 20.

30. On the employment of bureaucratic agencies in population elimination programs, see Richard L. Rubenstein, *The Cunning of History,* pp. 22–35.

31. Guy Sacerdoti, "How Hanoi Cashes In," *Far Eastern Economic Review,* June 15, 1979, pp. 24–26; "Pointing the Finger at Hanoi," *Far Eastern Economic Review,* August 3, 1979 (unsigned article), pp. 20–21; Richard Nations, "Hanoi's Test of Civilization," *Far Eastern Economic Review,* August 3, 1979; Grant, op. cit., pp. 102–4, 110.

32. Wain, op. cit., pp. 102–5; Grant, op. cit., pp. 110ff.

33. "Pointing the Finger at Hanoi," *Far Eastern Economic Review,* August 3, 1979, pp. 20–1.

34. Mary Lee, "Ill Winds Over Fragrant Harbour" in *Far Eastern Economic Review,* May 25, 1979, pp. 14–18. (Hong Kong means "fragrant harbor" in Chinese.)

35. Emily MacFarquar, op. cit., p. 24. See also K. Das and Guy Sacerdoti, "Economics of a Human Cargo," *Far Eastern Economic Review,* December 22, 1978, p. 10.

36. Grant, op. cit., pp. 116–23.

37. On the Thai pirates, see Bernard Nossiter, "Thai Piracy Against Boat People Seems Relentless," *New York Times,* May 7, 1980; "Vietnamese Refugees: From One Horror to Another," *The Economist,* February 9, 1980, p. 63; Barbara Crossette, "Pirates Continue Brutal Attacks on Vietnam Refugees," *New York Times,* January 10, 1982; "Excerpts From U.S. Account of Refugee's Ordeal," *New York Times,* January 10, 1982; Grant, op. cit., pp. 15, 18, 63–67; See editorial, "How Not to Deter Refugees: By Allowing Them to Be Murdered By Pirates," *The Economist,* May 29, 1982, p. 16.

38. See "The Tragedy of the KG 0729," *Far Eastern Economic Review,* December 22, 1978, p. 13; Grant, op. cit., p. 64; Wain, op. cit., pp. 83–4.

39. Crossette, loc. cit.

40. K. Das, "An Accidental Deterrent," *Far Eastern Economic Review,* April 22, 1979, pp. 22–23.

41. Grant, op. cit., p. 64; Wain, op. cit., p. 83.

42. Wain, loc. cit.; Crossette, loc. cit.

43. See Rubenstein, op. cit., pp. 12ff.

44. See Emily MacFarquar, op. cit., p. 20.

45. "The Khmers Who Couldn't Look Back" in *The Economist,* July 21, 1979, p. 21; Richard Nations, "The Incident that Jarred Waldheim," *Far Eastern Economic Review,* May 25, 1979, p. 20.

46. Wain, op. cit., p. 244ff.

47. Cited by Wain, op. cit., p. 163.

48. K. Das, op. cit., pp. 22–23; Grant, op. cit., p. 72; Wain, op. cit., pp. 7, 246.

49. Grant, op. cit., p. 73.

50. Emily MacFarquar, op. cit., p. 21.

51. On Pulau Bildong, see K. Das and Guy Sacerdoti, "Digging in for a Long Stay," *Far Eastern Economic Review,* December 22, 1978, pp. 11ff; MacFarquar, op. cit., p. 19; David Jenkins, "An Island in the Stream," *Far Eastern Economic Review,* May 25, 1979, pp. 14–20.

52. Wain, op. cit., p. 254.

53. See Mary Lee, "Free Port or Free-for-All," *Far Eastern Economic Review,* October 5, 1979. See also Mary Lee, "Ill Winds Over Fragrant Harbour," op. cit., pp. 14–18.

54. Grant, op. cit., p. 70.

55. Grant, op. cit., pp. 68, 70ff; Wain, op. cit., p. 233.

56. Michael Richardson, "How Many Died?" *Far Eastern Economic Review,* October 26, 1979.

57. See "Indonesia: Facing a Liquid Auschwitz," *Time,* July 2, 1979, pp. 38f; "Save Us! Save Us!" *Time,* July 9, 1979, pp. 28ff. "Agony of the Boat People," *Newsweek,* July 2, 1982, pp. 42–50; Wain, op. cit., p. 234.

58. Wain, op. cit., p. 280.

59. Wain, op. cit., p. 275.

60. Wain, op. cit., p. 309.

61. Grant, op. cit., pp. 153f.

62. See A. J. Ryder, *Twentieth-Century Germany from Bismarck to Brandt,* pp. 458–59.

63. John McBeth, "A Perilously Short Fuse," *Far Eastern Economic Review,* June 15, 1979, p. 26. Singapore's Foreign Minister, Sinnathamby Rajaratnam

observed, "A poor man's alternative to the gas chambers is the open sea;" cited by Wain, op. cit., p. 189.

64. The story of the St. Louis is told in Gordon Thomas and Max Morgan Witts, *Voyage of the Damned.*

65. Bernard Wasserstein, *Britain and the Jews of Europe, 1939–1945,* pp. 54ff.

66. Grant, op. cit., p. 79.

Chapter 9
Reflections on the Age of Triage

1 See Stuart W. Hinds, "On the Relation of Medical Triage to World Hunger: An Historical Survey," in George R. Lucas, Jr., and Thomas W. Ogletree, eds., *Lifeboat Ethics: The Moral Dilemmas of World Hunger,* pp. 31–4.

2. *Stedman's Medical Dictionary,* cited by Hinds, op. cit., p. 31.

3. Henry Beecher, *Research and the Individual,* pp. 209–10.

4. Peter Ritchie-Calder, "Triage = Genocide," *Center Report,* June, 1975. See also William and Paul Paddock, "The Thesis of Triage" in *Famine 1975: America's Decision: Who Will Survive?* pp. 206–29; Wade Green, "Triage: Who Shall Be Fed? Who Shall Starve?" *New York Times Magazine,* January 5, 1975; Alan Berg, "The Trouble with Triage," *New York Times Magazine,* June 15, 1975.

5. This view has been advanced most vigorously by the noted biologist, Garrett Hardin. See "Lifeboat Ethics: The Case against Helping the Poor," *Psychology Today,* September, 1974. See also Hardin, "Another Face of Bioethics: The Case for Massive 'Diebacks of Population,'" *Modern Medicine,* March 1, 1975, and Hardin, "The Toughlove Solution," *Newsweek,* October 26, 1981. See also Wayne Bartz, "Outrageous Solutions to the Population Outrage," in Edward Pohlman, ed., *Population: A Clash of Prophets,* p. 297.

6. Ritchie-Calder, loc. cit.

7. Hinds, op. cit., pp. 46ff.

8. For an important analysis of the welfare policies of the Reagan administration, see Francis Fox Piven and Richard A. Cloward, *The New Class War: Reagan's Attack on the New Welfare State and its Consequences.* For an indispensable guide to the politics of welfare, see Piven and Cloward, *Regulating the*

Poor: The Functions of Public Welfare. See Nick Kotz, "The War on the Poor," *The New Republic,* March 24, 1982.

9. This is evident when one considers the cuts being proposed in the 1983–1984 federal budget for programs such as the Aid to Families with Dependent Children and Food Stamps. These programs had already suffered severe cuts in the budget of the previous year. The 1982–1983 budget for AFDC was $6,600,000,000; the amount proposed for 1983–1984 is $5,500,000,000, a cut of 16.7 percent. The 1982–1983 budget for the Food Stamp program was $11,800,000,000; the amount proposed for 1983–1984 is $9,600,000,000, a decrease of 18.6 percent. When inflation is taken into account, the cuts are actually much more severe. See "Those Budget Cuts: Who'll Be Hit Hardest" in *U.S. News and World Report,* August 10, 1981.

10. See "Many Do Not Get Counted," *Time,* February 8, 1982, p. 29.

11. See "Reagan's Polarized America," *Newsweek,* April 5, 1982, pp. 17ff.

12. See William E. Tate, *The Enclosure Movement,* pp. 81ff.

13. See Anne McDougall, "Back to School at 35 and Over," *U.S. Government Special Labor Force Report: October, 1978* (Washington: U.S. Department of Labor and Statistics).

14. McDougall, loc. cit.

15. Ronald H. Miller, "A Decade of Data on Adult Learners," *College Board Review,* Winter 1979–1980.

16. See Derek C. Bok, "Student Aid and the Public Interest," *Harvard Magazine,* May-June, 1982, pp. 43–49, 74–79. (This is the President's Annual Report to the Board of Overseers of Harvard University.)

17. Ibid.

18. See "The Speedup in Automation," *Business Week,* August 3, 1981, pp. 58–67. I am indebted to Professor Theodore Chiricos of Florida State University for calling this special report to my attention. For an overall survey of the changing worldwide patterns of employment, see "Where Will the Jobs Come From?" *The Economist,* January 3, 1981, pp. 45–62.

19. "Speedup," op. cit., p. 61.

20. Booz, Allen, and Hamilton, Inc., *The Impact of Robotics on the Workforce and Workplace.* See also Barnaby J. Feder, "Robots Enter the Limelight," *New York Times,* March 4, 1982, and Phillip R. Lynch, "Deus Ex Machina," *New York Times,* April 26, 1982.

21. "Speedup," op. cit., p. 62.

22. See Emma Rothschild, "Reagan and the Real America," *The New York Review of Books,* February 6, 1981, p. 12. Ms. Rothschild has taken this figure from U.S. Department of Labor, *Employment and Earnings,* March 1980, Table B-1.

23. On the transfer of manufacturing operations by multinational corporations

see, Richard J. Barnet and Ronald E. Muller, *Global Reach: The Power of the Multi-National Corporations.* See especially the chapter entitled "The Obsolescence of American Labor," pp. 303–333. See also Iver Peterson, "U.S. Auto Makers Using More Mexico Plants," *New York Times,* July 19, 1982, Section 1, Page 1.

24. See Piven and Cloward, *New Class War,* pp. 37–9; George Gilder, *Wealth and Poverty;* Robert Pear, "Three Key Aides Reshape Welfare Policy," *New York Times,* April 26, 1982.

25. See James Tobin, "Reagonomics and Economics," *The New York Review of Books,* December 3, 1981, pp. 1–4 and Piven and Cloward, op. cit., pp. 26ff.

26. See Piven and Cloward, op. cit., pp. 134ff.

27. Patrick Colquhoun, *A Treatise on Indigence,* pp. 6–7. In fairness to Colquhoun, it is important to note that he distinguished between poverty, which is the necessity of working for a living, and indigence, which is the inability to make a living at all. By Colquhoun's definition, most Americans would be classified as paupers but not indigents. Colquhoun did not oppose relief for the indigent. For a discussion of Colquhoun, see J. R. Poynter, *Society and Pauperism: English Ideas on Poor Relief, 1795–1834,* pp. 200–207.

28. Colquhoun, loc. cit.

29. Sidney and Beatrice Webb, *English Poor Law History: Part I, The Old Poor Law,* p. 403. This is Vol. 7 of the *Webbs' English Local Government.*

30. See Ken Auletta, *The Underclass;* see also "The American Underclass," *Time,* August 29, 1977 and "The Blackout Coverstories: Night of Terror," *Time,* July 25, 1977. See Joseph Treaster, "Crime at an Early Age: On the Violent Streets of Luis Guzman," *New York Times,* November 9, 1981.

31. G. W. F. Hegel, *Philosophy of Right,* trans. T. M. Knox, (first German edition was published in 1820), addition to par. 244.

32. Adam Smith, *The Wealth of Nations,* (Penguin edition), p. 119.

33. Piven and Cloward, *Regulating the Poor,* pp. 200ff; see Wayne D. Rasmussen, "The Mechanization of Agriculture," *Scientific American,* Vol. 247, No. 3 (September 1982), pp. 76–89.

34. See Piven and Cloward, op. cit., pp. 222ff.

35. Kai Erikson, *Wayward Puritans,* pp. 3ff. In his chapter "On the Sociology of Deviance," Erikson cites Emile Durkheim, *The Rules of Sociological Method,* trans. S. A. Solovay and J. H. Mueller, p. 67, who held that, by virtue of its capacity to define the boundaries of acceptable behavior, crime is "an integral part of all healthy societies." See also Jeffrey H. Reiman, *The Rich Get Richer and the Poor Get Prison: Ideology, Class, and Criminal Justice,* pp. 35–43.

36. For an important study on the relationship between unemployment and crime, see Theodore G. Chiricos and William M. Norton, "Unemployment, Welfare and Property Crime," unpublished paper to be presented at the Annual Meeting of the American Sociological Association, San Francisco, September

1982. See also Theodore G. Chiricos, "Rates of Crime and Unemployment: A Critical Review," presented at the annual meeting of the American Sociological Association, Toronto, September 1981.

37. Leonard Levin, *Triage.*
38. Levin, op. cit., p. 193.
39. Levin, op. cit., p. 194.
40. Levin, op. cit., p. 136.
41. Allen Tate, "The Problem of the Unemployed: A Modest Proposal," in *The American Review,* Vol. 1, No. 2 (May 1933). This article was called to my attention by Mr. Bill Moss, formerly a graduate student at Florida State University. On contemporary apprehension by American blacks that they may some day be targeted for extermination as a surplus population, see Samuel F. Yette, *The Choice: The Issue of Black Survival in America.* It is interesting to note that the title of the paperback edition was changed to "...*The Issue of Black Extermination in America."* For a sociological examination of the same theme, see Sidney M. Wilhelm, *Who Needs the Negro?* pp. 270–337.
42. Jonathan Swift, *A Modest Proposal for Preventing the Children of Poor People From Being a Burthen to Their Parents or Country, And for making them Beneficial to the Publick,* (1st ed. 1729).
43. See Elizabeth Hall and Paul Cameron, "Are We in Love with Death?" in *Psychology Today,* April 1976.
44. For a chilling view of the tradeoff between lives and profits in the construction and maintenance of modern airliners, see Paul Eddy, Elaine Potter, and Bruce Page, *Destination Disaster: From the Tri-Motor to the DC10: The Risk of Flying.* The authors are investigative reporters for *The Sunday Times* (London). See also "Ford Study: Death, Injury Cheaper than Fixing Cars," *Tallahassee Democrat,* October 14, 1979. This was a *Chicago Tribune* wire-service dispatch to the *Tallahassee Democrat.*
45. Cited in Allan Chase, *The Legacy of Malthus,* p. 6.
46. Lee Mays, "Reagan Expert Under Attack For Ties To Nazi War Criminal," *St. Petersburg Times,* April 25, 1982. The story is identified as having originated in the *Los Angeles Times.*
47. See C. B. Macpherson, *The Political Theory of Possessive Individualism: Hobbes to Locke,* pp. 222, 232.
48. As a member of the Commission on Trade, in 1697 Locke wrote that unemployment was caused by "nothing else but the relaxation of discipline and the corruption of morals." H. R. Fox Bourne, *The Life of John Locke,* Vol. 2, p. 578. I am indebted to Macpherson, op. cit., p. 223 for this reference. In fairness to Locke, it must be remembered that those who believed in the Protestant work ethic found it equally difficult to understand the worklessness of the overprivileged nobility and the underprivileged poor. Honest labor

constituted the means by which one fulfilled one's calling and served God in the world. Those who did not work were without a worldly means of serving God and were, at the very least, morally suspect. Thus, the Puritan theologian William Perkins (d. 1602) held that both the idle nobility and unemployed paupers were without a proper calling. Of the workless indigent, Perkins complained: "It is a foule disorder in any Commonwealth, that there should be suffered rogues, beggars, vagabonds; for such kind of persons commonly are of no civill societie or corporation, nor of any particular Church; and are rotten legges, and armes that droppe from the body." Cited by David Little, *Religion, Order, and Law,* pp. 119, 121.

49. R. H. Tawney, *Religion and the Rise of Capitalism,* p. 267; cited by Macpherson, op. cit., p. 228.

50. Christopher Hill, *Puritanism and Revolution,* pp. 228–29.

51. The colleague is Professor Leo Sandon, Director of the American Studies Program of Florida State University.

52. Howell Raines, "Reagan Order Tightens the Rules on Disclosing Secret Information," *New York Times,* April 4, 1982; "Excerpts from Executive Order on Secrecy Rules," *New York Times,* April 4, 1982; James C. Goodale and Lawrence M. Martin, "Will They Classify Even the Alphabet?" *New York Times,* April 11, 1982.

53. Max Weber, "Bureaucracy," *From Max Weber: Essays in Sociology,* ed. H. H. Gerth and C. Wright Mills, p. 233.

54. See Max Weber, *Sociology of Religion,* trans. Ephraim Fischoff, p. 148.

55. According to Andrew Carnegie, "neither the individual nor the race is improved by alms-giving," in "Wealth," *The North American Review,* Vol. 39 (June 1889), p. 663; cited by George Bedell, Leo Sandon, Jr. and Charles J. Wellborn, *Religion in America.* See also Walter I. Trattner, *From Poor Law to Welfare State: A History of Social Welfare in America,* pp. 50–55.

56. The term "preterition" refers to the passing over of the non-elect or non-election to salvation. The preterite are therefore those rejected by God. For the influence of Calvinism on non-Protestants, see E. Digby Baltzell, *Puritan Boston and Quaker Philadelphia: Two Protestant Ethics and the Spirit of Class Authority and Leadership,* pp. 417–32.

57. This point is made by David Bakan, *The Duality of Human Existence,* p. 35.

58. Hans-Guenter Zmarzlik, "Social Darwinism in Germany Seen as an Historical Problem," *Republic to Reich: The Making of the Nazi Revolution,* ed. Hajo Holborn, pp. 442ff. On Social Darwinism as a legitimating ideology for imperialism, see Hannah Arendt, *The Origins of Totalitarianism,* pp. 158–266.

59. See J. D. F. Peel, *Herbert Spencer: The Evolution of a Sociologist.* According to Peel, Spencer was "in no way the apologist of capitalist interest." However, Spencer's "misgivings about industrial capitalism" were ignored by his business admirers. See Peel, op. cit., pp. 214–15.

60. Cited by Richard Hofstadter, *Social Darwinism in American Thought,* p. 45.

61. Hofstadter, loc. cit.

62. Zmarzlik, op. cit., p. 440.

63. See Michael Walzer, *The Revolution of the Saints: A Study in the Origins of Radical Politics,* p. 76.

64. Charles Darwin, *On the Origin of the Species,* p. 62.

65. Charles Darwin, *The Variations of Animals and Plants under Domestication,* (London: John Murray, 1868), Vol. 1, p. 10; cited by Anthony Flew in his introduction to *Thomas Malthus, An Essay on the Principle of Population,* p. 50 (Penguin ed.).

66. Malthus, op. cit., pp. 205ff.

67. Malthus, op. cit., pp. 193ff. For an analysis of the Neo-Malthusian character of Reagonomics, see Robert Lekachman, "Malthusiasm," *New York Times,* March 30, 1981.

68. Herbert Spencer, *Social Statics,* pp. 414–15.

69. Ibid.

70. Hofstadter, op. cit., p. 52.

71. William Graham Sumner, "The Concentration of Wealth," in *Social Darwinism: Selected Essays of William Graham Sumner,* ed. Stow Person.

72. A. G. Keller and M. R. Davie, ed. *Essays of William Graham Sumner,* Vol. 2, p. 56.

73. H. Richard Niebuhr, *The Social Sources of Denominationalism,* p. 96.

74. See Peter Berger, *The Sacred Canopy: Elements of a Sociological Theory of Religion,* pp. 29–51.

Chapter 10
Is There a Way Out?

1. Lester C. Thurow, *The Zero-Sum Society: Distribution and the Possibilities for Economic Change.*

2. Thurow, op. cit., pp. 205f. See also Wassily W. Leontief, "The Distribution of Work and Income," *Scientific American,* Vol. 247, No. 3 (September 1982), pp. 188–204.

3. U.S. Department of Commerce, *Survey of Current Business,* Vol. 59, No. 7 (July 1979), p. 16; cited by Thurow, op. cit., p. 206.

4. I follow C. B. Macpherson's description of possessive individualism as a conception of the individual as "essentially the proprietor of his own person

or capacities, owing nothing to society for them." See Macpherson, op. cit., pp. 3, 263–64. For a conservative view of the problematics of individualism, see Robert A. Nisbet, *The Quest for Community*, pp. 224-248.

5. H. Richard Niebuhr, *The Social Sources of Denominationalism*, p. 82.

6. See Roderick MacFarquar, "The Challenge of Post-Confucian Asia," *The Economist*, February 9, 1980; Roy Hofheinz, Jr. and Kent E. Calder, *The East Asia Edge*, pp. 22–26; Richard Tanner Pascale and Anthony G. Athos, *The Art of Japanese Management: Applications for American Executives*, pp. 85ff.

7. See Peter Berger, op. cit., pp. 74ff.

8. The best known exponent of this view is Robert N. Bellah, "Civil Religion in America," *Daedalus*, Vol. 96, No. 1 (Winter 1967).

9. Berger, op. cit., p. 137.

10. John Locke, *Second Treatise*, from *Two Treatises of Government*, ed. Peter Laslett, Section 124.

11. John Locke, "A Letter Concerning Toleration," in *Main Currents in Western Thought*, ed. Franklin LeVan Baumer.

12. For an informed discussion of the problem of reconciling religious faith with critical historical methods of studying religious texts, see Van Harvey, *The Historian and the Believer: The Morality of Historical Knowledge and Christian Belief*.

13. See Richard L. Rubenstein, *After Auschwitz*, p. 9.

14. See Montgomery Watt, *Muhammed at Mecca*, pp. 151ff.

15. See George E. Mendenhall, *The Tenth Generation: The Origins of the Biblical Tradition*, p. 19ff., and Moshe Greenberg, *The Hab/Piru*, American Oriental Series, Vol. 39.

16. See Gerhard von Rad, *Old Testament Theology*, Vol. 1, pp. 8-9, 20.

17. After God reveals himself to Moses as the God of the Israelites' forefathers, Moses is depicted as asking him, "If I go to the Israelites and tell them, and they ask me his name, what shall I say?" (Exod. 3:13). This would indicate that the name, if not the actuality, of the Hebrew God, was previously unknown. The same point is implicit in Exodus 6:2, 3, where God is depicted as saying to Moses, "I am the Lord, and I appeared to Abraham, Isaac and Jacob as God almighty. But I did not let myself be known to them by the name Yahweh."

18. Richard J. Bernstein, *Praxis and Action: Contemporary Philosophies of Human Activity*, p. 77.

19. G. W. F. Hegel, *Philosophy of Right*, trans. T. M. Knox, Preface, pp. 12-13.

20. For the phrase, "the wisdom of ripeness," I am indebted to Shlomo Avineri Hegel's *Theory of the Modern State*, p. 128.

21. G. W. F. Hegel, *Reason in History*, trans. Robert S. Hartman, p. 27.

BIBLIOGRAPHY

I. Books

Ackerman, Nathan, and Jahoda, Marie. *Anti-Semitism and Emotional Disorder* New York: Harper and Brothers, 1950.

Adorno, T. W., et al. *The Authoritarian Personality.* New York: Harper and Brothers, 1950.

Arendt, Hannah. *The Origins of Totalitarianism.* New York: Harcourt Brace, 1951. *The Human Condition.* Chicago: University of Chicago Press, 1958.

Arlen, Michael J. *Passage to Ararat.* New York: Farrar, Strauss and Giroux, 1975.

Auletta, Ken. *The Underclass.* New York: Random House, 1982.

Avineri, Shlomo. *Hegel's Theory of the Modern State.* Cambridge: Cambridge University Press, 1972.

Aydelotte, Frank. *Elizabethan Rogues and Vagabonds.* Oxford: Clarendon Press, 1913.

Bahmueller, Charles F. *The National Charity Company.* Berkeley: University of California Press, 1981.

Bakan, David. *The Duality of Human Existence.* Chicago: Rand McNally, 1966.

Baltzell, E. Digby. *Puritan Boston and Quaker Philadelphia: Two Protestant Ethics and the Spirit of Class Authority and Leadership.* Boston: Beacon Press, 1982.

Barnet, Richard J., and Ronald Muller. *Global Reach: The Power of the Multi-National Corporations.* New York: Simon and Schuster, 1974.

Barron, John, and Paul, Anthony. *Murder of a Gentle Land: The Untold Story of Communist Genocide in Cambodia.* New York: Readers Digest Press, 1977.

Bedell, George, Sandon, Jr., Leo, and Wellborn, Charles J. *Religion in America.* New York: Macmillan, 1975.

Bedoukian, Kerop. *The Urchin.* London: John Murray, 1978.

Beecher, Henry. *Research and the Individual.* Boston: Little, Brown, 1971.

Ben-Sasson, H. H. (ed.) *A History of the Jewish People.* Cambridge, Mass.: Harvard University Press, 1976.

Berger, Peter. *The Sacred Canopy: Elements of a Sociological Theory of Religion.* Garden City, N.Y.: Anchor Books, 1967.

Berger, Peter. *Pyramids of Sacrifice: Political Ethics and Social Change.* New York: Basic Books, 1974.

Bernstein, Richard J. *Praxis and Action: Contemporary Philosophies of Human Activity.* Philadelphia: University of Pennsylvania Press, 1971.

Billington, James H. *The Icon and the Axe: An Interpretive History of Russian Culture.* New York: Vintage Books, 1970.

Bonar, James. *Malthus and His Work.* 1st ed. 1885. London: Frank Cass, 1966.

Booz, Allen, and Hamilton, Inc. *The Impact of Robotics on the Workforce and Workplace.* Pittsburgh: Carnegie-Mellon University, 1981.

Borkin, Joseph. *The Crime and Punishment of I. G. Farben.* New York: Free Press, 1978.

Bourne, H. R. Fox. *The Life of John Locke.* 1st ed. 1876. Aalen: Scientia Verlag, 1969.

Boyajian, Dickran H. *Armenia: The Case for a Forgotten Genocide.* Westwood, N.J.· Educational Bookcrafters, 1972.

Bracher, Karl Dietrich. *The German Dictatorship.* New York: Praeger, 1973.

Bruce, Maurice. (ed.) *The Rise of the Welfare State: English Social Policy, 1601-1971.* London: Weidenfeld and Nicholson, 1973.

Bryce, Viscount James. *The Treatment of the Armenians in the Ottoman Empire 1915-16: Documents Presented to the Secretary of State for Foreign Affairs by Viscount Bryce.* 1st ed. London 1916. Beirut: G. Doniguian and Sons, 1972.

Byrnes, R. F. *Pobedonostsev.* Bloomington: Indiana University Press, 1968.

Carlebach, Julius. *Karl Marx and the Radical Critique of Judaism.* London: Routledge and Kegan Paul, 1978.

Carr-Sanders, A. M. *World Population.* Oxford: Oxford University Press, 1936.

Carus-Wilson, E. M. *Essays in Economic History.* London: Edward Arnold, Vol. 1 (1954), Vol. 2 (1962), Vol. 3 (1962).

Chadwick, Edwin. *The Papers of Sir Edwin Chadwick.* London: University College, 1978.

Chase, Allan. *The Legacy of Malthus: The Social Costs of the New Racism.* New York: Alfred A. Knopf, 1977.

Churchill, Winston S. *The Second World War.* London: Cassell, 1951, Vol. 4.

Cippola, Carlo M. *The Economic History of World Population,* 6th ed. Harmondsworth, Middlesex: Penguin Books, 1975. Cippola, (ed.) *The Fontana Economic History of Europe,* Vol. 3, *The Industrial Revolution.* London: Fontana/Collins, 1973.

Colquhoun, Patrick. *A Treatise on Indigence.* London: J. Hatchard, 1806.

Conquest, Robert. *The Great Terror: Stalin's Purge of the Thirties.* Rev. ed. Harmondsworth, Middlesex: Penguin Books, 1974.

Cowherd, Raymond Gibson. *Political Economists and the English Poor Laws: A Historical Study of the Influence of Classical Economics on the Formation of Social Policy.* Athens: Ohio University Press, 1977.

Crankshaw, Edward. *The Shadow of the Winter Palace: The Drift to Revolution, 1825-1917.* Harmondsworth, Middlesex: Penguin Books, 1978.

Darwin, Charles. *On the Origin of the Species by Means of Natural Selection: Or the Preservation of Favoured Races in the Struggle for Life.* 1st. ed. 1859. New York: Modern Library, 1936.

Dawidowicz, Lucy. *The War against the Jews, 1933-1945.* New York: Bantam Books, 1975.

Day, William. *An Inquiry into the Poor Laws and Surplus Labour, and Their Mutual Reaction.* London: J. Fraser, 1833.

Durkheim, Emile. *The Rules of Sociological Method.* Trans. Sarah A. Solovay and J. H. Mueller. Glencoe, Ill.: Free Press, 1958.

Eddy, Paul, Potter, Elaine, and Page, Bruce. *Destination Disaster: From the Tri-Motor to the DC10: The Risk of Flying.* New York: Ballantine Books, 1978.

Edsall, Nicholas C. *The Anti-Poor Law Movement, 1834–44.* Manchester: Manchester University Press, 1971.

Edwards, R. Dudley, and Williams, T. Desmond. (eds.) *The Great Famine: Studies in Irish History, 1845–52.* New York: New York University Press, 1957.

Eliot, Gil. *The Twentieth Century Book of the Dead.* New York: Charles Scribner's Sons, 1972.

Erikson, Kai. *Wayward Puritans.* New York: John Wiley, 1966.

Evans, Christopher. *The Micro Millennium.* New York: Washington Square Press, 1979.

Ferenc, Benjamin B. *Less than Slaves: Jewish Forced Labor and the Quest for Compensation.* Cambridge, Mass.: Harvard University Press, 1979.

Festinger, Leon. *A Theory of Cognitive Dissonance.* Evanston: Row, Peterson, 1957.

Festinger, Leon, Riecken, Henry W., and Schachter, Stanley. *When Prophecy Fails.* Minneapolis: University of Minnesota Press, 1956.

Finer, Samuel Edward. *The Life and Times of Sir Edwin Chadwick.* London: Methuen, 1952.

Fitzgerald, Stephen, *China and the Overseas Chinese.* Cambridge: Cambridge University Press, 1972.

Friedlander, Saul. *Pius XII and the Third Reich: A Documentation.* Trans. Charles Fullman. New York: Alfred A. Knopf, 1966.

Frolich, Paul. *Rosa Luxemburg.* New York: Monthly Review Press, 1972.

Gazlay, John G. *The Life of Arthur Young: 1741–1820.* Philadelphia: American Philosophical Society, 1973.

Gilbert, Martin. *Exile and Return: The Jewish Struggle for a Jewish Homeland.* Philadelphia: J. P. Lippincott, 1978.

Gilder, George. *Wealth and Poverty.* New York: Basic Books, 1981.

Gonner, Edward C. K. *Common Land and Enclosure.* Introd. G. E. Mingay. 1st ed. 1912. London: Frank Cass, 1966.

Grant, Bruce, et al. *The Boat People: An "Age" Investigation with Bruce Grant.* Victoria, Australia: Penguin Books, 1979.

Great Britain. *The Act for the Amendment of the Poor Laws.* (4 and 5 William 4, C, 76.) London: Saunders and Benning, 1836.

Great Britain, Treasury. *Correspondence Explanatory of the Measures Adopted by Her Majesty's Government for the Relief of Distress*

Arising from the Failure of the Potato Crop in Ireland: Presented to Both Houses of Parliament by Command of Her Majesty. London: W. Clowes and Sons, 1846.

Greenberg, Louis. *The Jews in Russia.* 2nd ed. New York: Schocken Books, 1976.

Greenberg, Moshe. *The Hab/Piru.* New Haven: American Oriental Society, 1955 (American Oriental Series, Vol. 39).

Griffith, Grosvenor Talbot. *Population Problems in the Age of Malthus.* 1st ed. 1926. London: Frank Cass, 1967.

Grunberger, Richard. *Red Rising in Bavaria.* New York: St. Martin's Press, 1973.

Halevy, Elie. *The Growth of Philosophical Radicalism.* Clifton, N.J.: A. M. Kelley, 1972.

Hamerow, Theodore S. *Restoration, Revolution, Reaction: Economics and Politics in Germany, 1815-1871.* Princeton: Princeton University Press, 1958.

Hammond, John, and Hammond, Barbara. *The Village Labourer: 1760-1832: A Study in the Government of England before the Reform Bill.* 1st ed. 1911. Abridged ed. London: Longmans Green, 1920. *The Town Labourer, 1760-1832: The New Civilisation.* London: Longmans Green, 1936. *The Age of the Chartists, 1832-1854, A Study of Discontent.* London: Longmans Green, 1930. *The Bleak Age.* London: Longmans Green, 1934.

Handlin, Oscar. *The Uprooted.* 2nd ed. enlarged. Boston: Atlantic, Little, Brown, 1973. *A Pictorial History of Immigration.* New York: Crown Publishers, 1972.

Hansen, Marcus Lee. *The Atlantic Migration, 1607-1860.* Cambridge, Mass.: Harvard University Press, 1971. *The Immigrant in American History.* New York: Harper Torchbooks, 1964.

Hartwell, R. M. *The Industrial Revolution and Economic Growth.* London: Methuen, 1971. Hartwell et al. *The Long Debate on Poverty: Eight Essays on Industrialisation and 'The Condition of England.'* London: Institute for Economic Affairs, 1972.

Harvey, Van. *The Historian and the Believer: The Morality of Historical Knowledge and Christian Belief.* New York: Macmillan, 1966.

Hasbach, Wilhelm. *A History of the English Agricultural Labourer.* Trans. Ruth Kenyon. London: P. S. King and Son, 1908.

Hay, Malcolm. *Europe and the Jews: The Pressure of Christendom on the People of Israel for 1900 Years.* Boston: Beacon Press, 1961.

Hayter, W. G. *Proposals for the Redemption of the Poor's Rates by Means of Emigration.* London: 1817.

Heer, David. *Society and Population.* Englewood Cliffs, N.J.: Prentice-Hall, 1968.

Hegel, G. W. F. *Jenaer Realphilosophie I, Die Vorlesungen von 1803/4.* ed. J. Hoffmeister. Leipsig: Felix Meiner, 1932. *Jenaer Realphilosophie II: Die Vorlesungen von 1805/6.* ed. J. Hoffmeister. Leipsig: Felix Meiner, 1931. *Phenomenology of Spirit.* Trans. A. V. Miller. New York: Oxford University Press, 1979. *Philosophy of Right.* Trans. T. M. Knox. Oxford: Oxford University Press, 1942. *Reason in History.* Trans. Robert S. Hartman. Indianapolis: Bobbs-Merrill, 1972.

Heller, Celia S. *On the Edge of Destruction: Jews of Poland Between Two World Wars.* New York: Columbia University Press, 1977.

Hilberg, Raul. *The Destruction of the European Jews.* Chicago: Quadrangle Books, 1967.

Hildebrand, George C., and Porter, Gareth, *Cambodia: Starvation and Revolution.* New York and London: Monthly Review Press, 1976.

Hill, Christopher. *Puritanism and Revolution: Studies in Interpretation of the English Revolution of the 17th Century.* London: Secker and Warburg, 1958. *The World Turned Upside Down: Radical Ideas During the English Revolution.* 1st ed. 1972. Harmondsworth, Middlesex: Penguin Books, 1975.

Hobbes, Thomas. *Leviathan.* ed. C. B. Macpherson. Harmondsworth, Middlesex: Penguin Books, 1968.

Hobsbawm, Eric J. *The Age of Revolution, 1789–1848.* 1st ed. 1962. New York: Mentor Books, 1978.

Hobsbawm, Eric, and Rude, George. *Captain Swing.* New York: Pantheon, 1968.

Hofheinz, Jr., Roy, and Calder, Kent E. *The East Asia Edge.* New York: Basic Books, 1982.

Hofstadter, Richard, *Social Darwinism in American Thought.* Boston: Beacon Press, 1955.

Horkheimer, Max, and Adorno, T. W. *Dialectic of Enlightenment.* Trans. John Cumming. New York: Herder and Herder, 1972.

Hovannisian, Richard. *Armenia on the Road to Independence.* Berkeley: University of California Press, 1967. *The Armenian Holocaust: A Bibliography Relating to the Deportations, Massacres of the Armenian People, 1915–1923.* Cambridge, Mass.: Armenian Heritage Press, 1978.

James, Patricia. *Population Malthus: His Life and Times.* London: Routledge and Kegan Paul, 1979.

Joffroy, Pierre. *A Spy for God: The Ordeal of Kurt Gerstein.* New York: Universal Library, 1969.

Johnson, Stanley C. *A History of Emigration: From the United Kingdom to North America, 1763–1912.* 1st ed. 1912. London: Frank Cass, 1966.

Johnston, H. J. M. *British Emigration Policy, 1815–1830: "Shoveling Out the Paupers."* Oxford: Oxford University Press, 1972.

Kayser, Louis Elmer. *The Grand Social Enterprise.* New York: AMS Press, 1967.

Kazarian, Haigaz K. *Minutes of Secret Meetings Organizing the Turkish Genocide of the Armenians.* Boston: Commemorative Committee on the 50th Anniversary of the Turkish Massacres of the Armenians, 1965.

Kelly, J. T. *Thorn on the Tudor Rose: Monks, Rogues, Vagabonds, and Sturdy Beggars.* Jackson: University Press of Mississippi, 1977.

Kerridge, Eric. *Agrarian Problems of the Sixteenth Century.* London: Allen and Unwin, 1969.

Kieniewicz, Stephan. *The Emancipation of the Polish Peasantry.* Chicago: University of Chicago Press, 1969.

Kline, David. *The New Face of Kampuchea.* Chicago: Liberator Press, 1979.

Kuper, Leo. *Genocide: Its Political Use in the Twentieth Century.* New Haven: Yale University Press, 1982.

Landes, David S. *The Unbound Prometheus: Technological Change and Industrial Development in Western Europe from 1750 to the Present.* Cambridge: Cambridge University Press, 1969.

Langer, William L. *New Illustrated Encyclopedia of World History.* New York: Harry Abrams, 1975. 2 vols.

Lansbury, George. *My Life.* London: John Constable, 1928.

Lasswell, Harold D., Lerner, Daniel, and Rothwell, C. E. *The Comparative Study of Elites: An Introduction and Bibliography.* Hoover Institute Studies. Stanford: Stanford University Press, 1952.

Lekachman, Robert. *Public Service Employment: Jobs for All.* New York: Public Affairs Committee, 1972.

Lekachman, Robert. *Greed Is Not Enough: Reagonomics.* New York: Pantheon Books, 1982.

Leon, Abram. *The Jewish Question: A Marxist Interpretation.* New York: Pathfinder Press, 1970.

Levin, Leonard. *Triage.* New York: Dial Press, 1972.

Levy, Hermann. *Large and Small Holdings: A Study of English Agricultural Economics.* Trans. Ruth Kenyon. 1st ed. 1911. London: Frank Cass, 1966.

Littell, Franklin H. *The Crucifixion of the Jews.* New York: Harper and Row, 1975.

Little, David. *Religion, Order, and Law.* New York: Harper and Row, 1969.

Locke, John. *Two Treatises of Government.* Ed. Peter Laslett. Cambridge: Cambridge University Press, 1960.

Loewenstein, Rudolph M. *Christians and Jews: A Psychoanalytic Study.* New York: Delta Books, 1961.

Löwith, Karl. *From Hegel to Nietzsche: The Revolution in Nineteenth Century Thought.* Trans. David E. Green. New York: Holt, Rinehart and Winston, 1964.

Lucas, George R., and Ogletree, Thomas W. (eds.) *Lifeboat Ethics: The Moral Dilemmas of World Hunger.* New York: Harper and Row, 1976.

Lukacs, Jr., Georg. *The Young Hegel: Studies in the Relations Between Dialectics and Economics.* Trans. Rodney Livingstone. Cambridge, Mass.: MIT Press, 1976.

Macdonagh, Oliver. *Ireland: The Union and Its Aftermath.* London: Routledge and Kegan Paul, 1977.

Macpherson, C. B. *The Political Theory of Possessive Individualism: Hobbes to Locke.* Oxford: Oxford University Press, 1962.

Malthus, Thomas Robert. *An Essay on the Principle of Population.* Ed. Philip Appleman, New York: W. W. Norton, 1976. Ed. Anthony Flew. 1st ed. 1798. Harmondsworth, Middlesex: Penguin Books, 1970. *The Pamphlets of Thomas Malthus.* New York: A. M. Kelley, 1970.

Marx, Karl, and Engels, Friedrich. *Marx and Engels on the Population Bomb: Selections from the Writings of Marx and Engels Dealing with the Theories of Thomas Robert Malthus.* Ed. Ronald L. Meek. Berkeley: Ramparts Press, 1971.

Massing, Paul. *Rehearsal for Destruction: A Study of Political Anti-Semitism in Imperial Germany.* New York: Harper and Brothers, 1949.

May, Arthur J. *The Hapsburg Monarchy, 1867–1914.* Cambridge, Mass.: Harvard University Press, 1951.

McCord, Norman. *The Anti-Corn Law League, 1838–1846.* London: Allen and Unwin, 1968.

McEvdy, Colin, and Jones, Richard. *Atlas of World Population History.* Harmondsworth, Middlesex: Penguin Books, 1978.

Mendenhall, George E. *The Tenth Generation: The Origins of the Biblical Tradition.* Baltimore: Johns Hopkins University Press, 1973.

Mendes-Flohr, Paul R., and Reinharz, Jehuda. (eds.) *The Jew in the Modern World: A Documentary History.* New York: Oxford University Press, 1980.

Middlebrook, Martin. *The First Day on the Somme.* New York: W. W. Norton, 1972.

Mitchell, Allan. *Revolution in Bavaria.* Princeton: Princeton University Press, 1965.

Mommsen, Wolfgang J. *The Age of Bureaucracy: Perspectives on the Political Sociology of Max Weber.* Oxford: Basil Blackwell, 1974.

Moore, Jr., Barrington. *Social Origins of Dictatorship and Democracy: Lord and Peasant in the Making of the Modern World.* Boston: Beacon Press, 1966.

More, Thomas. "Utopia" [trans. Ralphe Robyson, 1st ed. 1516], in *Three Renaissance Classics.* Ed. Burton A. Milligan. New York: Charles Scribner's Sons, 1953.

Morgenthau, Henry. *Ambassador Morgenthau's Story.* Garden City, N.Y.: Doubleday and Page, 1919.

Mosse, George. *Toward the Final Solution: A History of European Racism.* New York: Harper and Row, 1978.

Nazer, James. *The First Genocide of the Twentieth Century.* New York: T and T Publishing Company, 1968. *The Armenian Massacre.* New York: T and T Publishing Company, 1970.

Nelson, Benjamin. *The Idea of Usury: From Tribal Brotherhood to Universal Otherhood.* 2nd ed. Chicago: University of Chicago Press, 1969.

Nicholls, George. *A History of the English Poor Laws.* London: Frank Cass, 1967. 3 vols. *A History of the Irish Poor Laws.* New York: A. M. Kelley, 1967.

Niebuhr, H. Richard. *The Social Sources of Denominationalism.* 1st ed. 1929. Hamden, Conn.: Shoestring Press, 1954. *Radical Monotheism and Western Culture.* 1st ed. 1943. New York: Harper and Row, 1960.

Nisbet, Robert A. *The Quest for Community.* New York: Oxford University Press, 1969.

Osborne, John W. *William Cobbett: His Thought and Times.* New Brunswick, N.J.: Rutgers University Press, 1966.

Oxley, Geoffrey W. *Poor Law Relief in England and Wales, 1601–1834.* Newton Abbot: David and Charles, 1974.

Paddock, William and Paul. *Famine 1975: America's Decision: Who Will Survive?* Boston: Little, Brown, 1971.

Parekh, Bikhu C. (ed.) *Jeremy Bentham, Ten Critical Essays.* London: Frank Cass, 1974.

Parsons, Talcott. *The Structure of Social Action.* New York: McGraw Hill, 1937. 2 vols.

Pasquale, Richard Tanner, and Athos, Anthony G. *The Art of Japanese Management: Applications for American Executives.* New York: Simon and Schuster, 1981.

Peel, J. D. F. *Herbert Spencer: The Evolution of a Sociologist.* New York: Basic Books, 1973.

Petersen, William. *Malthus.* Cambridge, Mass.: Harvard University Press, 1979.

Piven, Frances Fox, and Cloward, Richard A. *The New Class War: Reagan's Attack on the New Welfare State and Its Consequences.* New York: Pantheon Books, 1982. *Regulating the Poor: The Functions of Public Welfare.* New York: Pantheon Books, 1971.

Pohlman, Edward. (ed.) *Population: A Clash of Prophets.* New York: New American Library, 1971.

Polanyi, Karl. *The Great Transformation: The Political and Economic Origins of Our Time.* 1st ed. 1944. Boston: Beacon Press, 1957.

Ponchaud, François. *Cambodia Year Zero.* Trans. Nancy Amphoux. New York: Holt, Rinehart and Winston, 1978.

Pope, Liston. *Millhands and Preachers.* 1st ed. 1942. New Haven: Yale University Press, 1972.

Pound, John. *Poverty and Vagrancy in Tudor England.* London: Harlow, Longman, 1971.

Poynter, John Riddoch. *Society and Pauperism: English Ideas on Poor Relief, 1795-1834.* London: Routledge and Kegan Paul, 1969.

Pridham, Geoffrey. *Hitler's Rise to Power: The Nazi Movement in Bavaria, 1923-1933.* New York: Harper and Row, 1974.

Reiman, Jeffrey H. *The Rich Get Richer and the Poor Get Prison: Ideology, Class, and Criminal Justice.* New York: John Wiley, 1979.

Reuther, Rosemary. *Faith and Fratricide: The Theological Roots of Anti-Semitism.* New York: Seabury Press, 1974.

Rogger, Hans, and Weber, Eugen. (eds.) *The European Right: A Historical Profile.* Berkeley: University of California Press, 1966.

Rose, Michael E. *The English Poor Law 1780-1930.* Newton Abbot: David and Charles, 1971.

Rosenberg, Alfred. *Race and Race History.* Ed. Robert Pois. New York: Harper and Row, 1974.

Rosenblum, Nancy. *Bentham's Theory of the Modern State.* Cambridge, Mass.: Harvard University Press, 1978.

Rubenstein, Richard L. *After Auschwitz: Radical Theology and Contemporary Judaism.* Indianapolis: Bobbs-Merrill, 1966. *The Cunning of History: Mass Death and the American Future.* New York: Harper and Row, 1975.

Ryder, A. J. *Twentieth-Century Germany from Bismarck to Brandt.* New York: Columbia University Press, 1972.

Sachar, Howard M. *The Course of Modern Jewish History.* New York: Delta Books, 1970.

Salaman, Redcliffe N. *The History and Social Influence of the Potato.* Cambridge: Cambridge University Press, 1949.

Sarkisyanz, Manuel. *A Modern History of Transcaucasian Armenia.* Privately printed by author. Nagpur, India: Udyama Commercial Press, 1975. (Distributed by E. J. Brill, Leiden.)

Scholem, Gershom. *Sabbatai Sevi: The Mystical Messiah.* Princeton: Princeton University Press, 1973.

Schorsch, Ismar. *Jewish Reactions to German Anti-Semitism, 1870-1914.* New York: Columbia University Press, 1972.

Schorske, Carl. *Fin-de-Siècle Vienna: Politics and Culture.* New York: Alfred A. Knopf, 1980.

Scott, Franklin D. (ed.) *World Migration in Modern Times.* Englewood Cliffs, N.J.: Prentice-Hall, 1968.

Shawcross, William. *Sideshow: Kissinger, Nixon and Kissinger and the Destruction of Cambodia.* New York: Pocket Books, 1979.

Slater, Gilbert. *The English Peasantry and the Enclosure of the Small Fields.* 1st ed. 1907. New York: A. M. Kelley, 1968.

Smith, Adam. *The Wealth of Nations.* Ed. Anthony Skinner. 1st ed. 1776. Harmondsworth, Middlesex: Penguin Books, 1974.

Soames, Jane Nickerson. *Homage to Malthus.* Port Washington, N.Y.: Kennikat Press, 1975.

Solzhenitsyn, Alexander. *The Gulag Archipelago: 1918-1956.* Trans. Thomas P. Whitney. London: Collins/Fontana, 1974. *The Gulag Archipelago Three.* New York: Perennial Library, 1976.

Spencer, Herbert. *Social Statics.* New York: D. Appleton and Co., 1864.

Stephen, Leslie. *The English Utilitarians.* 1st ed. 1900. New York: A. M. Kelley, 1968.

Sumner, William Graham. *Essays of William Graham Sumner.* Ed. A. G. Keller and M. R. Davie. New Haven: Yale University Press, 1963. 2 vols. *Social Darwinism: Selected Essays of William Graham Sumner.* Ed. Stow Person. Englewood Cliffs, N.J.: Prentice-Hall, 1963.

Swift, Jonathan. *A Modest Proposal for Preventing the Children of Poor People from Being a Burthen to Their Parents or Country,* in *Prose Works of Jonathan Swift.* 1st ed. 1729. Ed. H. Davis. Oxford: Oxford University Press, 1955.

Tal, Uriel. *Christians and Jews in Germany: Religion and Politics and Ideology in the Second Reich, 1870-1914.* Ithaca: Cornell University Press, 1975.

Tate, William Edward. *The Enclosure Movement.* New York: Walker, 1967.

Tawney, R. H. *The Agrarian Problem in the Sixteenth Century.* London: Longmans Green, 1912. *Religion and the Rise of Capitalism.* London: John Murray, 1926.

Thirsk, Joan. (ed.) *The Agrarian History of England and Wales, 1500-1640.* Cambridge: Cambridge University Press, 1967. Vol. 4.

Thomas, Brinley. *Migration and Economic Growth: A Study of Great Britain and the Atlantic Economy.* Cambridge: Cambridge University Press, 1954.

Thomas, Gordon, and Witts, Max Morgan. *Voyage of the Damned.* New York: Stein and Day, 1974.

Thompson, E. P. *The Making of the English Working Class.* 1st ed. 1963. New York: Vintage Books, 1966.

Thurow, Lester C. *The Zero-Sum Society: Distribution and the Possibilities for Economic Change.* New York: Basic Books, 1980.

Toynbee, Arnold. *Lectures on the Industrial Revolution of the Eighteenth Century in England.* London: Rivingtons, 1884.

Trattner, Walter I. *From Poor Law to Welfare State: A History of Social Welfare in America.* New York: Free Press, 1974.

Trevelyan, Sir Charles Edward. *The Irish Crisis.* London: Longman, Brown, Green and Longman, 1848 (reprinted from the Edinburgh Review, No. 175, January 1848).

Trevelyan, Charles E., and Northcote, Stafford H. *Papers Relating to the Reorganisation of the Civil Service Presented to Both Houses of Parliament.* London: Eyre and Spottiswood, 1855.

Trevelyan, George Otto. *Life and Letters of Lord Macaulay.* London: Longmans, Green, 1878.

Trollope, Anthony. *The Three Clerks.* 1st ed. 1858. Oxford: Oxford University Press, 1925.

Ulam, Adam B. *Stalin: The Man and His Era.* New York: Viking/Compass, 1973.

Vital, David. *The Origins of Zionism.* Oxford: Oxford University Press, 1975.

Vogel, Ezra. *Japan as No. 1: Lessons for America.* Cambridge, Mass.: Harvard University Press, 1979.

Von Rad, Gerhard. *Old Testament Theology.* London: S.P.C.K., 1953. Vol. 1.

Wain, Barry. *The Refused: The Agony of the Indochinese Refugees.* New York: Simon and Schuster, 1982.

Waite, Robert L. *The Psychopathic God: Adolf Hitler.* New York: New American Library, 1978.

Wakefield, Edward Gibbon. *A Letter from Sidney and Other Writings.* 1st ed. 1829. London: Dent, 1929.

Walker, Mack. *Germany and the Emigration, 1816-1885.* Cambridge, Mass.: Harvard University Press, 1964.

Walzer, Michael. *The Revolution of the Saints: A Study of the Origins of Radical Politics.* Cambridge, Mass.: Harvard University Press, 1965.

Wasserstein, Bernard. *Britain and the Jews of Europe, 1939-1945.* Oxford: Oxford University Press, 1980.

Watt, Montgomery. *Muhammed at Mecca.* Oxford: Oxford University Press, 1953.

Webb, Sidney and Beatrice. *English Poor Law History: Part I, The Old Poor Law* and *Part II, The Last One Hundred Years,* published in 2 vols. Hamden, Conn.: Archon Books, 1963. These are part of the larger work, *English Local Government,* 1st ed. 7 vols. (London 1927).

Weber, Max. *Ancient Judaism.* Trans. H. H. Gerth and Don Martindale. Glencoe, Ill.: Free Press, 1952. *Economy and Society.* Ed. Guenther Roth and Claus Wittich. New York: Bedminster Press, 1968. 3 vols. *From Max Weber: Essays in Sociology.* Ed. H. H. Gerth and C. Wright Mills. New York: Oxford University Press, 1946. *Sociology of Religion.* Trans. Ephraim Fischoff. Boston: Beacon Press, 1956.

Wilhelm, Sidney. *Who Needs the Negro?* Garden City, N.Y.: Anchor Books, 1971.

Wilson, Bryan. *Religion in Sociological Perspective.* Oxford: Oxford University Press, 1982.

Winch, Donald. *Classical Political Economy and Colonies.* Cambridge: Harvard University Press, 1965.

Winslow, Gerald R. Winslow. *Triage and Justice.* Berkeley: University of California Press, 1982.

Wischnitzer, Mark, *To Dwell in Safety: The Story of Jewish Migration Since 1800.* Philadelphia: Jewish Publication Society, 1948.

Woodham-Smith, Cecil. *The Reason Why.* New York: McGraw-Hill, 1953. *The Great Hunger: Ireland, 1845-1849.* 1st ed. 1962. New York: E. P. Dutton, 1980.

Yelling, J. A. *Common Field and Enclosure in England, 1450-1850.* London: Macmillan, 1977.

Yette, Samuel F. *The Choice: The Issue of Black Survival in America.* New York: G. Putnam, 1971.

II. Articles and Pamphlets

Armengaud, André. "Population in Europe, 1700–1914," in Carlo M. Cippola (ed.), *The Fontana Economic History of Europe*, Vol 3, *The Industrial Revolution*. London: Fontana/Collins, 1973.

Bartz, Wayne. "Outrageous Solutions to the Population Outrage" in Edward Pohlman (ed.), *Population: A Clash of Prophets.*

Beardwood, Roger. "The Southern Roots of the Urban Crisis," *Fortune,* August 1968.

Bellah, Robert N. "Civil Religion in America" *Daedalus,* Vol. 96, No. 1 (Winter 1967).

Berg, Alan. "The Trouble with Triage," *New York Times Magazine,* June 15, 1975.

Berk, Stephen M. "The Russian Revolutionary Movement and the Pogroms of 1881–1882," *Soviet Jewish Affairs,* Vol. 7, No. 2 (1977).

Blum, Jerome. "English Parliamentary Enclosure," *Journal of Modern History,* Vol. 53, No. 3, pp. 477–504. September 1981.

Business Week. "The Speedup in Automation," August 3, 1981.

Calhoun, John. "Population Density and Social Pathology," *Scientific American,* February 1962.

Carnegie, Andrew. "Wealth," *The North American Review,* Vol. 39, June, 1889.

Chanda, Nayan. "A Fairy Tale of Kampuchea," *Far Eastern Economic Review,* July 20, 1979.

Chiricos, Theodore G. "Rates of Crime and Unemployment: A Critical Review," unpublished paper presented at the annual meeting of the American Sociological Association, Toronto, September 1981.

Chiricos, Theodore G., and Norton, William M. "Unemployment, Welfare and Property Crime," unpublished paper to be presented at the Annual Meeting of the American Sociological Association, San Francisco, September 1982.

Coleman, D. C. "Labour in the English Economy of the Seventeenth Century," *English Historical Review,* 2nd series, Vol. 8 (1956), p. 3.

Crossette, Barbara. "Pirates Continue Brutal Attacks on Refugees," in *New York Times,* January 10, 1982.

Das, K. "An Accidental Deterrent," *Far Eastern Economic Review,* April 22, 1978.

Das, K., and Sacerdoti, Guy. "Digging in for a Long Stay" and "Economics of a Human Cargo," *Far Eastern Economic Review,* December 22, 1978.

Davis, Kingsley. "The Migration of Human Populations," *Scientific American,* September 1974.

Donaldson, Peter J. "In Cambodia, A Holocaust Clearly," *New York Times,* April 22, 1980.

Economist, The. "The Whole Case of Ireland and the Irish Poor Law," February 17, 1849. "The Poor of Ireland," June 28, 1851, "The Drug for Irish Maladies," October 4, 1851. "The Irish Priesthood and the Irish Laity," June 19, 1852. "Effects of Emigration on Production and Consumption," February 12, 1853. Vol. 11, pp. 168–69. "The Khmers Who Couldn't Look Back," July 21, 1979. "Vietnamese Refugees: From One Horror to Another," February 9, 1980. "Where Will the Jobs Come From?," January 3, 1981. "Haiti," July 4, 1981. "Taiwan's Car Industry," March 6-12, 1982. "How Not to Deter Refugees: By Allowing Them to be Murdered by Pirates," May 29, 1982.

Eitzen, D. Stanley. "Two Minorities: The Jews of Poland and the Chinese of the Philippines," *Jewish Journal of Sociology,* Vol. 10, pp. 221-38, (December 1968).

Encyclopaedia Judaica. Articles: "Berlin," Vol. 4, p. 644. "May Laws," Vol. 11, pp. 1147-48. "Pobedonostsev," Vol. 13, p. 663. "Pogroms," Vol. 13, pp. 695–98. "Poland," Vol. 13, pp. 735–49. "Population," Vol. 13, pp. 889–92. "Vienna," Vol. 16, p. 1247.

Enloe, Cynthia. "Ethnic Diversity: The Potential for Conflict," in Guy J. Pauker, Frank H. Golay, and Cynthia Enloe, *Diversity and Development in Southeast Asia: The Coming Decade.* New York: McGraw-Hill, 1980.

Ettinger, S. "Anti-Semitism as Official Policy in Eastern Europe," in H. H. Ben-Sasson (ed.), *A History of the Jewish People.*

Everitt, Alan. "Farm Labourers," in Joan Thirsk (ed.), *The Agrarian History of England and Wales, 1500-1640.* Vol. 4.

Far Eastern Economic Review. "The Tragedy of the KG 0729," December 22, 1978. "The Kampuchean Holocaust," July 20, 1979. "Pointing the Finger at Hanoi," August 3, 1979.

Feder, Barnaby J. "Robots Enter the Limelight," *New York Times,* March 4, 1981.

Fenichel, Otto. "The Psycho-Analysis of Anti-Semitism," *American Imago,* Vol. 1 (1940).

Festinger, Leon. "Cognitive Dissonance," *Scientific American,* October 1962.

Gershman, Carl. "After the Dominoes Fell," *Commentary,* May 1978.

Ghosh, R. N. "Malthus on Emigration and Colonization: Letters to Wilmot-Horton," *Economica,* February 1963.

Ginzberg, Eli. "The Mechanization of Work," *Scientific American,* September 1982.

Goodale, James C., and Martin, Lawrence M. "Will They Classify Even the Alphabet?" *New York Times,* April 11, 1982.

Gouldner, Alan. "Stalinism: A Study of Internal Colonialism," *Telos,* 34 (Winter 1977-1978).

Green, Wade. "Triage: Who Shall Be Fed? Who Shall Starve?" *New York Times Magazine,* January 5, 1975.

Grenier, Richard. "The Horror, The Horror," *The New Republic,* May 26, 1982.

Hall, Elizabeth, and Cameron, Paul. "Are We in Love with Death?" *Psychology Today,* April 1976.

Handlin, Oscar. "Does Economics Explain Racism?" *Commentary,* July 1948.

Hardin, Garrett. "Lifeboat Ethics: The Case against Helping the Poor," *Psychology Today,* September 1974. "Another Face of Bioethics: The Case for Massive 'Diebacks of Populations,'" *Modern Medicine,* March 1, 1975. "The Toughlove Solution," *Newsweek,* October 26, 1981.

Hartwell, R. M. "Economic Change in England and Europe, 1780-1830," in *The New Cambridge Modern History.* Cambridge: Cambridge University Press, 1965. Vol. 9.

Himmelfarb, Gertrude. "Bentham's Utopia: The National Charity

Company" *The Journal of British Studies,* Vol. 10, No. 1 (November 1970).

Hinds, Stuart W. "On the Relation of Medical Triage to World Hunger: An Historical Survey" in George R. Lucas, Jr., and Thomas N. Ogletree, *Lifeboat Ethics: The Moral Dilemmas of World Hunger.*

Jenkins, David. "An Island in the Stream," *Far Eastern Economic Review,* May 25, 1979.

Kotz, Nick. "The War on the Poor," *The New Republic,* March 24, 1982.

Langer, William. "Europe's Initial Population Explosion," *The American Historical Review,* Vol. 69, No. 1 (October 1963), pp. 1–17. "American Foods and Europe's Population Growth, 1750–1850," *Journal of Social History,* No. 1 (Winter 1975), pp. 57–66.

Lee, Mary. "Ill Winds over Fragrant Harbour," *Far Eastern Economic Review,* May 25, 1979. "Free Port or Free-for-All," *Far Eastern Economic Review,* October 5, 1979.

Leontief, Wassily. "What Hope for the Economy?" *New York Review of Books,* August 12, 1982. "The Distribution of Work and Income," *Scientific American,* September 1982.

Locke, John. "A Letter Concerning Toleration" (1689), in Franklin LeVan Baumer, *Main Currents in Western Thought.* New York: Alfred A. Knopf, 1970. "Report on the Poor," in H. R. Fox Bourne, *The Life of John Locke,* Vol. 2, pp. 377–91.

Lynch, Phillip R. "Deus Ex Machina," *New York Times,* April 26, 1982.

MacFarquar, Emily. "The Survivors Who Seek Their Place in Paradise," *The Economist,* July 21, 1979.

MacFarquar, Roderick. "The Challenge of Post-Confucian Asia," *The Economist,* February 9, 1980.

Marshall, Dorothy. "The Old Poor Law, 1662–1795," E. M. Carus-Wilson, *Essays in Economic History,* Vol. 1.

May, Clifford D. "Mexico City: Omens of the Apocalypse," *Geo,* May 1981.

Mayer, Arno. "The Lower Middle Class as Historical Problem," *Journal of Modern History,* Vol. 47, No. 3 (September 1975).

Mays, Lee. "Reagan Expert under Attack for Ties to Nazi War Criminal," *St. Petersburg Times,* April 25, 1982.

McBeth, John. "A Perilously Short Fuse," *Far Eastern Economic Review,* June 15, 1979.

McDougall, Anne. "Back to School at 35 and Over," *U.S. Government Special Labor Force Report,* U.S. Department of Labor and Statistics, October 1978.

Miller, Ronald H. "A Decade of Data on Adult Learners," *College Board Review,* Winter 1979–1980.

Nations, Richard. "The Incident that Jarred Waldheim," *Far Eastern Economic Review,* May 25, 1979. "Hanoi's Test of Civilization," *Far Eastern Economic Review,* August 3, 1979. "Battle for the Hearts and Stomachs," *Far Eastern Economic Review,* December 7, 1979.

Newsweek. "Agony of the Boat People," July 2, 1979. "Reagan's Polarized America," April 5, 1982.

New York Times. "Thousands of Aliens Held in Virtual Slavery in U.S.," October 19, 1980. "Excerpts from U.S. Accounts of Refugee's Ordeal," January 10, 1982. "Robots Enter the Limelight," March 4, 1982. "Excerpts from Executive Order on Secrecy Rules," April 4, 1982.

Nossiter, Bernard. "Thai Piracy against Boat People Seems Relentless," *New York Times,* May 7, 1980.

Pear, Robert. "Three Key Aides Reshape Welfare Policy," *New York Times,* April 26, 1982.

Pierson, George W. "The M-Factor in American History," *American Quarterly,* Summer Supplement 1962.

Raines, Howell. "Reagan Order Tightens the Rules on Disclosing Secret Information," *New York Times,* April 4, 1982.

Rasmussen, Wayne D. "The Mechanization of Agriculture," *Scientific American,* September 1982.

Richardson, Michael. "How Many Died?" *Far Eastern Economic Review,* October 26, 1979.

Ritchie-Calder, Peter. "Triage = Genocide," *Center Report,* June 1975.

Rosenberg, Hans. "Political and Social Consequences of the Great Depression of 1873–1896 in Central Europe," in James J. Sheehan (ed.), *Imperial Germany.* New York: Franklin Watts, 1976.

Rothschild, Emma. "Reagan and the Real America," *New York Review of Books,* February 6, 1981.

Rousset, Pierre. "Cambodia: Background to the Revolution," *Journal of Contemporary Asia,* Vol. 7, No. 4 (1977), pp. 513–28.

Rubenstein, Richard L. "Response to the Issue on Judaism and Psycho-

History of the *Journal of Psycho-History,*" *Journal of Psycho-History,* Spring 1979.

Sacerdoti, Guy. "How Hanoi Cashes In," *Far Eastern Economic Review,* June 15, 1979.

Salaman, Redcliffe N. "The Influence of the Potato on the Course of Irish History" (Tenth Finlay Memorial Lecture Delivered at University College, Dublin). Dublin: Browne and Nolan, 1944.

Schell, Jonathan. "The Fate of the Earth: I. A Republic of Insects and Grass," *The New Yorker,* February 1, 1982.

Tallahassee Democrat. "Ford Study: Death, Injury Cheaper than Fixing Cars," October 14, 1979.

Tate, Allen. "The Problem of Unemployment: A Modest Proposal" in *The American Review,* Vol. 1, No. 2 (May 1933).

Tawney, R. H. "Poverty as an Industrial Problem" (Inaugural Lecture Delivered on October 22, 1913, at the London School of Economics and Political Science). London: The Ratan Tata Foundation, 1913.

Thirsk, Joan. "Enclosing and Engrossing" and "The Farming Regions of England," in Joan Thirsk (ed.), *The Agrarian History of England and Wales, 1500–1640,* Vol. 4.

Time. "The Blackout [Coverstories]: Night of Terror," July 25, 1977, and "The American Underclass," August 29, 1977. "Indonesia: Facing a Liquid Auschwitz," July 2, 1979. "Save Us! Save Us!," July 9, 1979. "Many Do Not Get Counted," February 8, 1982.

Tobin, James. "Reagonomics and Economics," *New York Review of Books,* December 3, 1981.

Treaster, Joseph. "Crime at an Early Age: On the Violent Streets of Luis Guzman," *New York Times,* November 9, 1981.

U.S. News and World Report. "Those Budget Cuts: Who'll Be Hit Hardest," August 10, 1981.

Weber, Max. "Bureaucracy," "Science as a Vocation," "The Social Psychology of the World Religions," and "Capitalism and Rural Society in Germany," in H. H. Gerth and C. Wright Mills (eds.) *From Max Weber: Essays in Sociology.*

Weinraub, Bernard. "In Vietnam Tears as the Past Is Remembered," *New York Times,* December 27, 1981.

Yahil, Leni. "Select British Documents on the Illegal Immigration to Palestine (1939–1940)," in *Yad Vashem Studies.* Vol. 10. Jerusalem: 1974.

Young, Arthur. "An Inquiry into the Propriety of Applying Wastes to the Better Maintenance and Support of the Poor," in *Annals of Agriculture.* London: H. Goldney, 1801. Vol. 36, pp. 497-658. This article was also published as a pamphlet: Bury St. Edmunds: Rackham, 1801.

Zmarzlik, Hans-Günter. "Social Darwinism in Germany Seen as a Historical Problem," in Hajo Halborn (ed.), *Republic into Reich: The Making of the Nazi Revolution.* New York: Pantheon Books, 1972.

INDEX

Abdul Hamid (Sultan of Ottoman empire), 12–14, 144
Act of Elizabeth (England, 1601), 64, 65, 67
Act of Union (England and Ireland, 1801), 103, 125
Adorno, Theodore, 56
Agnes (ship), 119–120
Agrarians, 211
Agriculture: rationalization of, in Soviet Union, 19, 20–22, 23; rationalization of, in U.S., 22, 23
Alexander II (Czar of Russia), 140
Ambros, Otto, 213
Andover scandals (England, 1845), 79–80
Anglican Church, 47, 99
Anti-Semitism: factors causing, in modern Europe, 146–150; historical antecedents of, 131–145; Hitler on, 160; psychological interpretations of, 130–131; theological issues relating to, 128–129. *See also* Jews
Aristotle, 57
Arlen, Michael, 16
Armenian genocide, 11, 12–19, 125, 144, 239
Association of Southeast Asian Nations (ASEAN), 183, 185, 187, 188, 192
Auschwitz, 74, 126, 161, 213
Automation, computerized, and population redundance, 200–202
Automobile industry, American vs. Japanese, 27

Bacon, Francis, 57
Bakan, David, 217
Balkan War (1912), 17
Barth, Karl, 239
Beach people, 183, 184–185. *See also* Ethnic Chinese refugees
Becher, J. T., 70
Beecher, Henry, 196
Bentham, Jeremy, 68, 121, 122; his principle of "less eligibility," 70, 73, 74–75, 204; his proposals for relief of the poor, 72–75

Berger, Peter, 123
Berliner Tageblatt, 18–19
Bessborough, Lord, 107
Bey, Taalat, 14, 15, 18–19
Billingsley, John, 48
Billington, James, 143
Bishton, J., 48
Bismarck, Otto von, 144
Black Death (1347), 37–38
Board of Agriculture (England), 49
Board of Public Works for Ireland, 108, 110
Boat people, *see* Ethnic Chinese refugees
Bolshevism, 30, 154, 214
Bracher, Karl Dietrich, 153
British Labour Party, 80
Brougham, Lord, 104
Bryce, Viscount James, 15–16
Business Week magazine, 201

CAD/CAM (computer-aided design and computer-aided manufacturing), 200
Calvinism, 51, 214; role of, in emergence of capitalism, 231–232; and Social Darwinism, 216–223
Cambodia, *see* Kampuchea
Canada, Irish immigration to, during famine, 117, 118, 119–120
Caprivi, Leo von, 151–152
Carnegie-Mellon University, 201
Castro, Fidel, 86
Chadwick, Sir Edwin, 69–70, 77, 78, 80, 204; and Poor Law Reform (1834), 75, 113
Charles I (King of England), 45
Child labor, in pre-industrial England, 67–68, 73
Chimney sweeps, children used as, in England, 68
China, People's Republic of, 31, 174, 185, 194
China, Republic of (Taiwan), 30, 32
Chinese, ethnic, *see* Ethnic Chinese refugees
Chinese Exclusion Act (1882), 146, 157

Richard L. Rubenstein is Distinguished
Professor of Religion and founder and
director of the Center for the Study
of Southern Culture and Religion at
Florida State University. He is also
the author of six other books, including *The Cunning of History* and *The
Religious Imagination* (published
by Beacon Press), for which he was
awarded a *Portico d'Ottavia* Literary
Award.